THE DRAGON EMPRESS

Marina Warner was born in London of an Italian mother and an English father. Her history and criticism has focussed mainly on female symbolism – *Alone of All Her Sex: the Myth and the Cult of the Virgin Mary* (1976); *Joan of Arc: the Image of Female Heroism* (1981); *Monuments and Maidens: the Allegory of the Female Form* (1985) – and is currently finishing a study of fairytale, called *From The Beast to The Blonde*. She has also written novels. Her current novel, *Indigo*, was published last year; *The Lost Father* (1988) was a Regional Winner of the Commonwealth Writers' Prize and winner of the Macmillan Silver P.E.N. Award. She has recently published *The Mermaids in the Basement* her first collection of short stories.

She lives in London with her husband, the artist John Dewe Mathews, and one son.

BY MARINA WARNER

Fiction

In a Dark Wood
The Skating Party
Indigo
The Mermaids in the Basement

Non-fiction

The Dragon Empress:
Life and Times of Tzu'hsi 1835–1908
Empress Dowager of China

Alone of All Her Sex:
the Myth and the Cult of the Virgin Mary

Joan of Arc:
the Image of Female Heroism

Monuments and Maidens:
the Allegory of the Female Form

'Marina Warner, a very bright young journalist, has done some painstaking research to illustrate the whole period afresh with a spirited narrative, every line bristling with brilliant detail about the Manchu court and about the European bigwigs who, with Chinese reformers and revolutionaries hardly allied to them, finally overturned the Ch'ing Dynasty. Miss Warner has boundless curiosity and prevails on experts to provide material largely from contemporary Chinese sources, in the form of transcripts and paraphrases ... this is a lively, colourful and delightfully fair piece of historical biography'

Hugh Porteus, *Observer*

'Miss Warner's biography does not try to engage our sympathies on its subject's behalf and is all the better for that. Tz'u-hsi ruled over four hundred million people for forty-seven years, from 1861 to 1908, growing her fingernails six inches long and surrounding herself with a court of eunuchs – so unlike our own dear Queen Victoria. She started as a humble concubine of the fifth class in the harem of the Emperor Hsien-feng, but never really looked back from the moment the Chief Eunuch carried her into the Emperor's bedroom in a scarlet rug. The picture of court life is endlessly fascinating. Goodness knows whether Miss Warner has got all her facts right, but even if only half of them are correct, I still find myself gasping at her wit, her industry and her command of beautiful, plain English'

Auberon Waugh,
Harper & Queen

'This astonishing young author has put together a fresh and fascinating account that reveals China's last imperial reign as surely the most absurd government ever to have charge of a major nation. I read every word'

Barbara W Tuchman

ACKNOWLEDGMENTS

My deepest thanks to : William Shawcross, Professor Ivan Morris, who very kindly read the manuscript; to Sheila Murphy who encouraged me throughout and patiently typed the manuscript; to Man-shih Yang who read the Chinese sources for me; to Beatrix Miller for the most valuable gift of all – time; and to Christopher Falkus and Enid Gordon for their help and enthusiasm.

M W 1972

Marina Warner

THE DRAGON EMPRESS

Life and Times of Tz'u-hsi
1835–1908
Empress Dowager of China

VINTAGE

VINTAGE
20 Vauxhall Bridge Road, London SW1V 2SA

London Melbourne Sydney Auckland Johannesburg
and agencies throughout the world

First published in Great Britain by
by Weidenfeld & Nicolson 1972

Vintage edition 1993

2 4 6 8 10 9 7 5 3 1

Printed and bound in Great Britain by
Cox & Wyman, Reading, Berkshire

ISBN 0 09 916591 0

NOTE ON REREADING
THE DRAGON EMPRESS, 1993

In an old snapshot one looks so much fatter or so much thinner than one ever remembers being; and how hard it is to own up at a distance to those clothes, to that hairstyle, to that look. Were thighs really shrink-wrapped like that? Was pink-and-white gingham with broderie anglaise trimmings really it in those days?

The Dragon Empress wasn't the first book I wrote, but the first I had published, because the subject – a wicked woman in power – was of interest to many people, and it was the era of plenty (the early Seventies) when books were richly illustrated and sold internationally in 'co-editions'. I had been writing poetry and a novel, but these were somehow not so saleable. Tz'u-hsi drew me then for personal reasons, and some of these have now faded and indeed embarrass me. My interest in the culture of China still stands, but I am no longer looking, as I was then, for models of female authority. In that, I was in step with the feminism of the times. Heroines and leaders, rulers and fighters, regardless of intrinsic merit or ability – let alone virtue – were the necessary opponents of history as it was taught. An entry for 'Women' in the index of standard studies of different periods would normally lead the reader to a paragraph on 'droit de seigneur' or death in childbirth.

The postwar generation, following the lead of American reformers, wanted to challenge this peripheral condition. Although Simone de Beauvoir was an inspiration, her deep pessimism did not offer the promise that others held out – the French were content to describe matters as they are, but the Americans and the Australians (Germaine Greer), true to the principles of undefeated democratic individualism, wanted to describe them how they might be in order to bring about change. My excursion into China took place in this climate, looking for other ways of being, other types of situation. Following the *philosophes* of the eighteenth century (whom I had studied) who had found in Confucian despotism an ideal rule of enlightenment, I turned East, and attempted a variety of feminist Chinoiserie.

The events of the Seventies and, especially, the Eighties, revealed that women in power are not identical with women's interests. Although Margaret Thatcher was certainly not solely responsible for disillusion with the idea of female rule, writers on women's history no longer examined the lives of queens with enthusiasm. The best analyses concentrated on the reasons for women's subordination: on victims, not heroines. Or rather, heroic victims, like the mystical self-starving saints of the middle ages or the artists and poets – Artemisia Gentileschi and Sylvia Plath. This era has not yet passed; Linda Colley is one of the few brilliant historians who is still openly interested in élite women, their influence and political power.

The most recent biography of Tz'u-hsi, *Dragon Lady* by Sterling Seagrave (1992), takes a revisionist line: his empress is a nice, dull old thing who knows nothing of scheming or struggles or poison or *coups de main*. Her nefarious legend arose in the teahouses of Peking and the gossip of amahs and eunuchs, and was peddled by charlatans like Sir Edmund Backhouse and unscrupulous swashbuckling gentlemen of the press like The Times correspondent Morrison of Peking. Seagrave's Tz'u-hsi is a victim of orientalist storytelling, which concocted a vicious Eastern female potentate – a Chinese Cruella de Vil – to meet its hearers' fantasies.

Yet Chinese who were brought up on stories of Tz'u-hsi's wickedness hardly believe in the same wily Oriental bogey as westerners, though the culture of wicked stepmothers and wanton tyrants (the Empress Wu, Madame Mao) seems held in common. And Backhouse, prodigious fraud that he was, was nonetheless reporting surmise and adapting tales he heard in Peking at the time – so the image of Tz'u-hsi cannot be altogether pinned on Westerners' prejudice. The case hangs, for until a Sinologist works on new documents, the Empress Dowager will remain screened from historical view – in the same way as she ruled in life from behind a yellow curtain.

In 1991, a Chinese film, *Raise the Red Lantern*, was released in the West. Made by Zhang Yimou, who began directing during the thaw before the Tien An Men catastrophe, and has since fallen foul of the present government, this quiet, intense and beautiful film followed the fortunes of a young student who is inducted into a nobleman's palace as his Fourth Wife; the red lanterns of the title are raised by servants outside the apartment of the woman he chooses to be his partner that night. The ritual stirs up profound anxiety in each of the wives and sets them viciously against one another. Loneliness, suffocation, intrigue and emptiness are the terms of a sentence in the Confucian ménage, and in the end the heroine hangs herself. Zhang Yimou set the action in the Twenties, after the fall of the Ch'ing, in the period of the warlords, but the film may have been banned because it contains an implicit attack on all tyranny.

The high crimson-purple walls of the palace where the wives are imprisoned, its innards of individual cells and reptilian tiled roofs and tight courtyards, convey a much larger social allegory about enclosing systems which stifle thought and excite violence. The ritual with the red lanterns was never practised in a Chinese polygamous household, but it provides a vivid and frightening image of the arbitrariness of power.

Tz'u-hsi was one who survived the red lantern: she would have found her way about that household without much difficulty.

Marina Warner, 1993

CONTENTS

ILLUSTRATIONS

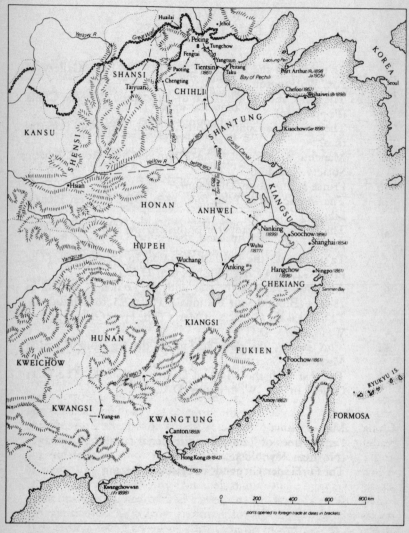

China, showing the treaty ports and the date of their opening; the march of the Taiping rebels to Nanking and then to Peking; and Tz'u-hsi's flight and return, 1900–02

FOREWORD

When Marco Polo was in prison in Genoa, the rumour soon spread that a Venetian captive was telling the most marvellous tales, so marvellous that people suspected he might be romancing. As a child, I felt the same about China: the ancient civilisation of the Far East existed for me as some kingdom of fantasy, so civilised and refined did it appear, with its language written in symbols, its immeasurable antiquity, its scholar-poets writing with brushes to wise rulers from pavilions wreathed in clouds. I collected Chinese objects, from the first Chinese shops opening in post-war London (reproductions of horses prancing and rolling, a pair of chopsticks, a tasselled lantern). My favourite image, hung above my bed, was of the princess who flew away to the moon when she was threatened by a demon king. He was her husband, the Archer God, and she had stolen from him the plant of immortal life; hence his fulminations and furious red face. In her flight, her long ribbons and the sash of her robes streamed and spiralled around her. For a long time, China seemed to me the kind of place where such an escape was a possibility.

In Paris, in 1964, I made friends with Irene Andreae, the first Chinese I had ever met. She was doing a thesis at the Sorbonne on a Jesuit missionary at the Ming court, and she continued my fascination with the country where she was born by telling me many more stories, and by disentangling legend from history. It was from her that I heard about Tz'u-hsi, the power behind the Throne at the end of imperial China, and the struggle of the many millions of Chinese then and now. I was going up to Oxford, and I considered reading Chinese but was afraid that the difficulty of the language might defeat me. After Oxford, I applied for a scholarship to America to study Chinese, but not surprisingly I was turned down. I stayed a Sinophile, but an outsider, and wrote this book without an insider's skills. I travelled to the Far East to research it, and saw streets in Macao where the coffin makers work in a Confucian spirit on splendid caskets still offered, with gorgeous grave-clothes, by properly filial children to their parents. I visited the spoils from the Imperial City Chiang Kai-shek took with him when he fled to Taiwan in 1949. The nearest I came to Tz'u-hsi herself was when I met a teacher of Mandarin at the Chinese university of Hong Kong. She had been married when she was young to the brother of the last emperor of China, Tz'u-hsi's deathbed nominee, and had been repudiated by him at the orders of the Japanese who wished to ally him instead with a Japanese princess and beget an heir to their puppet state of Manchukuo. The world of the Chinese emperors, so remote in custom and magnificence, is not so distant from our own: the last inmates of the Forbidden City were expelled in 1924, when the world of *Ulysses*, rapid communications, and Mussolini was already here.

In 1975, I went to China for the first time, to Peking, where Tz'u-hsi lived most of her life, and I saw her apartments in the palace. Confucianism was under ferocious attack, and in the Forbidden City we were shown a conspicuous example of its folly: a gold stupa encrusted with gems so huge it looked like a piece of a mountain. The Ch'ien-lung emperor had had it made as a reliquary for his mother's hair. The time during which Tz'u-hsi dominated the affairs of state was described in the historical museum in Yenan, where we travelled after, as a period of 'semi-colonial semi-feudalism'.

Seeing Mao's China (he was then still alive) made me realise that a country's history does not fall into neat chapters, as history writers make it appear to do, and that there was a much greater continuity between the nineteenth century past and the intractable problems of the twentieth century. Oddly, I would not have written this book, if I had learned what going to China taught me, that the implications of Tz'u-hsi, who epitomises an era and its government, did not end when the world she had known was overturned, as I, like a teller of tales, thought that it had. Also, when I was researching the book, Hugh Trevor-Roper had not been given at Basel airport Sir Edmund Backhouse's autobiography, which he then described in *A Hidden Life* (1976). Backhouse's phantasmagoria about the love affairs of the Empress cast doubt, retrospectively, on his veracity as her principal biographer, with J. O. P. Bland, in *China Under the Empress Dowager*, a crucial source until Trevor-Roper's revelations. Backhouse crystallised the rhetoric of oriental despotism in translation, with phrases like 'In token of our leniency . . . (so and so) is hereby permitted to commit suicide. . .' In conversation with me, Hugh Trevor-Roper also called into question the two volumes of memoirs by the Princess Te-Ling. Were they ghosted, or forged? How much, if anything, did Backhouse fabricate in his much more substantial book? At this stage, it is hard to disentangle. When Marco Polo's stories of China began circulating, people did not believe what they heard was true; but on verification by later historians and archaeologists, Marco Polo has largely been vindicated. The thirteenth century was a more sceptical age than ours, contrary to what one might expect; we live in credulous times, when the irrational and the mythic have gained acknowledgement as fundamental forces over our lives. Tz'u-hsi, the monstrous and powerful empress of so many millions is perhaps a bit of 'une fable convenue', as Voltaire said of history itself, since the chief sources reporting her statements and her character may have found in her the realisation of their own fantasies. If I were writing this book now, I would enquire further into other 'wicked ladies' in Chinese history – the Empress Wu, Chiang Ching – and try and understand how Tz'u-hsi was perceived within a tradition of termagants.

Tz'u-hsi's fabulous presence moved through times of great consequence, and it was this tragic crisis, reverberating through a civilisation I deeply admire, that I tried to catch in this book over a decade ago.

1984

Chapter One

THE MINOR
MANCHU'S DAUGHTER

Walls within walls within walls not only encircled the Middle
Kingdom, but contained each city, and within each city each
quarter, and within each quarter each palace and each mansion. The
snaking fortifications of the Great Wall guarded the Kingdom from
the northern invader; forty-foot-high and fifty-foot-thick walls
encompassed Peking's Inner, or Tartar, City and in turn enclosed
the high, blind, purple-stained walls of the Imperial City at whose
hidden heart lay the Forbidden City itself, where the Son of Heaven,
the emperor of China, was secluded. From this embattled cell,
Tz'u-hsi, the daughter of a minor Manchu mandarin, ruled China
for nearly fifty years.

Tz'u-hsi was born Lan Kuei (Little Orchid) in 1835, on the tenth
day of the tenth moon, which fell that year on 29 November. China
was Chung Kuo, the Middle Kingdom, and at its centre at that time
was the Tao-kuang (Glory of Right Principle) Emperor, of the
Ch'ing, or Manchu dynasty, who had inherited the empire from his
father, the Ch'ia-ch'ing (High Felicity) Emperor, when the latter
expired struck by lightning in 1821. But China's glory was on the
turn, and from 1835 onwards Tz'u-hsi's fortunes grew as her
country's perished. That year China was still at its greatest extent,
ringed like Saturn by countries eager and accustomed to pledge their
dependence on the Son of Heaven and bring him the tribute of
vassals: Annam, Laos, Siam, Burma to the south; Nepal to the west;
Korea, the Ryukyu Islands and Sulu guarding the long, exposed
ocean front to the east and south-east; and the Mongol, Manchurian
and Turkestan tribes to the north and north-west. All acknowledged
China suzerain by the last half of the eighteenth century; all were to
be lost by the beginning of the twentieth, as the Chinese empire,
with Tz'u-hsi as ruler, cracked like thin ice at contact with not only
Western firepower, but also, more fatally, with Western commercial, industrial and economic ethics and above all individual instincts
of competition, which could not be absorbed into the Confucian
framework. But when Tz'u-hsi was born, not a fume of all this
clouded Chinese eyes. The Eastern giant seemed invulnerable,
self-sufficient, long sovereign of all within its experience, not by

might but by the right of culture, brilliantly and civilly administered by principles developed for itself and by itself.

The capital of the Celestial Empire, Peking, rose among groves of white pines in a level plain, less than a hundred miles south of the Great Wall, against grassy banks of hills that climb in waves to the north and to the west, in whose fertile and misty hollows nestled temples and palaces: the fabled Yuan Ming Yuan (the 'Round Bright Garden') with its lakes and pagodas, the loveliest of the many summer palaces of the emperors and their families. On one of the clear bright days of the Peking climate when the sand storms from the Gobi desert were for once stilled, these palaces could sometimes be glimpsed, but from the approaches to Peking itself only the topmost brilliant yellow glazed eaves of the massive gatehouses of the Tartar City scaled the height of the City walls, and above them the peak of Prospect Hill, and above all the bizarre bulb of the White Dagoba. No towers otherwise pierced the horizon, for out of respect for the emperor, and for the *feng shui*, the spirits of wind and water, nothing was built higher than his dwelling place.

When travellers first entered Peking through the south gate of the Outer or Chinese City, the raised causeway was flanked by woods filled with gloomy crows cawing, and 'muddy, swampy land, untilled and bare, over which wander[ed] a few thin sheep, plucking at the scanty tufts of rank grass'.[1] The vast grounds of the Temple of Heaven – 640 acres – and of the Temple of Agriculture – 320 acres – stretched out on either side. Only at the foot of the Ch'ien Men, the central gate of the Tartar City, did the throng and bustle begin. The sixty-foot-broad street, central artery of Peking's chequerboard layout, preserved since Kubla Khan founded the city of Khanbalic on the same site in 1267, then led on straight to the Wu Men (The Gate of the Zenith) of the Imperial City. All along it mat-shed booths and shops huddled three rows deep; flags announcing their wares streamed in a typical Peking breeze; beggars in organized gangs buttonholed passers-by; rope dancers twirled and spun; clairvoyants sold almanacs of lucky days, and told fortunes with a throw of the *I Ching*; pedlars shuffled past carrying yoked paniers of sweets and needles and tea and toys and rice cakes and paper patterns and doughnuts and fans, each with his own drum or pipe or whistle so that the Chinese woman, whom it hurt to hobble on bound feet, could distinguish him from behind her walls and send out for his goods. Nightsoil merchants collected manure – human and animal – parsimoniously in jars and carried it off to the country; craftsmen mended porcelain with rivets; chiropodists and barbers, puppeteers and story-tellers, scribes and quacks jostled and crowded; acrobats and jugglers performed, sometimes with bears and monkeys, or gave a legend or an old tale in fanciful masks and every variety of wig and costume. Smells of roasting meats and game, of ginseng and soy, of garlic and tobacco hung in the streets as the travellers' coolies drew them on. Peking carts – wheelbarrows drawn by one man or more – tangled with each other; donkeys and mules staggered by under mountainous loads; sly-eyed camels from Mongolia swayed past. When a mandarin was passing, his attendants cleared the way with flicks of their bamboo rods, laying about them quite unceremoniously; the number of his retinue and outriders, the colour of his cart (green for a mandarin of the first and second ranks; blue for the third and fourth), the button in his round cap and the *p'u tzu*, the embroidered plaque on his breast,[2] all proclaimed his standing. Higher officials, ministers and princes rode in sedans, while imperial yellow was reserved for the Son of Heaven and his retainers alone.

The teeming crowd was ragged and rundown, squalid and diseased. Even the officials' resplendent robes were soiled; the city guards, who patrolled the streets at night with a large rattle and a lantern after the city gates were closed, were in tatters; men picked lice out of their hair, and even 'the highest officers of state made no hesitation of calling their attendants in public to seek in their necks for those troublesome animals, which, when caught, they very composedly put between their teeth'.[3] The streets were muddy, dirty, watered for sewage day and night, and often flooded in heavy rain; the houses were dilapidated, and even the grandest presented slovenly walls to the outside world, reserving their enchanted gardens and arbours for the eyes of their inmates only. From Prospect Hill, an artificial mound built to obstruct the descent of the noxious and unpropitious spirits of the north on to the Forbidden City, this secret, tranquil, elegant Peking was revealed. For from above, Peking looked like a magic forest, filled with flowering trees and exotic shrubs, more wooded than the countryside itself, and showing through the foliage the gleaming old gold of the imperial yellow tiles of the Forbidden City, the bright enamels of the temple roofs, gatehouses and palaces, and the vivid explosion of scarlet and emerald and azure of Chinese architecture's open pavilions and ornate upturned eaves.

In this capital city Tz'u-hsi played as a child. It is not known when she first arrived in Peking, for some writers say she was only three, others – and this seems more convincing – that she was adolescent

The Imperial Clan

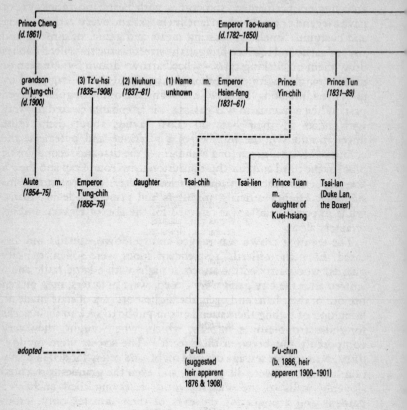

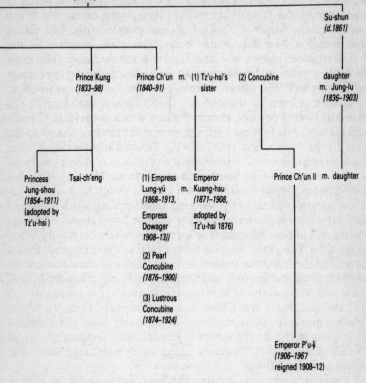

Ulgungga
(d.1846)

Su-shun
(d.1861)

Prince Kung
(1833–98)

Prince Ch'un
(1840–91) m.

(1) Tz'u-hsi's
sister

(2) Concubine

daughter
m. Jung-lu
(1836–1903)

Princess
Jung-shou
(1854–1911)
(adopted by
Tz'u-hsi)

Tsai-ch'eng

(1) Empress
Lung-yü
(1868–1913,

Empress
Dowager
1908–13))

(2) Pearl
Concubine
(1876–1900)

(3) Lustrous
Concubine
(1874–1924)

Emperor
Kuang-hsu
(1871–1908,
adopted by
Tz'u-hsi 1876)

Prince Ch'un II m. daughter

Emperor P'u-ji
(1906–1967
reigned 1908–12)

The Family of Tz'u–hsi

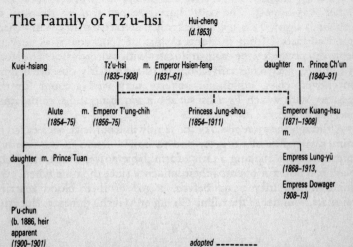

Hui-cheng
(d.1853)

Kuei-hsiang

Tz'u-hsi   m. Emperor Hsien-feng
(1835–1908)   *(1831–61)*

daughter m. Prince Ch'un
(1840–91)

Alute   m. Emperor T'ung-chih
(1854–75)   *(1856–75)*

Princess Jung-shou
(1854–1911)

Emperor Kuang-hsu
(1871–1908)
m.

daughter m. Prince Tuan

Empress Lung-yü
(1868–1913,

Empress Dowager
1908–13)

P'u-chun
(b. 1886, heir
apparent
(1900–1901)

adopted ----------

when she came to live there, with her mother, her two brothers and her sister, in a kinsman's house in Pewter Lane, Hsi-la-hu-tung, a side street in the Tartar City to the east near the canal, which ran parallel to the Imperial City's high and purple walls. Her father Hui-cheng, a Manchu of the Yehe Nara clan, enrolled in the Bordered Blue Banner, was an official of some mediocrity, for even the later elevation of his daughter to the highest power in the empire failed to pluck his career from obscurity. For two years after Tz'u-hsi was born he worked as a clerk, a junior mandarin in the Board of Civil Appointments in Peking, which supervised China's bureaucracy. His first provincial post was at Luhan in Shansi to the west of the capital and later, during Tz'u-hsi's girlhood, he was transferred to Anhwei, where he rose to the authoritative position of *taotai* or intendant of the Southern Anhwei circuit.[4] Because Tz'u-hsi always hated the harsh northern winters of Peking, because memories of the atmosphere of the seething nature-loving south flavoured her later outlook, it seems unlikely that she left Anhwei when she was three, but that she learned to love Wuhu where her family lived, built on the Yangstze, the river whose mighty drive through China carves out the Yangstze gorges, shaggy crags and pinnacles luxuriant with ferns and grasses, and then descends into a bright, broad, richly-watered swathe of viridian, fertile ground for mosquito and rice, until it meets the China seas at Shanghai. There at Wuhu Tz'u-hsi grew up, in 'summers of a still, damp heat, not a sign of movement in the air for weeks together, and a temperature of 90 degrees at midnight'.[5] Servants stood watch over their masters at night and fanned them.

Tz'u-hsi's family were not rich; in China, that probably means her father was honest. The court later gossiped that on the way to Peking as a girl, Tz'u-hsi, mistakenly delivered a paltry sum – three hundred taels – from the local magistrate, pocketed it as heaven-sent, and rewarded the magistrate later with a viceroyalty. The story is folklore, such as usually clings to rulers of fairly obscure origin, but nevertheless, childhood poverty may well account for the rapacity with which Tz'u-hsi set about acquiring and accumulating later on in life.

Although the sacredness of the family in Confucian society led to joint ownership of property and to united action in the family's interests, often making a clan a formidable power block, the Yehe Nara had not consolidated their influence since the time when, two hundred and fifty years before, a girl of their blood married Nurhaci, founder of the ruling Ch'ing or Manchu dynasty. But after

6

Tz'u-hsi's arrival at court and rise to power, she concentrated titles, wealth and power on her immediate relations, manipulated the succession to create her sister's son emperor, and so contrived the eclipse of the direct imperial Aisin Gioro line by the Yehe Nara. But she confessed: 'I was not a bit happy with my parents. I was not the favourite. My sisters had everything they wanted, while I was, to a great extent, ignored.'[6]

As a young girl, Tz'u-hsi had long eyes, a broad forehead and a firm, rounded chin which was to develop later into quite a jowl. But these heavy features were enlivened by an alert and vivacious expression and a smile that flashed across her face with winning suddenness. Her anger was, however, as swift, and wilfulness, such as she always displayed when in power, is a characteristic that usually develops early: she was probably a headstrong and capricious adolescent. She was only five foot high, with delicate well-shaped hands and nails that she grew four inches long on her third and little finger, as the snobbery of otium demanded. They were shielded with jade or filigree nail-protectors – and someone who once clasped her hand remarked it was like clutching a handful of pencils. Her silky, full and raven hair was never cut, and her scalp was massaged with scented oils and pomades. Like all Manchu girls she was gaudy, her face whitened to a death mask pallor, her cheeks rouged into two spots of high colour, her bottom lip painted in a scarlet tear-drop to resemble a cherry. Sometimes she added blush to her eyelids, and outlined the eye with kohl. The white lead used in Chinese makeup was poisonous: an American lady doctor, consulted by a Manchu girl who complained of semi-paralysis of the face, prescribed less powder and paint and the girl recovered. Tz'u-hsi herself once remarked enviously on the whiteness of European complexions, for her own was very sallow. But she added that their hairiness – Oriental women have no down, and the men hardly any beard – was repellent. Nevertheless she had a clear opinion of herself: 'A lot of people were jealous of me, because I was considered to be a beautiful woman at that time.'[7]

But the standard of beauty was not very high. As in Europe at an earlier date, disfiguring diseases like smallpox and goitre were rife, and medicine was primitive. Those who survived without a 'visit of the celestial flowers', as smallpox was propitiatingly called, were very few: Tz'u-hsi was one. A young Englishman commented: 'All Chinamen and Manchus of rank seem to have a "monstrosity" of some sort: either a fearful goitre; or one side of the face totally different from the other; or a strange squint or four or five teeth run together in one piece, like a bone; or a big dinge in the forehead. . . . In those days everyone was deeply pockmarked. . . . Ch'ung-lun (an official at the Board of Foreign Affairs) did me the honour to wet his finger and rub my cheeks to see if I was painted.'[8]

A poem survives which celebrates Tz'u-hsi's beauty, but it was written by a flatterer who never saw her. Custom forbade writings about the emperor and his entourage; also, descriptions of beauty rarely conjure a face precisely. The only legendary beauty who can be disentangled from the host of *femmes fatales* of the Chinese emperors' court was the famous Fragrant Pearl of the T'ang dynasty, who, having been nourished on rose-petals and scented herbs and precious essences as a child, exhaled heavenly aromas as she moved.

As in all civilizations which require that women of quality should be wives, mothers and beauties only, toilette was a major pre-occupation, and Tz'u-hsi from puberty onwards imbibed, consumed, rubbed on and massaged in every form of charlatan or authentic recipe to keep herself young and beautiful. Above her mask-like visage her hair was gathered up from the nape into an enormous, weighty decoration of jewels, shaped like flowers and insects, which fanned out on either side and hung down with tassels of pearl. The heavy headdress flattered her oriental features, accentuating the highness of the cheekbones and the fragility of the neck until a Manchu girl looked like a spring tree bowed with blossom.

The Manchu costume, the same for men and for women, was loose and fastened at the side, worn over a tunic and pantaloons. It was embroidered with flowers and animals, fantastic emblems and symbolic beasts, studded and threaded with as many precious stones and pearls and as much gold as its owner could buy, and designed in the most lively and triumphant contrasts of colour. The Manchu shoes, hung with strings of pearl and encrusted with stones – for women, for the men wore thick-soled, fur-lined boots – were raised on a high central wedge like a streamlined clog, making Tz'u-hsi five foot six altogether.

Women rarely received any education at all, and indeed one court lady described later how she had taught herself: 'My mother was opposed to having her daughters learn to read, but like most wealthy families, she had old men come into the palace to read stories or recite poetry for our entertainment. I not infrequently followed the old men out, bought the books from which they read, and then bribed some of the eunuchs to teach me to read them.'[9] But

Tz'u-hsi's father Hui-cheng was not an anachronistic progressive, nor did he have the money to employ literate servants or the pedigree to entitle him to eunuchs, and therefore the education that Tz'u-hsi had undoubtedly acquired by the age of sixteen was the fruit of her own resourcefulness and diligence. Immured in the boredom and decorum of a young girl's life, she must have pestered any literati with whom she came into contact with the almost tiresomely childlike and irrepressible curiosity she displayed throughout her life, until she had mastered, without formal tuition, the rudiments of reading and writing – no mean feat in a country where women, even of the noblest birth, were usually illiterate, and therefore a significant reflection on Tz'u-hsi's industry and dedication.

When Tz'u-hsi was eighteen, her father was cashiered for deserting his post before the onslaught of the Taiping rebellion. From then on he vanishes, and the date of his death, in a country dedicated to filial piety and to the worship of fathers after death, is not even recorded into the copious court annals.[10] As a daughter Tz'u-hsi could not perform the Confucian ceremonies at his grave, and as a woman she adopted her husband's family as her own when she married. Naturally Tz'u-hsi was only too ready to exchange her insignificant father for the august lineage of the Ch'ing emperors, and only too happy to forget him when she rose at court. From her point of view, Hui-cheng's only importance was that he was a Manchu and a Bannerman. For, ever since a statute of 1661, young Manchu girls were eligible for service in the Forbidden City either as maidservants or, more vitally, as concubines for the emperor. When therefore the Tao-Kuang Emperor died in 1851 and his young son Hsien-feng succeeded, the Captain of the Bordered Blue Banner sent the names of Hui-cheng's daughters to the Chief Eunuch at the Forbidden City, that they might be summoned to the Son of Heaven's side.

For Tz'u-hsi and her father belonged to the ruling race: in 1644 the hordes of Manchu cavalry and infantry swept from Manchuria into Peking. They were divided (then, and in Tz'u-hsi's day) into eight military companies or Banners, Bordered and Plain, White, Yellow, Red and Blue. The last Ming emperor, 'his left foot bare', fled his palace in Peking and hanged himself from a tree overlooking the Forbidden City's golden tiled roofs. Although the Bordered Blue was one of the 'inferior' banners, it nevertheless gave Tz'u-hsi, the daughter of a Manchu Bannerman, access to the court and its exclusively Manchu harem.

The new dynasty in 1644 assumed the supreme power over its Manchu 'slaves' and its Chinese 'subjects', by taking over the existing bureaucracy, the traditions and ethics of the Ming whom it had deposed, and by appointing the Chinese who came over to its side (many of whom it enrolled as Chinese Bannermen) to the important posts of the empire. Although until the end of the seventeenth century the change of dynasty was marked by blood-shed and struggle, Han Chinese[11] of all classes – gentry, literati and peasants – accepted the Ch'ing with that practical fatalism that Confucius's inspiration and hero, the Duke of Chou, formulated when his Chou empire ousted the Shang-Yin in the twelfth century BC: the philosophy that a dynasty ruled by the Mandate of Heaven, and that when rebellion and natural disasters, floods and famine plagued a country, as they had during the declining years of the Ming, they signalled the exhaustion of Heaven's will that the dynasty should continue to rule. If another leader or another dynasty then arose and brought harmony and relief to the people, the Mandate of Heaven had been transferred and the country could accept him calmly and even joyfully as its ruler.

But by their own designs the Manchus were always to remain foreigners. Even their language, which they made all Chinese officials learn, conducting all the business of government bi-lingually, was not even related to Chinese, but belonged to the mysterious Ural-Altaic group, which includes Finnish and Hungarian, and it was written in adapted Mongol script. Just as they adopted Chinese traditions to govern China so they could have been assimilated if they had wished. But they chose instead to practise a form of racialism, to accentuate the differences and give them ballast in legislation and privileges. Intermarriage was in theory forbidden to the emperor, for the succession had to be pure. Tz'u-hsi, as a Manchu girl, therefore had an *entrée* to the harem. However, the emperor and other Manchus and Mongols sometimes took unofficial Chinese concubines. Manchu princes and nobles who were directly descended from the original victorious generals formed a privileged élite in a country otherwise devoted to egalitarianism and equal opportunity for all. Living off stipends from the Imperial Treasury and revenue from lands allotted to them, the Manchu princes and nobles inherited prerogatives without responsibility and enjoyed leisured days, removed by caste from the necessity to toil. The Bannermen, descendants of the soldiers who had fought under the princes, were also segregated by privilege from the mass of the Chinese people: at the conquest, Chinese land had been confiscated on their behalf, and in Tz'u-hsi's day they still lived off incomes – pittances, but nevertheless unearned – from the land granted them by the government. No Manchu of whatever class could take up a trade or become a merchant, for such despised activities were beneath even the meanest of them. Their military careers were secure and hereditary, as from birth they were enrolled in the standing Banner army; and their progress through the mandarinate was assisted, for they were entitled to pass directly to the second qualifying stage of the traditional examinations that controlled all official appointments, and there was a special examination in Manchu for them. The bilingual bureaucracy ensured their privilege: Manchu scribes and translators were obviously in great demand.

In a population of four hundred million there were only five million Manchus, but they were represented in the civil service in a far greater proportion. During the Ch'ing dynasty, from 1644 to 1912, including the fifty years Tz'u-hsi was in power, the office of viceroy of a province (an immensely powerful appointment, as each of China's eighteen provinces was almost autonomous) was held by an equal number of Manchus and Chinese. Of the governors, who in some provinces were subordinate to viceroys, but in others were independent,[12] there was a fairer ratio of almost two Chinese appointments to one Manchu, but of the offices on the government boards and other crucial organs in Peking, which were the equivalent of ministries, the converse is true.[13] Manchus were preferred to Chinese beyond any question of merit, and Tz'u-hsi was to continue the custom: when a Mongol Bannerman, Ch'ung-ch'i came first in the metropolitan examinations in 1865, becoming 'senior wrangler', the highest honour in an empire of scholars, he broke an unwritten rule of the dynasty: Bannermen did not dazzle in the examinations because they did not need to.

Tz'u-hsi, even as a little girl at Wuhu in the south of China, far removed from the stronghold of Manchu privilege in Peking and the north, was nevertheless brought up to believe unthinkingly in a Manchu hegemony. Throughout her life she harped, sometimes playfully, sometimes earnestly, on the distinctions. She always asked officials their racial origins, and made patronizing remarks about Chinese. The manners of the occupying race were ingrained in her from childhood, and although she was quick to see the talents of a Chinese and to give him an important post, she later allowed her favourites, like the handsome Manchu general Jung-lu, to soar to the most powerful positions in the empire even though he had not taken the lowest qualifying examination required of a Chinese, and when she decreed in 1901 that a shrine should be built to the memory of the Viceroy Li Hung-chang, the perspicacious statesman who handled China's foreign affairs for thirty years, he was the first Han Chinese in the history of the dynasty to receive such an honour.

Sumptuary laws distinguished the races and emphasized the conquest of the outsiders from Manchuria. In 1644 they had immediately ordered their new subjects to shave their heads, leaving the queue or pigtail to grow from the crown, as a symbol of their submission to Ch'ing rule. From that date on males over the age of fourteen therefore adopted the style, and the queue often reached their knees. The queue was a powerful image: it stereotyped 'the Chinaman' for centuries in the West, and even inspired George Washington and George III, in an excess of chinoiserie, to wear docked versions themselves. In China its potency as a badge of subjection continued. The Taiping rebels of the 1850s and 1860s, when Tz'u-hsi was first empress, wore their hair loose and wild; and after Tz'u-hsi's death, in the 1910s and 1920s, cutting the pigtail was an open gesture of repudiation of the Manchus.

Manchu women, tall and strong and mountain-bred, had ridden at the side of their men and herded flocks in the harsh northern landscape. They had never therefore bound their feet, like the tender and sheltered Chinese. From the age of five or six, bandages were bound tightly round the feet of a Chinese girl, forcing the heel under the instep to meet the crumpled toes until the whole foot measured not more than three inches in length. In her tiny embroidered shoes, with beribboned pantaloons falling prettily over the swollen and deformed ankles, or in elegant spats, the Chinese girl minced along daintily on the arm of one of her sons or one of her servants. This was the famous 'lily walk', for the undulation of her figure as she tottered on her cramped and crippled feet was celebrated in millennia of prose and verse, even though, when the bandages were renewed, the stench of compressed flesh was appalling. But bound feet were not only thought seductive, but also became a symbol of caste, for the peasantry and the coolie class could not afford to immobilize their daughters. They urgently needed their labour. Manchu women often longed to adopt the erotic and status-giving deformation, and intermittent imperial edicts had to remind them that foot-binding was strictly against Manchu laws and traditions. Tz'u-hsi herself never succumbed, for she had naturally tiny feet, and marvelled, when she first saw Europeans, at the size of theirs.

Tz'u-hsi's emphasis on the differences between the ruling race and its subjects throughout her life echoed the statecraft that earlier emperors had used to keep the Chinese submissive; it was rooted in her family tradition and her childhood education, although by her day it was political myopia, only serving to polarize hostility artificially towards the dynasty, long after they had absorbed in many ways the thoughts and customs of the once vanquished race. For when Tz'u-hsi was born the Manchus had become physically indistinguishable from the Chinese, and the learning of the language was for many an arduous task. Tz'u-hsi herself spoke a little, but her first language was Chinese. Even at court, where a pretence was maintained (for the emperor always spoke Manchu in audience), the lingua franca had however become Chinese, and although the documents, edicts and business of government continued to be bilingual, for many officials – including Manchus – the language was an obscurantist formality. Tz'u-hsi indeed even prided herself on the purity of her Chinese, affected not to understand coarser accents than her own and turned away in scorn when she heard corrupt pronunciation.

After two centuries of colonizing the Chinese, the Manchus had themselves been colonized. Each dynasty in the many conflicts of China's long history had established itself by force, but each one had successively fallen under the spell of Chinese wisdom and of Confucian pacifism. The Manchus, originally hardy, tough-living northern archers, hunters and warriors, had gradually yielded to the Chinese hero-image of the scholar poet, or literatus, and had polished their native warlikeness with the soft cloth of a more sophisticated ideal until their military traditions had been abandoned for intellectual aspirations, and the hierarchy of an army for the etiquette of an academy. In the *Tao Te Ching*, a more esoteric work than Confucius's *Analects*, there is nevertheless this fundamentally Chinese and Confucian concept: 'To think them [weapons] lovely means to delight in them, and to delight in them means to delight in the slaughter of men. And he who delights in the slaughter of men will never get what he looks for out of those that dwell under heaven.'[14] The Manchu Bannermen Tz'u-hsi knew as a child were steeped in these peaceable and scholarly ideals; though they were required to keep up their warlike skills, though they qualified in picturesque military examinations of weight-lifting, stone-throwing and archery at full gallop, the army was neglected, disorganized and effete, and the profession of soldier held in such contempt that no man of ability ever took up a military career. Forbidden to take up professions, the Bannermen were a notorious gang in China's main cities: unemployed, rowdy, arrogant and often down-at-heel. 'As a class they are indolent, ignorant and proud.'[15]

Yet Tz'u-hsi's head was so filled as a child with tales of earlier Manchu prowess, of the hunting exploits of early Ch'ing emperors wheeling on their stocky long-haired Mongol ponies over the dynasty's homelands, that the evidence of their degeneracy before her eyes shocked her and gave her longings that their former Manchu spirit be regained. The vernacular poetry and drama of the Chinese streets were also comparatively untempered by the ideal of the meditative scholar, so that alongside the wisdom and insights of the sages Tz'u-hsi also absorbed the exploits of folk heroes and legendary soldiers, which inspired in her a primitive, instinctual excitement at virile, ready men and at martial valour that marked her out as a true atavistic Manchu.

When the Tao-kuang Emperor died and was succeeded by his son Hsien-feng (of Universal Plenty), at twenty years old,[16] the new Son of Heaven, the Imperial Household first heard of Tz'u-hsi, the young and vivacious daughter of their race. The same year, 1851, or early during the next, when Tz'u-hsi was fifteen or sixteen, the imperial couriers, heralds calling before them, rode up Pewter Lane in imperial-yellow carts to the house where Tz'u-hsi and her family were living and delivered their summons. The Hsien-feng Emperor was choosing his harem for the day when the mourning period of two years and three months for his father would be over[17] and Tz'u-hsi and her sister were commanded to appear.

Chapter Two

CONCUBINE, FIFTH RANK

One of sixty girls eligible for service in the palace, Tz'u-hsi, attired in the finest robes and jewels her family could buy or borrow, entered the emperor's palace. In procession, the girls flowed across the grey-green, still breadth of a moat, and passed into the Imperial City and the maze of halls and pavilions, temples and living quarters, pagodas and garden retreats of the Purple Forbidden City beyond. To the north lay the labyrinthine apartments of the Hsien-feng Emperor and his eunuch retinue; to the west the lovely contrived wilderness of the Sea Palaces, situated on the shores of three artificial lakes and sprinkled with pleasure domes.

For a sixteen-year-old girl like Tz'u-hsi, approaching this awesome precinct, potent image of the inaccessible divinity of its single male resident, was a terrifying experience. Yet for someone of Tz'u-hsi's background, concubinage was a natural outcome, and the imperial summons was final. While the force of numbers created by polygamy and the Confucian emphasis on the sacredness of parental authority gave the women of a household – the mothers, wives and mothers-in-law – tyrannical powers, a daughter had no voice in the decision of her future. But Tz'u-hsi never questioned this paradox on which she was to capitalize so greatly later, but accepted her position in full awareness of the political power within a concubine's grasp.

Tz'u-hsi and her companions, seated cross-legged in sedan chairs, filed through a smaller gate to the side of the T'ien An Men (the Gate of Heavenly Peace) the auspicious southern entrance of the palace. South was the source of the emperor's celestial energy: he always faced south on his throne, entered each city by the south gate when travelling, and on his death bed turned his face to the south. Only when he sacrificed at the Altar of Heaven, when he was the worshipper, not the worshipped, did he face northwards. The Wu Men (the Gate of the Zenith), set with four great towers, now rose before the Manchu girls. Passing through it, they entered the Forbidden City itself. It was also called 'Purple' after the character for the polar star, symbol of the palace around which the cosmos revolved, confused with its homophone, the character for purple, colour of the Imperial City's walls. Within it each building stood

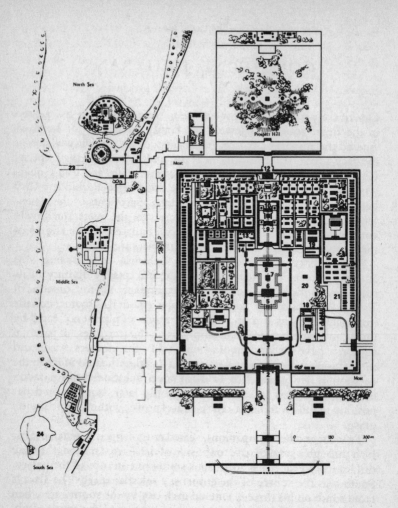

The Forbidden City and Sea Palaces of Peking

free, on raised terraces fringed by balustrades, carved in the white marble that the Ming emperors had brought from distant Yunnan to glorify their Peking domain.

The concubines-elect exchanged their own servants for palace eunuchs and, leaving their chairs behind, proceeded on foot across the wide courtyard up a side flight of white marble stairs. The central stairway was reserved, as were all the central gates, for the exclusive passage of the emperor. On its carved floating marble carpet, on which the Imperial five-clawed dragon, wreathed in clouds, pursued the ever-fleeing jewel of omnipotence. On either side before them roe the vermilion, uptilted temples to the Tutelary Gods and the Imperial Ancestors, where the Son of Heaven sacrificed every anniversary of a past emperor's birth and death. Buildings like these were ablaze with colour, their brackets and rafters carved with *feng*, the 'phoenix' or crested pheasant, female complement of the male dragon; with cranes, symbols of longevity; with flying bats, emblems of happiness, through a Chinese pun; snarling, grotesque lion dogs and tortoises stood guard on their thresholds against evil spirits. Inside they were decorated with embroidered hangings of peonies in full bloom, or over-ripe pomegranates and luscious peaches, of lotus and spiky blossom, all signifying good fortune, and the light filtered through lattice screens and reflected in the sombre cloisoné urns and bronze incense-burners.

The Manchu girls were escorted ceremoniously on over the dusty courtyards, across the Golden Water River, which divided the space in a flowing arc, and on over one of the five bridges that spanned it, standing for the five virtues of the Confucian canon. They probably passed through the Gate of Correct Conduct to the west of the T'ai Ho Men (the Gate of Supreme Harmony) and on across another huge courtyard, the largest within the Forbidden City, and skirted the Throne Hall of Supreme Harmony, which stood on the Dragon Pavement Terrace, for its columns and massive many-tiered roofs rose above a pure expanse of white marble, open to the sky and approached by a triple flight of steps rising in shallow gradations. There Tz'u-hsi and her companions were led to the left, and into the Nei Wu Fu, the offices of the Imperial Household Department, where they were expected.

When the Empress Dowager, the Hsien-feng Emperor's step-mother, arrived, accompanied by the Chief Eunuch, Tz'u-hsi curt-sied profoundly with the others. The five lucky characters of her birth, which formed her horoscope, were examined. No union in China could be ratified without consulting them – but matchmakers always saw to it that they harmonized when necessary. She was inspected for blemishes, defects and illness; questioned in Chinese and Manchu to ascertain she had at least a grasp, if shaky, of both; and examined in a few elementary passages of the classics. In the early days of the dynasty, when girls entered the palace at the age of thirteen, they were first appointed attendants, and then from amongst them the emperor selected his wives. But by Tz'u-hsi's day, dignity, decorum, a Manchu pedigree, and the emperor's mother, not Eros, governed the choice. Hsien-feng was not even present at the selection of his seraglio.

In spite of Tz'u-hsi's probable dreams of power, the summons to the palace by no means gave direct access to the throne, or even to the Son of Heaven's bed. It was perfectly possible to become a concubine and never meet the emperor, and concubinage often meant nothing more than waiting on the Empress Dowager as a servant in all but rank. Many Manchus therefore dreaded their daughters' departure. Outside the Forbidden City a Manchu girl could make a prosperous, happy marriage – inside, she might remain a virgin. When an emperor died his wives could not remarry, or return to their families. In the sombre recesses of the Forbidden City lived generations of imperial concubines as if they had been called to the monastic life: in 1924, when the court was finally driven out, three old ladies who had been the secondary wives of emperors were found living there in forgotten seclusion. Only the notorious Empress Wu of the T'ang dynasty, had survived the short reign of her first husband to become his son's consort as well. It could even be a healthier prospect to become a palace attendant, for they left the Forbidden City at the age of twenty-five, after a few years' employment, often assigned a generous dowry and an arranged husband.

On 14 June 1852, immediately after the mourning period for Tao-kuang had expired, Tz'u-hsi was appointed *Kuei Jen* (Honourable Person), a concubine of the fifth and lowest rank, and called the Concubine Yi. Her sister was rejected and she later married outside the palace. Of the sixty girls, twenty-eight were elected, including a gentle fifteen-year-old girl called Niuhuru after the clan to which she belonged. The Niuhuru was a prestigious clan: the mothers of the Ch'ien-lung and Hsien-feng Emperors, as well as Tz'u-hsi's own mother, all came from it. The girl Niuhuru's family was enrolled in the superior Yellow Banner and so, as her ancestry was more august, she was appointed *Pin*, concubine one rank above Tz'u-hsi. In a matter of weeks she became Hsien-feng's consort and

18

was crowned his empress, and it was she whom Tz'u-hsi befriended, instinctively attaching herself to success, for the younger girl was to become her colleague and rival for over twenty years.

The household into which Tz'u-hsi was now enrolled contained about six thousand people whose single lodestar and only male inhabitant was the emperor, around whom about three thousand eunuchs and three thousand women revolved. Among the myriad servants the concubines were but a handful, for although their number had swelled to seventy under some emperors, the harem fluctuated and was to dwindle to two or three by the end of the dynasty. Tz'u-hsi was given at least four eunuchs and as many maids to look after her personally; she was allotted apartments of her own, near the other concubines, but distinct from them – the communal gynaeceum of the Ottoman Empire was much too sensual and intimate for China; she was measured for court robes and shoes, and given jewellery and ornaments. In Anhwei her father, in recognition of the honour done his daughter, received, in this penultimate year of his life, bolts of silk, ounces of gold and silver, a horse or two elaborately saddled and bridled and an exquisite tea-set from the grateful throne.

The life Tz'u-hsi led in her new surroundings was thoroughly organized: the Imperial Household office's various boards constituted in themselves an autonomous bureaucracy which reflected the intricate ramifications of the bureaucratic empire itself. Departments supervised the vaults of gold and silver bullion and the stores of furs, porcelain, silk and tea; others collected the rents on Bannermen's property, provided the sacrificial meats and fruits for religious ceremonies, controlled the eunuchs, ordered court theatricals, looked after the kennels where the famous Pekingese were bred, maintained the fabric of the palaces and temples, saw to the court's supplies, tended the palace herds and flocks, paid each Bannerman his honorarium. And attached to these departments were subsidiaries: the palace stud, the imperial armoury, the imperial buttery, the imperial weaving and dyeing office, bureaus to look after the emperor's boats, wardrobe, gardens, game, printing office, library, and silkworms. Schools educated his sons and nephews, the Imperial Clan Court disciplined his relations, and the police bureaux dealt justice to his eunuchs.[1]

This autocrat's anthill, Tz'u-hsi vividly realized early on, was infiltrated and dominated by the eunuchs who were its menials. They had existed originally to safeguard the authenticity of the succession, and, as in all polygamous countries, to guarantee the chastity of the harem and consequently the emperor's honour. From the age of sixteen onwards, eunuchs were Tz'u-hsi's most constant companions and intimate friends. During her own reign two Chief Eunuchs, An Te-hai and Li Lien-ying, were notorious for their presumption of power and the influence and the graft which she allowed them to practise. But in giving them a *sans-gêne* in the palace she was not unique, for eunuchs were treated as invisible underlings, allowed far greater freedom of manner in the emperor's presence than the Grand Councillors themselves, and therefore able to insinuate themselves more poisonously into the currents of intrigue. As Tz'u-hsi had lived outside the Forbidden City until the age of sixteen, it seems that this love of castratis' company, formed in part *faute de mieux*, was also in part genuinely felt. Her love of obedience was flattered by their fawning, and the virility of her character was accentuated by their lack of it.

The acquisition of power by sybaritical women and eunuchs had contributed to the decay of the Ming dynasty. The Ch'ing had therefore introduced laws to curtail eunuch power, had forbidden them to hold office or high rank, to collect rents or be received in audience. The great K'ang-hsi Emperor in the seventeenth century had called them pitilessly 'equivalent to the meanest of insects'[2] and had forbidden the castration of Manchus by statute in 1684. Although none of the restrictions had been waived, by the middle of the nineteenth century eunuchs were again on the rise both in numbers and in powers, and so, the only Chinese with whom the Son of Heaven was consistently in contact were the most ignorant and ignominious class.

Traditionally the emperor had three thousand eunuchs, the princes thirty each, the emperor's children and nephews twenty each, his cousins and the descendants of the Tartar princes who helped Nurhaci found the dynasty ten each. They had been recruited into the palace through the princes who provided five fully trained eunuchs every five years for 250 taels each (about £75); but this method had never furnished enough, and by the reign of Hsien-feng a register had been opened in which the names of candidates were inscribed. That the state had any charms at all seems incomprehensible, but the squalor, misery and abject poverty in which many Chinese lived, combined with their reverence for the emperor, made the lure of his service extremely powerful. Within there were riches, luxury, food in the belly and money in the palm – it was an overwhelming bribe. Often only the knife lay between one form of beggary and another.

For although a palace eunuch was only given ten taels a month and daily rice, he was entitled to a cut on all money that passed through his hands, and jewels, jade, fur, silk, antiques, paintings, vases were sent as gifts and tribute to the emperor in such quantities that a little pilfering, or even a great deal, went by quite unnoticed. Many of these presents were offered by officials to request an imperial audience, and were appropriated by the emperor's Privy Purse, which meant, when Tz'u-hsi was empress, by herself; but a fifth at least went to the eunuchs. Therefore, as they were allowed to leave the Forbidden City provided they returned by sunset, many were able to establish their own houses in Peking from the splendid proceeds of their position. Occasionally they 'married' and adopted children to save face. Sometimes the rôle even became hereditary: a man married, had children, and left his family to become a eunuch; in turn his children married, had children and became eunuchs. Their face-saving devices were necessary because eunuchs were whole-heartedly despised. A common saying was 'he stinks like a eunuch, you get wind of him at five hundred yards'.[3] They were nicknamed 'crows', because of their harsh, high-pitched voices; and they were so sensitive to their mutilation that the mention of a teapot without a spout or a dog without a tail offended them deeply, while, unlike some Chinese men, they showed exceptional modesty when urinating in the street.

The castrations were carried out near the gate of the Imperial City. The operation cost six taels – a derisory sum. The surgeon asked the parents, if the victim were still a child, if they consented; if he were grown up, they asked him if he were certain, just before the descent of the knife or the scissors. For three days afterwards the patient could not drink, but if on the third day he was able to pass water, all was well. The wound then took three months to heal completely. The casualty rate was three to four per cent; retention and incontinence were likely to arise, and a eunuch often suffered from evil-smelling discharges all his life. If castrated young they never became hirsute, and their voices never broke but developed into a rasping falsetto; if castrated after the age of puberty they lost all their facial and body hair and their voices were high, but less of a screech. They became slack-bellied and flaccid, their faces shrunken and wizened, and they suffered from premature ageing. At forty a eunuch looked like a man of sixty.

The family who performed the castrations jealously guarded their hereditary rôle because, while the operation was cheap, they hired out the testicles or sold them back at an exorbitant rate to their client (from whom they had stolen them while he lay unconscious), for at the annual inspections which were carried out in the Imperial City by the Chief Eunuch each one was required to prove himself by producing his remains, bottled and labelled. Also, according to Confucian doctrine, mutilation of the body reflected the imperfection of the spirit. All eunuchs desired to be buried whole, so that their spirit could enter eternal life intact. The same superstition led the relatives of condemned men to bribe the executioner to sew on their victim's head immediately after the fall of the sword, and made the commuting of the death sentence from decapitation to strangulation an act of clemency. A man who offered himself for emasculation forfeited his family and burial with his ancestors – a heavy penalty in the ancestor-worshipping society of China. Eunuchs were therefore buried in their own cemetery outside Peking, and they worshipped in their own temple.

The Chief Eunuch was chamberlain of the household and responsible for the thousands of gardeners, carpenters, cooks, cabinet-makers, painters, glaziers, tailors, laundrymen, scullions, cleaners and sweeps under him. Each eunuch was apprenticed to a master and his eventual success or promotion depended on the favour in which his master was held. On his master's death, a young eunuch might be forgotten in the sluices until the day he himself died, but if he was apprenticed to the Chief Eunuch he might rapidly acquire influence. He could hold one of forty-eight grades, but he was not allowed to hold any official rank higher than the fourth, although Tz'u-hsi raised Li Lien-ying, the favourite of her middle and old age, to the second rank. The post of lama at the ancient occult Buddhist temples in the Forbidden City was coveted, as no vocation was necessary and the temple offerings made it immensely lucrative; and the rôle of actor was also highly desirable, for theatricals, particularly under Tz'u-hsi, were the staple recreation of the court. Eunuchs were in general illiterate; a handful, like Li Lien-ying acquired erudition and posed as scholars. They were often affectionate and gay, but also feather-brained and foolish; they rushed up to ladies-in-waiting after being given an order, for they had already forgotten it, and showed all the characteristics of recidivist delinquents, repeatedly committing petty offences, remaining incorrigible and seemingly impervious to the brutal punishments meted out to them. Everywhere the ruler went, so did an imperial yellow satin bag of birch wands. If a eunuch committed an offence, he was immediately beaten; if he tried to escape he was beaten once, and then, when the scabs had begun to form, a second time; if he tried again, he was put in the Chinese stocks, the *cangue*, a wooden collar which shackled the hands to the neck, for two months; if again, he was banished to Mukden, the ancient capital of Manchuria. If he was caught stealing, he was instantly decapitated.

When P'u-i, the last of the Ch'ing dynasty, decided in 1923 to abolish the office of eunuch altogether, he had them rounded up without warning by troops in one courtyard and driven from the palace. Subsequently they were allowed back in ones and twos to collect their belongings. It was not extreme hard-heartedness that made the last emperor so peremptory: had the eunuchs been given notice they would have picked the Imperial City clean. Only a few months before, when the emperor had asked for the inventory of one of the treasure stores, it had mysteriously burned down overnight; and when one of the wives of a preceding emperor died, her apartments were looted unrestrainedly by the eunuchs, who went unpunished because her spirit would have lost face if the plundering were admitted publicly.

Such venality was increased by Tz'u-hsi's long indulgence of eunuchs' foibles, for as soon as she entered the Forbidden City in 1852, she understood that these her servants were her most useful tools. During her reign the effeminate, homosexual atmosphere of the court increased, although there were no longer a group of painted célestes as there had been under Ch'ien-lung. But she favoured and befriended eunuchs with increasing love because, as her multiplying powers confined her more and more within the lonely barriers of the absolute ruler, she could trust no one wholeheartedly. Any of the princes or officials or ministers might turn against her and bring about her downfall; but the eunuchs, cut off from all social position and family background, were totally dependent on their monarch, and therefore totally loyal. Their fate was bound up in hers and so they became, in her court, her favourite tale-bearers and agents.

But in the 1850s Tz'u-hsi was of course only on the threshold of her later career. From her apartments she may only have caught tantalizing glimpses of the young Hsien-feng Emperor as he was carried past on his palanquin, or of the emperor's gifted brother Prince Kung, or of the Grand Councillors as they left the morning audience. She only eavesdropped on palace gossip about affairs of state, and frustratingly, day after day, she was ignored among the other girls in his harem, and the gaiety of palace pleasures and pursuits. For Hsien-feng, discouraged by the insurmountable problems of internal rebellion, tricky relations with foreign powers and the depleted treasury he had inherited from his father the Tao-kuang Emperor, was losing himself more and more in his hedonist's Eden, his ring of summer palaces in the hills eighteen miles to the west of Peking. There, he escaped the Son of Heaven's onerous and tiresome responsibilities, boated on his lakes, banqueted in his palaces, wandered among his exotic groves and shrubberies and experienced more orgiastic pleasures than his seraglio of well-brought-up, young and demure Manchu girls could provide. Inspired by the eunuchs' ambivalent sexual leanings, he slipped out with them into the dives of the Outer City, to frequent its bawdy houses and its opium dens, its pornographic peep-shows, its dancers and singers, its transvestite actors, and above all, its forbidden, lily-footed Chinese women.

But Tz'u-hsi, low-ranking concubine as she was, managed to exploit her position profitably. For the first time in her life she had well-stocked libraries within her reach, cabinets of state annals and collections of works of art. Although forbidden to entertain any men intimately or informally, she must at this time have seconded some scholar-official who worked in the palace to interpret the classics to her, to help her improve her calligraphy, of which she was later so proud, and to expound China's history to her, for at no other time in her life did she have either the money or the time to learn the philosophy and historical precedents that formed the basis of her later orthodox genius.

As a young girl Tz'u-hsi would have absorbed the outlook and doctrine contained in the Confucian classics, but now she studied more closely Confucius' collected saying in the *Analects*, the *Book of Odes*, and the *Book of History* which he may have edited, the writings of Mencius, Confucianism's most brilliant and persuasive thinker, and the historical records of the Twenty-Four Dynasties. No distinction existed in China between religious and secular teachings, as between the Gospels and the Ancients in Western philosophy, so that in China scholars were moral preceptors and their works and interpretations had scriptural validity.

The vision in these works that Tz'u-hsi now pored over focused on Heaven, the emperor and the family, all interconnected by an explicit set of duties and prescribed relationships. Heaven (*T'ien*) the force that ordered the cosmos, was no personal god. Although emperors slaughtered animals in sacrifice at the Temple of Heaven until 1915, they were not idolaters, but worshipped an abstract concept of universal harmony in nature. The doctrine of the Mandate of Heaven, on which their rule depended, turned on two of the most attractive aspects of Confucian philosophy: that a good ruler, inspired by *jen* (benevolence) holds the welfare of his subjects closest to his heart; and that this rule, maintained not by force but by solicitude and moral persuasion, is rewarded from heaven by tranquillity and order within the empire. But Confucianism was a pragmatic philosophy of government, and Tz'u-hsi learned rapidly that the emperor's love of his people was underlined, just as was a parent's in the family, by disciplinary threats. Confucius himself had believed in the uplifting and improving values of *hsing* (punishments) and his followers had developed this aspect of his teaching. As in all absolute despotism, few channels of protest were open to the subjects of the Ch'ing emperors and as dissent endangered even eminent officials, the only route was often rebellion, and rebellion was severely and summarily punished. Each of the many revolts that convulsed the rule of the Ch'ing in Tz'u-hsi's day, including the titanic upheaval of the Taiping rebellion, signified the lapse or imminent withdrawal of the Mandate of Heaven, but each time the mandate was fought for and grimly and bloodily retrieved, at Tz'u-hsi's order, for Confucianism also taught, in its practical way, that if a revolt could be crushed, as the mighty Taipings were, such a defeat proved that Heaven did not lend its support.

The fabric of Chinese society was the family, and the sacredness of the parent-child relationship extended after death to become ancestor-worship. *Hsiao* (filial piety) saturated Chinese thought and behaviour for almost two millennia. Parents were honoured, loved, obeyed without question, and no consideration for their comfort and happiness was too extreme. The heroes of the *Book of Filial Piety* sleep on icebound lakes to melt them for their mothers' favourite fish, or romp and frolic at advanced ages like children to make their ancient parents feel young again. Families spent hard-earned savings on luxurious funerals, extravagant sacrifices in the ancestral temple, while no present was more handsome than a noble and expensive coffin – even to a living parent. Although the eldest son alone could perform the Confucian rites before the ancestral tablets and daughters were therefore unwanted – many were even exposed to die as infants by the poor – the overwhelming authority that a mother enjoyed over the family could put the instruments of tyranny in a woman's hands. Chinese literature, comic and serious, abounds with fiendish mothers-in-law who torment their sons' wives, with mothers who sap their sons' lifeblood, with grandmothers who hold the family pursestrings in an iron claw. Tz'u-hsi, cavalier as she was about her own parents, and her own father in particular, was excessively punctilious about the ancestors she acquired by marriage into the imperial family, and about observing the correct rules of filial conduct – when it suited her. It suited her admirably, for instance, to exploit later the Confucian doctrine of *hsiao* all her worth, in order to justify the rule that she was to exercise over China for nearly fifty years.

For the Chinese family, hoarding its wealth to consolidate itself, fostering its own interests, a constricted, self-centred, incestuous unit, constituted a microcosm: the bond between parent and child radiated outwards, a model for the relationships between friends, colleagues, officials in the ever-widening circles of the well-defined hierarchy of Chinese society, at whose very core stood the emperor. In the mirror of the emperor the people glimpsed the way, so that the respect he showed his mother (and Tz'u-hsi was to become the mother of an emperor) was the paradigm for the behaviour of all his subjects. The *Book of Filial Piety* declares: 'In order to prevent the people from treating their parents with cruelty, the Emperor first sets an example by showing a dear love to his mother.' For a good son was a good subject, and a good subject mined his natural potential as deeply as he could in the service of his family, the emperor and China. In an eloquent allegory, Mencius unfolded his deep-rooted faith in human beings' fundamental goodness and educability: he describes a mountain, once luxuriant and thickly forested, now bare of trees and grass, not through a defect of its own nature, but through improper care and cultivation. 'Given the right nourishment, there is nothing that will not grow, and deprived of it, there is nothing that will not wither away.'[4]

So, in theory, Chinese society was mobile, and everyone could become, through education and government examinations, a member of the all-important pressure group of scholar-officials or gentry-literati, whose advice was taken by the emperor for the government of the empire. Apart from the hereditary Manchu élite, to whom Tz'u-hsi belonged, inherited office or privilege was unknown. When an Englishman who visited China in the eighteenth century explained that 'a great deal of the legislative body of the [English] nation were entitled to their rank and situation by birth' the Chinese 'laughed heartily at the idea of a man being born a legislator when it required so many years of close application to enable one of their countrymen to pass his examination for the very lowest order of state officers'.[5]

The fluidity of Chinese society was however determinedly regulated by lock-gates called *li*, elaborate and complex rules of conduct or etiquette prescribed as social norms in order to create harmony between man and nature. All official and personal relationships – between ruler and subject, prince and minister, father and son, husband and wife, between brothers and between friends – were formalized, and everyone within the hierarchy was made thoroughly aware and sensitive to the requirements and procedure of his position. All encounters were managed by the book, and the Western stereotype of the inscrutable smiling Chinaman may have developed because, in the many disagreeable clashes with the West over the unequal treaties, the Chinese remained decorous and polite, whatever the foreigners' show of temper. They preferred to avoid the issue rather than flout the exigencies of the *li* and cause the foreigners to lose face by a blunt refusal.

Deep in her studies of this resplendent ideal of a harmonious society, cushioned by the luxuries and ceremony of the isolated court, Tz'u-hsi forgot with amazing speed the world she had known outside. For in practice the Confucian vision was muddied: like Mencius's mountain, China and the Chinese people were untended, unwatered, unnourished, and all their native goodness a withered and barren bed. As a child and a growing girl Tz'u-hsi had been corrupted, seemingly to the point where she could no longer even distinguish between corruption and its opposite: she had seen rank being bought and sold, making a nonsense of the intellectual meritocracy; she had seen the rule of literati become an excuse for incompetent classics professors to bungle the eternal problems that beset China – wars, floods, poor harvests and consequent famine – when specialists were really needed to deal with them; she had seen the people experience the 'benevolence' of the despot in the extortions of his officials, in summary beheadings and cruel punishments for crime. Rebels were suspended in the streets in tiny cages, thieves were fettered in wooden *cangues*, felons bled from weals of floggings, and decapitated heads crawling with flies were spiked and exhibited on the city walls. Tz'u-hsi knew, as did everyone in China, that the Manchus were the ruling class, and the Chinese gentry and literati a self-perpetuating minority, since the peasants could not educate their children either because there was no temple school, or because they could not afford to spare them from the land. She had seen these things before she entered the Forbidden City, but her memories were fleeting, erased by the splendour of imperial life.

From her diligent studies of the classics in the Forbidden City, Tz'u-hsi acquired in her late teens and early twenties a superficial and useful coat of varnish, which for forty years was to serve her ends.

Her command of the well-chosen Confucian platitude or historical cliché could often confound ministers later; and she could always shame someone by outdoing them in the courtesies required by the *li*. But while her memories of squalor, poverty and graft evaporated, her spirit had not been refined by a long formal education in the classics, so she retained, under the veneer of literacy and of learning, the more primitive beliefs in Buddhism and magic with which she had been surrounded in the south and in Peking.

For the sober agnosticism of the Confucian sages was shot through in China by the two great mystical religions, Buddhism and Taoism, which by some gymnastic syncretism the people of China managed to combine, although the three philosophies contradicted each other flatly in many areas. The Buddhists advocated withdrawal from the world, from the family and from materialism; Confucianism enjoined active participation in society and praised material efforts to look after the family. The Taoists believed in the spontaneous expression of instincts untrammelled by education; Confucianism was founded on the belief that human nature needs to be improved by schooling. All three philosophies did however pursue an ideal harmony between man and the cosmic forces of nature, and it was this nature-worshipping but illogical amalgam that gave the streets and the landscape of China that Tz'u-hsi knew when she was young its particular flavour and atmosphere, while the haphazard superstitions countered the inhuman efficiency, the moral sententiousness of much of Confucianist doctrine.

The Chinese countryside was littered with gravemounds, seemingly at random, but in fact placed by careful geomantic considerations of the movements and actions of the *feng shui*, spirits of wind and water; when astrologers foretold a lucky day, the towns were jammed with weddings and with funerals; charms and spells were chanted in every temple; incense curled in the streets; a swarming pantheon of deities and spirits and gods and goddesses presided benignly over most houses and many shrines. Though the peasants and the common people were the most addicted to magic and charms, the emperor himself traditionally consulted astrologers for all his movements, and as high priest of all three religions, united all forces and beliefs, however disparate, within himself, the microcosm. Each year he drew the first furrow, sowed the first seed and reaped the first harvest in the Temple of Agriculture in Peking. When he had performed the rite, his labouring people followed suit. No matter how practical and educated Tz'u-hsi seemed as a young woman she never eradicated her worship of nature, her belief in portents, or her superstitious reliance on fate and the stars.

In 1855, three years after she had entered the Forbidden City, Tz'u-hsi's diligence and patience were rewarded. By the age of fifteen most emperors had produced an heir to the Dragon Throne. But Hsien-feng had only one daughter and therefore his step-mother, his ministers, and his courtiers pressed him unceasingly to pay more attention to his official wives and concubines. Niuhuru, his empress, whom Tz'u-hsi had befriended, had remained barren – fortunately for Tz'u-hsi – so Hsien-feng had to look elsewhere. His step-mother may have suggested Tz'u-hsi, as she had after all selected her herself; or the eunuchs, begged by the impatient girl, may have recommended a meeting; or, as the story-tellers say, Tz'u-hsi was singing to herself in her clear, animated voice an old song from her childhood in Anhwei when the emperor passed her pavilion and ordered the sweet singer to his side.

One day, the Chief Eunuch turned over the jade tablet on which the emperor wrote the name of the concubine with whom he wanted to sleep that night, and finding Tz'u-hsi's name inscribed, went to her apartments, undressed her, wrapped her in a scarlet rug and carried her on his shoulders to the Hsien-feng's bed. There he laid her down and removed the rug. Etiquette required that Tz'u-hsi should crawl up from the foot towards the emperor. In the emperor's chamber and at his door eunuchs were posted. At dawn the Chief Eunuch gathered Tz'u-hsi up again, carried her back to her rooms, and the date of her intercourse with the emperor was registered in a book and authenticated with his seal.

An esoteric Taoist sect had, in the first and second centuries AD, produced many handbooks of erotic lore – *The Manual of Lady Mystery*, *The Secret Codes of the Jade Room*, *The Art of the Bedchamber*, and *Important Guidelines of the Jade Room* – which, disguised as sapient commentaries on a faultless way to good health and long life, describe lavishly and lingeringly and infinitely poetically the art of sex and love. Doubtless, Hsien-feng knew from an early age this elegant and classical pornography and all its hundreds of picturesque variations: 'The Dragon Turns' (missionary position); 'The White Tiger Leaps' (woman taken from behind); 'The Fish Interlock their Scales' (woman on top); 'The Fish Eye to Eye' (lying alongside each other); Approaching the Fragrant Bamboo' (both standing); 'The Jade Girl Playing the Flute' (fellatio); 'Twin Dragons Teasing the Phoenix' (one woman taken by two men simultaneously); 'The Rabbit Nibbles the Hair', 'The Cicada Clings', 'The Monkey

Wrestles', 'The Seagull Hovers', 'The Butterflies Somersault', 'The Blue Phoenixes Dance in Pairs', 'The Rooster Descends on the Ring' were different positions and caresses all prescribed and copiously commentated. But Tz'u-hsi was unlikely to have been shown the books, and was probably, in Hsien-feng's bed, frightened, inhibited and a virgin – highly recommended by one of the Taoist sages, Peng-tsu: 'If a man wants to derive great benefit from intercourse it is best for him to find partners in inexperienced females. He ought to make love to virgins and this will restore his youthful looks. What a pity there are not many virgins available.'[6]

Jaded as he was from the more professional enticements of the capital without his walls, Tz'u-hsi did manage to excite the lethargic Hsien-feng, for in August 1855, Hsien-feng raised Tz'u-hsi one rank to *Pin*. Ostensibly her promotion commemorated the death of his step-mother, Tao-kuang's widow. It also fell however nine months before the birth of Tz'u-hsi's child.

On 27 April 1856 at the Yuan Ming Yuan, the Round Bright Garden, the greatest of the summer palaces, in a pavilion called the Library of the Topaz Wu-t'ung Tree (after the four rare trees with green bark and broad leaves which trumpeted as the wind blew through them), Tz'u-hsi, aged twenty, gave birth to a son: Tsai-ch'un, only male child of the Hsien-feng Emperor. Some chroniclers would have the baby smuggled in or substituted, or fathered by someone else. But Hsien-feng, though not conspicuously virile, was not sterile: he already had his year-old daughter, the Princess Jung-an, by one of his concubines, who later (in 1859) also bore him a son who died in infancy. Tz'u-hsi's mother was raised to the superior Yellow Banner as a reward. After the birth Tz'u-hsi claimed: 'I must say I was a clever woman, for I fought my own battles and won them too. When I arrived at court, the late emperor became very much attached to me. . . . I was lucky in giving birth to a son, as it made me the emperor's undisputed favourite.'[7]

But the emperor, or his advisers, were more wary than Tz'u-hsi later remembered: the mother of Hsien-feng's daughter had been created *Huang Kuei Fei*, concubine of the first rank, while Tz'u-hsi, on bearing the emperor a son, was only dubbed *Kuei Fei*, concubine of the second rank.

Chapter Three

LET THEM HAVE WAR

Hsien-feng, the Son of Heaven, was weary of the continual crises that beset his rule, grateful for his concubine's curiosity and dynamism, her enthusiasm for news and politics, and so at an early stage in their love affair, he let Tz'u-hsi 'classify his memorials'[1] and thus allowed her entry to the nerve-centre of power. His ministers bridled at a woman's interference, and her actions laid the foundations of later schisms; but the eunuchs, the vital go-betweens of the court, were quick to sense the prevailing wind and rally to the new favourite's side.

Tz'u-hsi's ignorance of the world beyond China was profound, and her outlook on foreign affairs echoed the Ch'ien-lung Emperor's haughty rejection of the first British embassy of 1793 under Lord Macartney, when the Son of Heaven had declared: 'There are well-established regulations governing tributary envoys from the outer States to Peking. . . . As a matter of fact, the virtue and prestige of the Celestial dynasty having spread far and wide, the kings of the myriad nations come by land and sea with all sorts of precious things. Consequently there is nothing we lack. . . .'[2]

To the Chinese and to Tz'u-hsi distinctions between Western countries were trifling: in the official documents. Europeans were 'barbarians from the Western Ocean'; in the vernacular they were 'red-haired barbarians', 'big-nosed hairy ones' or 'foreign devils'. In a record of the embassies to China in the Imperial Statutes, the 'country of the Western Ocean' sometimes described Portugal and sometimes I-ta-li-ya (the Papacy), while as late as the middle of the eighteenth century a scholar wrote in a learned work that France was the same as Portugal, Sweden and England were shortened names for Holland, that England was anyway a dependency of Holland,[3] and that the Spanish in the Philippines were the same people as the Portuguese in Macao and Malacca.

Ch'ien-lung had confined the Portuguese to Macao and the British to Canton, where they stifled their keen commercial instincts on a waterfront strip of thirteen warehouses, or 'Factories' – for they were factors or traders. There they had lived since 1757, packed tight, forbidden entry into the main walled city of Canton and permitted only to trade through government-appointed agents.

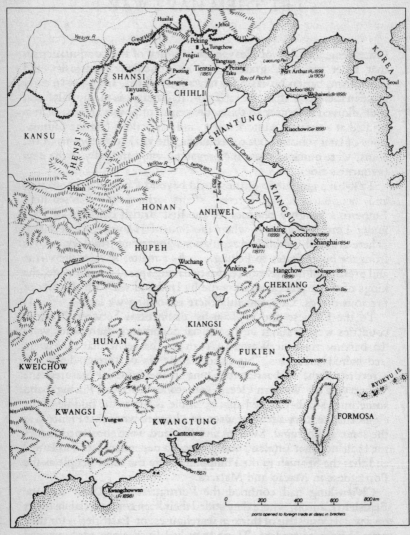

China, showing the treaty ports and the date of their opening; the march of the Taiping rebels to Nanking and then to Peking; and Tz'u-hsi's flight and return, 1900–02

England was an uncharted nonentity; yet when the Tao-kuang Emperor, Hsien-feng's father, had ordered the suppression of the illegal importation and trade in opium by the barbarian merchants at Canton in 1839, and dispatched his commissioner Lin Tse-hu to see to it, England defied the Middle Kingdom to defend the rich trade.[4] In the subsequent Opium War of 1839–42 China was irreparably defeated. The poppy continued to bloom in the fertile British plains of Bengal, to be shipped in junks and illicitly smuggled into the coves and creeks of the Cantonese waterfront, and to provide the bulk of the China traders' wealth. There has rarely been such self-righteousness combined with self-interest as the British mercantile class displayed.

In the 'unequal' Treaty of Nanking of 1842, opium, over which the two countries had fought, was not even mentioned. Four more strategic southern ports were opened to foreign trade and residence: Amoy, Foochow, Ningpo and Shanghai, as well as Canton; Hong Kong was ceded in perpetuity to Great Britain; and trade was made easier in many other ways. By the subsequent Treaty of the Bogue (1843) two momentous clauses were added: the British were given extraterritorial rights, putting their nationals beyond the reach of Chinese law; and in the 'most-favoured nation' clause it was agreed that one foreign power could claim a privilege granted to another. The Chinese sought, through extraterritoriality, to make the British responsible for the behaviour and discipline of their subjects in China, and through the 'most-favoured nation' clause to prevent one power from seizing rights and territory and concessions it would not wish another power to have, and so, through traditional Chinese diplomacy of 'using one barbarian to control another', to play off the traditional rivalries of the seaborne nations. But the practice was to turn out very different, for the first Opium War merely gave the cue for almost a century of unequal treaties.

Some Chinese did become inquisitive about the speck of a country that had humiliated them: in his pithy account of world geography and politics, an official noted in 1848 that while Americans were 'docile, good-natured, mild and honest', and did not have 'the fierce and cruel bearing of birds of prey', the English in India had 'stealthily encroached on the various states like silkworms eating mulberry leaves'.[5] But such well-informed caveats were rare, and when a missionary in the province of Shansi was greeted as His Excellency the Devil in the 1870s by a Chinese official, the confusion was a far more accurate reflection of the climate of combined vanity and ignorance in which Tz'u-hsi was nurtured.[6]

Tao-kuang, Hsien-feng's father, had sought desperately for redress against the injury and decay of his dynasty. He was thrifty, his robes were patched and worn, he had reduced palace spending; he had abolished the annual hunt of the Manchu emperors at their palace at Jehol and so begun the thinning of the warrior strain of his ancestors so marked in his dissolute son Hsien-feng; in 1841, almost at the height of Opium War with Great Britain, he had even reduced military expenditure in the province of Chekiang, near the troublespot of Canton in Kwangtung. His gestures, however ill-considered, were well-intentioned, for in 1835, while the resources of China remained the same, the population had exceeded four hundred millions for the first time.

Since Tz'u-hsi's arrival at court in Peking in 1852, the news from the south had been a chain of unchecked disasters. Myopia prevented the Chinese from grasping the implications of the treaties with foreign powers, but they could not blind themselves to the emergence of a spiritual leader, a member of the Hakka minority group who were treated as pariahs in Chinese society. For in the first year of Hsien-feng's reign, a Hakka peasant, Hung Hsiu-ch'uan, raised his standard in Yung-an, a walled city in the distant mountains of Kwangsi and on 25 September 1851 proclaimed himself T'ien Wang of Taiping T'ien-kuo, the Heavenly King of the Heavenly Kingdom of Great Peace. It was an open bid for the Dragon Throne.

Hung Hsiu-ch'uan's ambitions to become a scholar-official in the theoretically mobile society of China had been frustrated by failures in the local examinations. In 1836, when he was sixteen, he had been proselytized by one of the first Chinese converts to Protestantism and later, after failing once more in the civil service examinations at Canton, he had fallen violently ill, and in his delirium dreamed feverishly of an old man who 'wore a hat', and 'a tall and husky physique' and wore 'a black dragon robe, with a golden beard that flows down to his navel'.[7] Beside him sat a younger man, surrounded by girls of exquisite beauty and by attendants in dragon robes. Before Hung's eyes, Confucius, the sage himself, was bound and flogged as the source of evil teaching. Six years later, Hung rediscovered the Protestant leaflets he had been given and immediately identified the old man with God the Father, the younger man with God the Son, and concluded that he was the brother of Jesus Christ in a newly constituted Trinity, and that he, like Christ, had an earthly mission to redeem the oppressed. He had been taken up into heaven to 'slaughter the imps [the Manchus], tranquillize the people and save the world'.[8]

Hung then converted one of his relations and a schoolmate to the new religion in which he was God; and, on forsaking his native village where his high-handed destruction of Confucian tablets and shrines had scandalized his neighbours, he wandered through the mountains of Kwangsi as a pedlar, and visited Canton, making thousands of converts among the Hakka and Miao aborigine tribes. Members of secret anti-Manchu societies, malcontents, soldiers disbanded after the conclusion of the Opium War with England gathered to the visionary's side. Thus long-standing rebels, like the Triads who wished to restore the Ming, found common cause with Hung's distorted brand of Protestantism, exacerbated the religion's anti-Ch'ing drift and transformed this Peasants' Revolt into a cataclysm.

The Heavenly King founded a programme of radical reform: 'When you have money, you must make it public, and not consider it as belonging to one or another.'[9] The ownership of property was abolished and land was distributed equally, even to women; all money was yielded to a public treasury and administered for the Taiping followers' good; the sick, widowed and orphaned were cared for by the common funds; on the basis of the Christian brotherhood of man, the equality of all was proclaimed. As the Taiping King's followers swarmed through the poverty-stricken province of Kwangsi northwards, the alternative they offered became a powerful temptation. Actors, prostitutes, starving peasants, river porters, runners, the 'mean people' of China, excluded from the examinations by law, and therefore shackled to the bottom rung of the ladder, gathered to the Taiping cause to share in the share-out the rebels offered. As a badge of their revolt they refused to shave their heads and wear the Manchu queue, and therefore became known as the 'Long-Haired Banditti'.

The movement swelled through Kwangsi and spilled into Hunan and by 1853, Tz'u-hsi's second year at court, the rebels began following the course of the mighty Yangstze. They streamed through Hupeh and Anhwei, gathering men until they marched 250,000 strong. In March, with thousands of miles behind them and Wuchang and Anking on the Yangstze in their hands, they arrayed themselves before the walls of Nanking, the huge capital of Kiangsu, the most prestigious city of southern China, and viceregal seat of Liang-kiang, a region which comprised Anhwei, Kiangsi and Kiangsu, three of the empire's most crucial central provinces. On 21

March this revolutionary army captured, after only two days' siege, the strategic citadel and proclaimed it their Heavenly Capital.

At Nanking the Heavenly King disciplined his rabble of followers by the strictest measures in order to stamp out the vices prevalent in the regime he hoped to overthrow. Hung decreed that divination and fortune-telling, soothsaying, astrology and horoscopes were forbidden. He proscribed all opium, tobacco, alcohol and gambling. He segregated the women from the men, so strictly that men who employed women to wash or sew for them in camp were executed. He banned polygamy and prostitution, and punished adultery severely. In 1855 all men were ordered to marry to strengthen the rebels' stake in the future.

But as soon as Hung Hsiu-ch'uan had proclaimed himself the Heavenly King he established, in imitation of the ruling Manchus, a hegemony of his closest disciples and ennobled them with resonant titles: Tung Wang, King of the East, was his political right arm, but there were others – Kings of the North, South and West, as well as an 'Assistant King'. Soon, in spite of the professed equality of men, Hung apparelled himself in imperial yellow raiment, established a court around him as rigid and pompous as the Manchu court in Peking and demanded that he be addressed as Lord of Ten Thousand Years – a title reserved for the emperor. His Kings or Wangs followed his example, wearing motley finery and tiaras and setting up individual courts of their own, whose ceremonies grew more and more elaborate as the movement grew more powerful. The military, the despised dregs of Confucian society, who had carried the rebellion into the Yangstze valley, now became an élite, while craftsmen and traders and camp-followers were treated as the masses. The Heavenly King and his Wangs were not subject either to his laws or to the commandments of their adopted creed, for they soon acquired overflowing harems. Hung himself had eighty-eight wives, according to his son, who himself claimed to have had four at the age of nine. And in Canton the traffickers soon found the Taiping rebels the softest touch for opium in the southern delta.

In April 1853 the Heavenly King launched an expedition north, a throw for Peking itself. While Hung himself stayed behind in Nanking, inspiring the movement by accounts of his hallucinations and trances, his most talented general, Lin Feng-hsiang, then still in his twenties, led the soldiers towards the capital, while another general commanded troops marching in a westerly direction. It was immensely courageous, reckless strategy, these masses of peasant soldiery trooping up through China, harassed constantly by the increasingly panicky imperial armies, wavering once at the Yellow River after a series of setbacks, but then, after appealing to Nanking for reinforcements, pressing gallantly on, until they arrived within twenty miles of Tientsin, a gate to the capital only seventy miles beyond.

The scared eunuchs spread the news breathlessly throughout the court; Tz'u-hsi, an inconspicuous concubine in 1853, heard it; she was angered by their fears and cowardice and ashamed that the emperor even considered reviving his ancestsors' 'Annual Tour of Inspection' and vanishing into safety beyond the Great Wall to his hunting park at Jehol. Hsien-feng's Ministers prevailed upon him, however, to remain in Peking, and order war to the death on the rebels. The Tartar cavalry under the Mongol warrior Seng-ko-lin-ch'in attacked the Taipings unsuccessfully in their position ninety miles from Peking. But the rebels had marched seven months through China, and the weather they encountered in the north was raw beyond the endurance of southerners. As the winter approached they fell back on reinforcements in Shantung, and regrouped themselves. As the cold deepened, and their provisions diminished, they began to flee southwards towards milder weather and gentler pastures. As they straggled, they were cut off and slaughtered by the Ch'ing troops; in Shantung the remaining army joined battle and was massacred. By May 1855, Tz'u-hsi was cock-a-hoop at the news: the last bastion of the Taipings in the north, from which they had refused, after protracted battle, to be dislodged, was forced to surrender by Seng, who had tunnelled under the town's walls and then, by flooding it, literally flushed the rebels out.

In the south, Tseng Kuo-fan, a level-headed, dogged Chinese in his forties who had risen to become a general and scholar from poor peasant origins, had been commanded at the end of 1852 to raise a militia army in his native Hunan and attack the Taipings in their strongholds on the Yangstze river. Tseng's sober and thorough methods of drilling and training his recruits earned him a rebuke from the anxious and impatient capital, but he continued to take his time, preparing and hardening his men, until his Hunanese braves, as they came to be known, were the most streamlined fighting force in the empire. By 1855 Tseng was driving the weakened rebel lines back on to their own capital at Nanking, and through 1855–9, with Tz'u-hsi's new accents winging encouragement from Peking, was laying constant and relentless siege to the Taipings.[10] Some towns like Wuchang on the Yangstze changed hands three times before they were finally secured by the imperial forces. But by 1859 the

Taiping rebels found themselves confined to a riverine kingdom centred on Anking and Nanking in the valley.

Had the Taipings practised the forgiveness and mercy of Christianity they preached as fluently as their foreign exemplars, Nanking and the countryside around might have constituted an inexhaustible treasury of supplies and supporters. But the Taipings were locusts; a marching army on a long campaign, they had foraged as they moved and as often as not their foraging had been pure plunder and rapine, until the farming country through which they passed had become wasteland. The towns on the Yangstze were scarred by capture and recapture; their inhabitants, who often collaborated in order to survive, were stripped, according to the Taiping rule of communal ownership, of their property and livestock, and then lived to see it squandered by management and officials as corrupt as the Manchus the rebels had supplanted. One observer, Charles George Gordon, later Gordon of Khartoum, wrote: 'The people on the confines are suffering greatly and dying of starvation. . . . Words cannot express the horror the people suffer from the rebels, or the utter desert they have made of this rich province ... we are all impressed with the utter misery and wretchedness of these poor people.'[11]

When the bid for the north had failed, the Taipings lost the *élan* of idealism that had swept them to conquer the south, and fell to squabbling and rivalry amongst themselves. In 1856 the King of the East scored a victory against the imperial troops, which immediately unleashed internecine strife in Nanking. The Heavenly King, claiming divine inspiration, ordered the King of the North and the Assistant King to execute the King of the East for his presumption and treachery. He was instantly dispatched and in a bloodbath hundreds of his family, followers and camp were butchered with him. Punch-drunk, the King of the North then turned on the Assistant King, and the Heavenly King's own bodyguards. Hung retaliated promptly by murdering him, and then, fearing further repercussions, banished the Assistant King and concentrated the power in the incompetent and vainglorious hands of his close relatives. Debilitated by their own murderous quarrels, their own greed and intrigue, surrounded and besieged on all sides, the Taiping rebels were ready to be choked to extinction in the once flowering towns of Anking and Nanking, or so Tz'u-hsi and the ministers earnestly hoped in the court of Hsien-feng.

Tz'u-hsi's confidence in the mandate of the Ch'ing did not weaken as the rebels had marched victoriously through China; such unruliness among Chinese subjects merely appalled her. She never imagined the possibility of appeasement, or of investigating and correcting the source of such mighty unrest, and breathed fire, therefore, beside the arrogant Imperial Clansmen and councillors in her husband's court. She knew the countryside in which the Taipings were operating – the Yangstze Valley had been the scene of her childhood – and her familiarity made her indignation all the more fierce. But after 1855, when the Hsien-feng Emperor began to listen to her, her vehemence had yet another target. For 'aggressions from without' were now heaped upon 'calamities from within'.

Throughout the 1850s the West, and in particular the English and the French, confined in their treaty ports, grew more and more restless, and more and more convinced that their nineteenth-century equation – free trade plus Christianity equals 'civilization' – was essential to China. The Chinese and Tz'u-hsi did not agree, and finding foreign demands impudent and unthinkable, they precipitated the fatal wars with the Western Powers that laid in ruins the inalienable and pre-eminent Middle Kingdom Tz'u-hsi had once known. The first English treaty made after the Opium War had come up for revision in 1854, the treaties with France and with the United States in 1856. The approaches that the three countries' representatives made to the imperial commissioner Yeh Ming-ch'en at Canton at that time drew an impolite blank; the envoys, instructed by their governments not to use force, proceeded north, and met even stonier resistance to their request. The merchants in Hong Kong and in the new treaty ports champed impatiently at their restrictions, while in Canton (always a tinder box) the denial of entry into the Chinese walled city, as had been granted by treaty and was allowed in all the other ports open to foreigners, exacerbated the insult of the Chinese silence over the question of treaty revision. A luminous vision hung before the traders: four hundred million Chinese to whom wool and cotton and piece-goods and opium could be sold, four hundred million Chinese beyond the ports, debarred from the benefits of the spinning cotton-mills of Lancashire and the produce of the industrial revolution; four hundred million souls to save. The vision was narcotic: it exhilarated merchants and missionaries alike. The reality, that in 1851 the British had exported to China only £9 million worth of goods of which £6 million worth were in opium, did little to sober them. Yet the remaining £3 million only amounted to half the annual exports of manufactured goods to Holland, a country half the size of a Chinese province.[12] The implication, that the Chinese had no place for foreign goods in their society and no desire for them either was lost on the English: the Chinese millions would learn to need them or be taught to. Alongside the merchants, the French and the Americans shouted for treaty revision. Chinese souls should be free to practise Christianity, both Catholic and Protestant, they demanded. To the general uproar the diplomats added the thorny demand for an ambassador at Peking. As early as 1855 Palmerston was writing: 'The Time is fast coming when we shall be obliged to strike another blow for China. . . . These half-civilized governments such as those in China, Portugal and Spanish America all require a Dressing every eight to ten years to keep them in order. Their minds are too shallow to receive an Impression that will last longer than some such Period, and warning is of little use. They care little for words and they must not only see the stick but actually feel it on their shoulders before they yield.'[13]

On 8 October 1856 the *Arrow*, a small merchant ship owned by a Chinese living in Hong Kong and captained by an Englishman, was preparing to sail for Hong Kong from Canton when she was boarded in harbour by Chinese officers and men who promptly arrested the twelve members of her Chinese crew as pirates and summarily pulled down the flag she was flying. It was the Union Jack. She had been registered in the British colony, which allowed her to fly the British flag, making her British territory and giving her 'residents' extraterritorial rights. The Chinese on board were therefore released from Chinese authority until the British had examined them and handed them over.

The insult to Great Britain's flag immediately galvanized the *Arrow*'s young English captain, who was breakfasting peacefully with friends on another boat nearby and saw the incident clearly throughout. He rushed to his ship, rehoisted the Union Jack and hurried the news to Harry Parkes, the British consul in Canton. Parkes was a devout Christian, a hothead and one of the best Chinese linguists in British government service, for he had arrived in China as an orphan of thirteen to stay with his uncle, the Prussian missionary, Karl Gutzlaff, who had translated the New Testament into Chinese. Familiarity with Chinese had, however, convinced Parkes, in spite of a restive and self-lacerating conscience, that harsh, uncompromising tactics alone prevailed against Chinese obstinacy and vanity. He had a 'habit of *driving* the Chinese' wrote one contemporary, and added, 'I have heard more than one impartial observer speak of his treatment of Chinese officials on certain occasions as having been something "quite frightful"'.[14] In 1856, Parkes impetuously demanded an apology for the *Arrow* incident from the incommunicado and impassive commissioner, Yeh Ming-ch'en, and the immediate return of the prisoners. But to the Chinese, pirates on a Chinese boat only flew a British flag as a cover for their malpractices, and so Yeh refused to surrender the three suspects from the twelve-man crew and even denied that the flag had been flying at all. If he had known, as subsequently turned out, that the *Arrow*'s registration in Hong Kong had expired eleven days before and that therefore she was, in the strictest sense, no longer entitled to fly the Union Jack, Yeh would not have needed transparent lies as ammunition.

By 27 October the forts guarding the entrance of Canton harbour were in British hands in revenge for the series of outrages that Yeh had perpetrated on British pride, and the intransigent and foolhardy commissioner himself was being potted at every ten minutes by British cannon trained directly on his *yamen* or office. In December the Chinese rose in retaliation, set fire to the warehouses and the Factories on the waterfront reserved for foreigners and burned their rich imports to the ground. In spite of the loss the merchants were not entirely dismayed: the *Arrow* affair was fast growing into exactly the kind of stick they needed for a second blow for China. Since the French had heard in July that on 29 February 1856, the Abbé Chapdelaine, a missionary, had been executed at Chinese officials' orders in Kwangsi and his heart cut from his body, cooked and eaten – or so the French press gladly imputed – they too had found a pretext of their own to force the issue of treaty revision. 'The dreadful alliance', as the patriotic Parkes termed it, between England and France was struck.[15]

At first Palmerston's government was defeated in the Commons, so great was the disgust with his policy of a second war with China. But in the spring of 1857, after much electioneering about the horrors of the monster Commissioner Yeh, it was returned with an increased majority and Palmerston could with impunity send Lord Elgin as the British envoy to demand reparation, and if that were denied, to use force to press the question of a British representative's residence in Peking.

Lord Elgin, a son of the Elgin of the marbles, florid-complexioned, corpulent and hoary-headed, had gathered a varied and successful experience of Empire as Governor of Jamaica, and Governor-General of Canada. He looked old for his forty-five years. But the vigour of his mind showed itself throughout the China campaign, ordering imperialist strategy of the most ruthless sort and then spluttering into spleenful recriminations and truculence against himself and his job in his diary.

On his way to China, he was greeted in Singapore with news of the Indian Mutiny. Appealed to by his government, he relinquished the troops that were to support his demands for a settlement in China, and proceeded to Hong Kong, where he impotently kicked his heels, unable to continue north to Peking unarmed. Beset by the Governor of Hong Kong, Sir John Bowring, his loquacious justifications of Parkes's actions over the *Arrow* incident and his demands for vengeance, Elgin exploded in his journal: 'It is clear that there is here an *idée fixe* that nothing ought to be done till there has been a general massacre at Canton.'[16] Baron Gros, the French envoy, dawdled on his way east, further hampering Elgin's plans and freedom of movement, but finally joined him in October. After six months' enforced idleness, Elgin was compelled by Yeh's inflexibility and the merchants' bloodlust to launch an assault on Canton.

On 20 December 1857 the northern part of the city fell into British and French hands, and on 4 January Harry Parkes entered Yeh's *yamen* and found the commissioner scrambling to safety over his back wall. Yeh's incompetence had brought about his own fate; it was sad that it had also provoked China's. For, as Elgin wrote in a letter home: 'I made mild proposals to Yeh with the conviction that if they had been accepted I should have been torn to pieces by all who were ravening for vengeance and loot. But Yeh was my fast friend. . . . nothing would induce him to be saved. . . .'[17]

The first puppet government of modern times was set up to administer occupied Canton under Yeh's successor, with an American, French and British triumvirate in control – Parkes was the British member. Yeh himself, an embarrassing burden to his captors, was sent to Calcutta for want of something better to do with him. A year later he died in exile, having spent his last months composing irrelevant verses. Amongst his things at his *yamen* in Canton, a *planchette* was discovered: its sanguine predictions had probably accounted for Yeh's crass mishandling of the explosive situation. 'He would not fight,' went the Cantonese popular saying, 'he would not make peace, and he would not take steps for defence. He would not die, he would not surrender, and he would not flee. In his pretence at being a minister and a governor there was none like him in antiquity and there is almost none like him today.'[18]

Although the Manchu court in Peking had approved Yeh's haughtiness by decree more than once, it came to recognize his fault: 'The English for no good reason invaded our city of Canton,' wrote the emperor, 'and carried off our officials into captivity. We refrained at that time from taking any retaliatory measures, because we were compelled to recognize the obstinacy of the Viceroy Yeh had been in some measure a cause of the hostilities.'[19]

But Peking still did not grasp the extent of the foreign powers' bid for equality, and still saw them as subversive elements within the state. For the web of anti-foreign struggles in which Tz'u-hsi's first years at court were enmeshed was further complicated by the dangerous attraction foreigners felt for the philosophy of the Taiping rebels. The Taipings' professed Christianity attracted them; and the missionaries were awestruck at their theoretical celibacy, temperance and discipline. In the early 1850s, the West had flirted openly with the rebels under the very nose of the Ch'ing officials who were their hosts and responsible for their safety. Dr Hudson Taylor, founded of the China Inland Mission, commented happily: 'They chanted hymns and doxologies in a very solemn manner ... after which they all kneeled apparently with much reverence... a calm and earnest enthusiasm pervaded the entire body.'[20] Sir George Bonham, Bowring's predecessor as Governor of Hong Kong, sailed up the Yangstze in a British ship to Nanking, soon after the rebels had captured it, to visit them. He recommended neutrality, but his report was warm: 'The insurgents are ... anti-idolaters of the strictest order.'[21] The Chinese were infuriated: foreigners lived in China by the good grace of the emperor, and they insulted him by fraternizing with his enemies. Tz'u-hsi rightly suspected that if foreign governments decided to woo the insurgents at Nanking and were successful, they would have little scruple in fighting for the Dragon Throne on the Taiping side. In her eyes the foreign powers were therefore the equivalent of rebels.

In spite of the fall of Canton the court was not humbled or enlightened, but continued to want the *Arrow* affair treated as a local dispute involving provincial authorities only, so that its repercussions could not affect the whole of China. The Manchus in Peking, and Tz'u-hsi at Hsien-feng's elbow, although aware of many distinctions between the foreigners and rebels, could not eradicate their psychological disdain and consequent feeling that the French and English were flagrant violators of the authority of the Chinese emperor, and that their insistence, under the long shadow of the gunboat, on more freedoms within the empire and for a representative in Peking was a ludicrous impertinence which could never be allowed. Everybody, including imperial princes, made the *kowtow* – the three prostrations and the nine knockings – as a symbol of submission to the Son of Heaven; yet the foreign powers wanted their ruler's ambassador received as an equal. Although the issue between the two countries was clouded by a profusion of demands from both the merchant and missionary lobbies, the crucial clash lay here: the Chinese could not perform mental athletics and accept another power on an equal footing, but the British, in the flush of the great Victorian empire, were going to make them.

The prevarications of the Chinese were therefore of no avail. When Elgin and Gros insisted on making the *Arrow* affair a national matter, and began sailing northwards towards Peking with their fleet, the Chinese made one last attempt to bridle the barbarians: they reproved the two envoys for coming as far north as Shanghai and ordered them to return to Canton to negotiate. But the British and French, with twenty-six gunboats between them, accompanied by the Americans as 'impartial observers' and the Russians who had joined in for the spoils, defied the throne and by May 1858 they lay off the four Taku forts at the mouth of the Peiho, the access to the vulnerable capital only a hundred odd miles up river, where Tz'u-hsi was thundering war to the death on the barbarians into the ear of the somnolent and seedy Hsien-feng, her emperor and lord.

Chapter Four

NOT TO PILLAGE, BUT . . .

On 20 May 1858 the French and English assaulted the Taku forts. The Chinese gunners aimed high and wide, so it only took their attackers an hour and a half to capture and overrun them. 'It was a sickening sight,' wrote the young American missionary W.A.P. Martin, who accompanied the party as an interpreter. 'Trails of blood were to be seen in all directions . . . while the corpses of soldiers were roasting in their burning barracks.'[1] In Peking, the government, horrified at the collapse of their strategic sea defences and at the menacing proximity of the Allied forces, declared martial law; and Hsien-feng, cowed despite the counsels of war from Tz'u-hsi and his ministers, sent two of his highest-ranking Manchu officials to negotiate immediate terms of peace with Lord Elgin and Baron Gros.

Kuei-liang was controller-general of the Board of Punishments, 'a venerable man, of placid and benevolent expression, with a countenance full of intelligence though his eye was a good deal dimmed and his hand palsied from extreme age'.[2] Hua-sha-na, younger at fifty-three, was President of the Board of Civil Appointments, and a Mongol of high military rank 'with a martial air and something of the brusqueness of a soldier'.[3] Yet on arrival at Tientsin on 2 June, these elderly, eminent men were abused and dismissed by the furious French and British negotiators, on the grounds that they did not have seals from the emperor giving them plenipotentiary powers. But officials in China on missions within easy reach of the capital were not normally given seals, and the Americans, who treated the Chinese with pointedly democratic courtesy throughout, ignored the British quibble and accepted the Chinese argument that the emperor alone had plenipotentiary powers and that they, as his emissaries, had direct access to him.

The British negotiations had been entrusted to Frederick Bruce, Elgin's younger brother, and to the only fluent Chinese speakers in the party: Thomas Wade and Horatio Nelson Lay, both of whom were in their twenties. As Lay was working for the Chinese in their customs, his position as interpreter to the British was at the very least anomalous. Lord Elgin himself only saw the imperial commissioners twice, at the opening of the negotiations and at their close.

Even if he had been ignorant of the boorishness, bullying and ill temper of his representatives, he could not be excused, for his diary sings out his sincere horror of yoking China: 'No human power shall induce me to accept the office of oppressor of the feeble.'[4] His tolerance therefore of the brutal manners of his party was an alarming presage of his very Victorian ability to see the moral and practical point of a course of action that was personally repellent to him.

When Kuei-liang and Hua-sha-na returned with a seal that came up to British expectations, Wade and Lay resumed their apoplectic hectoring of the Chinese into submission. The British and the Chinese were equally misled by their habit of empire: the former confused the Middle Kingdom with a colony; the latter confused the makers of the British Empire with domestic rebels. In one contemporary's view, Wade and Lay's facility with the Chinese language made them 'treat the natives . . . with greater rudeness, or, as some would call it, energy, than is usual among other Englishmen in the East of similar social standing. The real cause of this I believe to be partial arrestment of moral development at the boisterous schoolboy stage, owing to a too early acquirement of power among people of a different moral code from that of their own countrymen'.[5]

Kuei-liang and Hua-sha-na had been ordered to come to a 'reasonable and mutually advantageous' peace and 'to agree to nothing detrimental to China'.[6] In the face of Wade and Lay's brashness it was a highly optimistic brief. On 23 June at Tientsin all seemed conceded by the Chinese. Every power except the British had concluded their treaties; as all contained the 'most-favoured nation' clause, they counted on Great Britain to wring the right of residence in Peking and the right to trade on the Yangstze and in the interior from the Chinese for their benefit. On 24 June, Kuei-liang and Hua-sha-na pathetically showed their death-warrants to the Russian and American envoys: if they yielded the two points, their lives were forfeit. They pleaded with Baron Gros to intervene, but Elgin would not be blackmailed: the heart of the matter was the right to have an ambassador in Peking, for nothing else so irreversibly implied the equality of nations. On 26 June, after the English threatened to march on Peking, the Treaty of Tientsin was signed. The right of residence at the capital and of audience with the emperor without the kowtow was granted; free trade in the interior was established; Christianity was to be tolerated and protected (the Chinese feared that if they refused, the foreign powers would ally themselves with the crypto-Christian Taipings); the import of opium was made legal for the first time; more ports were opened to foreign trade and residence; a foreigner was never again to be described in official documents as a Barbarian.

The elderly Kuei-liang, and Hua-sha-na were not executed, although the emperor and his entire court, including Tz'u-hsi, were stunned when they heard that they were going to receive in Peking, in audience, a foreigner who would not kowtow to the Son of Heaven. It was an omen, a potent omen, that the Mandate of Heaven was waning for the Ch'ing, for such lack of respect would demean the emperor and his rule in the eyes of his people. That the concessions over law and trade, religion and territory struck at China's sovereignty more radically and momentously than the refusal of an envoy to prostrate himself was not realized by the Chinese government at that time. One thing only rankled with the weak and dissolute Hsien-feng. Therefore on 22 October in Shanghai Kuei-liang and Hua-sha-na met Lord Elgin once again, ostensibly to fix the new tariffs. But their real business was more sensitive, and they deployed all the political arguments and displayed all their charm and even humility to convince Elgin to waive the right of residence. 'It would be an injury to China,' they pleaded, 'in many more ways than we find words to express,' and would cause 'the Chinese government to lose prestige in the eyes of the people'.[7] They even offered to abolish all tariff duties on all foreign trade altogether for this single concession, and Elgin, in a rush of magnanimity and in emotional exhaustion at the months of wrangling and argument, wavered and agreed. The *principle* of an equal ambassador was upheld, and the ambassador would, it was agreed, be received with all pomp the following year, 1859, when the time came to exchange the ratifications of the treaty; but he would not live, a permanent reminder of humiliation, in Peking, but in one of the treaty ports instead, Elgin conceded because residence in the capital, cut off from a supporting foreign colony, was a daunting prospect. Indeed the new Foreign Secretary, Lord Malmesbury, writing 'Peking would be a rat trap for the envoy if the Chinese meant mischief',[8] echoed the sentiments of the British cabinet, who even lowered the Chinese appointment from ambassador to minister. Their approval of Elgin's gesture was short-sighted, for Elgin had undone at one stroke the two-year-long tussle to break the Middle Kingdom's mighty solipsism. The once-crestfallen court was puffed up again; and the ignorance in which they all slumbered continued and deepened.

A year later, on 18 June 1859, the Chinese gunners under Seng-

47

ko-lin-ch'in, who were manning the Taku forts he had again rebuilt and reinforced, saw eighteen British and French gunboats and vessels appear at the mouth of the Peiho river. Frederick Bruce, Her Brittanic Majesty's new minister to China, and M. de Bourbulon, minister from the Emperor of the French, were arriving with the English Admiral Hope and a small fleet to ratify the Treaty of Tientsin as agreed the year before. The ships turned upstream under the gaze of the Taku soldiers, into direct line of fire from the ramparts. Within six days, eighty-nine of their men had been mown down and over half the landing force wounded, as the British laboured helplessly through the mud-flats before the forts in a desperate and ill-considered attempt to seize them as had been so simple the year before. Four of the shallow-draught gunboats in Frederick Bruce's magnificent escort to Peking were sunk, two were crippled. As he watched the slaughter, the American commodore could not bear his diplomatic neutrality and plunged into help tow back the wounded. Nevertheless, in the opinion of the American party, who had peacefully landed at Peitang north of the Taku forts on the shore in order to travel overland to Peking, as the Chinese had requested, 'without much baggage and with a moderate retinue'[9] the British were 'clearly in the wrong in the whole issue'.[10]

Frederick Bruce, Britain's first minister to China, lacked his brother's consideration and weight, and in 1859 he acted with haste. The emperor had sent commissioners, including Kuei-liang, to Shanghai and invited the envoys to a meeting; Bruce and Bourbulon had refused to see them but sailed on blandly to Peking. Nothing in the treaty the previous year suggested that the treaty powers had any right to travel to Peking up-river in several gunboats; Tientsin, the largest city on the Peiho near the shore was not a treaty port and therefore not open to foreigners; furthermore, after giving the order to attack the forts, Bruce had cut himself off from the admiral of his fleet so completely that he would have been unable to suspend the assault, even if he had wanted to, when he received on 25 June a letter from the viceroy of Chihli, Heng-fu, stating that the Chinese desired the British to follow the Americans' example. Bruce's rash and impetuous attack on the Taku forts that summer blew to smithereens the hardwon settlement of his brother. In England, when Elgin heard, he was 'quite overcome' by 'the dreadful news from China'. He wrote to his wife from Balmoral where he was staying: 'I never closed my eyes last night.'[11]

The court was jubilant at the signal triumph of Chinese arms over the barbarians, and the war party's star, identical with the hawkish

Tz'u-hsi at that time, rose in the ascendant. In order not to lose face the emperor had wanted by a show of force to channel the British and the French into the submissive ways of former tributary envoys. In the case of the Americans he had succeeded, for the United States envoy and his party bumped and ground democratically all the way to Peking in unsprung carts. But their mission also came to grief. The free and republican Americans, who did not even kneel to their own rulers, could perform the kowtow even less than the monarchist Europeans. Ward therefore returned to Peitang without seeing Hsien-feng; there the American Treaty of Tientsin was ratified on 16 August; and in the dynasty's annals, the American envoy was duly inscribed as 'the tribute-bearer Ward'. Bruce and Bourbulon would have obviously suffered the same fate if they had complied with the Chinese, and therefore Bruce's martial ardour was violently criticized, not so much because it had not been warranted as because it had failed.

For nine months the optimism of the Emperor, Tz'u-hsi and their entourage grew, for not a word came from the barbarians. But after nine months of parliamentary debate in England, Bruce was given freedom to proceed, and on 8 March 1860 he and the French minister Bourbulon issued an ultimatum. It included manifold demands for indemnities and for apologies, and declared that the events of the last year had rendered the Shanghai agreement over the question of residence null and void. Bitterly, the viceroy of Liang-kiang, a great Chinese official, lamented: 'He then says, that, although non-residence in the capital was conceded by Elgin, this concession has since been reversed by the Ruler of his nation, in consequence of the fight at Tientsin [sic]. This is a pretext for shifting and changing; but if the other side is at liberty to make alterations, we are also at liberty to make alterations.'[12]

A weary Lord Elgin and a self-pitying Baron Gros set out once again for China. En route, as a portent of disaster to come, they were shipwrecked. Delayed but unharmed, they continued east. In July 1860 they joined their countries' forces in China. For the third summer running, the English sailed up the China coast towards the massive Taku forts.

On 1 August 1860 the French and British landed a force of eighteen thousand men at Peitang on the shore of the Bay of Pechili and fought their way successfully to the ground behind the immense fortified earthworks that straddled the mouth of the river and the seaboard access to Peking. The mudflats and salt marshes which flanked Taku were staked with ironwork *chevaux de frise*, and defended by barrier after barrier of bamboo staves, while a complex of dykes and ditches networked the approaches to the river. Sinking knee-deep into the slime, painfully scrambling their way over pontoons, or when those failed, over ladders held in place by Chinese coolies hired and trained in Canton and brought up north as British auxiliaries, the Allies pressed on, until, by 21 August, the Taku forts had surrendered.

The first to fall, the upper north fort, was taken after fierce and courageous fighting under intensive bombardment on both sides; the slaughter of Chinese within the battlements was appalling: thirty-four British and French were killed in the attack; between twelve and fifteen hundred Chinese in the defence. In some cases the Chinese soldiers had been lashed to their guns by their officers. The French took the second northern fort, and in answer the southern forts both hoisted white flags. Seng-ko-lin-ch'in claimed that shells, hitting the powder magazines in both northern forts, had incapacitated them. He was recalled to Peking, but not disgraced. A more subtle tactic of withdrawing in order to lure on the enemy was adopted, as the unsuspecting Allies, glorying in their triumph – six Victoria Crosses were awarded for the action at Taku that August day – rode cheerfully through the man-high, waving fields of millet and sailed up the Peiho in three gunboats to Tungchow, a small walled town which they reached at the beginning of September and where they hoped to secure a new and reasonable peace.

It was one of fate's ironies therefore that the very day the Taku forts fell to the English and French and opened the way to Peking, Shanghai in the south was held for the imperial Ch'ing against the rebels by British soldiers. The decision of the foreigners to abandon their neutrality towards the Taiping rebellion and to maintain the rule of the Manchus in the south did nothing, however, to lessen the panic and vacillating alarm into which Hsien-feng, his ministers and Tz'u-hsi were thrown when they heard, as they boated and banqueted in the earthly paradise of the Yuan Ming Yuan, that the foreign armies were making straight and victoriously for the capital in the north. Hsien-feng veered violently between thoughts of war and longings for peace. Twenty-nine years old, inebriate and pleasure-loving, afflicted with dropsy in one leg, the Son of Heaven played for time. Kuei-liang was again sent to negotiate at Tientsin, with Heng-fu, viceroy of Chihli, and Heng-ch'i, an eminent and elegant Manchu official, who had known Parkes and other foreigners in Canton.

The English party's mood was blithe. Harry Parkes, who had

replaced Lay as interpreter with Wade, reported to Elgin that as his gunboat steamed up river, the locals 'gave proof of their good will in hauling, entirely of their own accord, at the hawsers or ropes that had occasionally to be landed, and also in bringing fresh fruit and vegetables to the boats'.[13] Bruce's original ultimatum of March was reiterated to the new commissioners: an apology, an indemnity of eight million taels (about £2,600,000) for each power (an increase over the four million taels British and the two million French indemnities of 1858), and of course ratification of the complete and unabridged Treaty of Tientsin. On 2 September the three negotiators capitulated unconditionally.

At Peking proud Manchu diehards, imperial clansmen, had Hsien-feng's ear: Prince Cheng and Prince I, led by the latter's forceful half-brother Su-shun, and Tz'u-hsi herself, whipped up the dithering emperor into a show of courage and decisiveness. Seng-ko-lin-ch'in also hardened his resolve, for he had had a fortnight to nurse his defeat at Taku and to take stock of the Allies' strength. Their force was puny compared to the thousands the Chinese could marshal to their side, and the Allies, thinking peace soon to be concluded, had left heavy artillery and large supplies of ammunition behind them. Also, Seng correctly surmised, they were scared of facing a Peking winter and running short of provisions.

On 6 September the impressionable Hsien-feng rallied and decreed: 'Who could have believed that all this time the barbarians have been darkly plotting and that they had brought with them an army of soldiers and artillery, with which they attacked the Taku forts from the rear, and having driven out our forces, advance upon Tientsin? Once more we ordered Kuei-liang to go to Tientsin and endeavour to reason with them, in the hope that they might not be lost to all sense of propriety. But these treacherous barbarians dared to advance their savage soldiery towards Tungchow and to announce their intention of compelling us to receive them in audience. Any further forbearance on our part would be a dereliction of duty to the Empire, so that we have now commanded our armies to attack them with all possible energy.... Hereby we make offer of the following rewards: for the head of a black barbarian [the British Sikh troops], 50 taels, and for the head of a white barbarian, 100 taels. Subjects of other submissive States are not to be molested, and whensoever the British and French repent them of their evil ways and return to their allegiance, we shall be pleased to permit them to trade again, as of old. May they repent while yet there is time.'[14] Ignorant warmongers were not the only Chinese delighted at Hsien-feng's declaration of war. Wen-hsiang, a leading and sober statesman, commented: 'We received an edict urging the army to exterminate the enemy. This was proclaimed in the capital and in the provinces, and court and countryside rejoiced equally.'[15]

On 7 September, the emperor followed his decree by instructing Kuei-liang at Tientsin that the added demands of the treaty powers could no longer be entertained. One cannot, he said, give 'gifts', 'while one's face is ashamed',[16] and anyway, the vast indemnity could probably not be raised in the exhausted country. He again expressed the fear that the powers would join the Taiping rebels and suggested that Tientsin might become a treaty port in exchange for the right of residence in Peking. Above all he voiced the indignation felt by the Chinese, a race who revered persuasion and discussion above all else, when treaties were continually exacted from them at the muzzle of a gun.

The commissioners twisted and turned and finally admitted they did not have the powers necessary to sign the new peace. Elgin, plunged ever deeper into the nightmare evasiveness of Chinese diplomacy, ordered an immediate march on Peking. The French and British swept forward with a speed that dazzled the Chinese, and reached Yang-tsun, thirty-two miles from the city walls, without a single incident. The court in fury and terror relieved Kuei-liang and Heng-fu of their task and appointed ever grander Manchus to negotiate: Mu–yin, President of the Board of War, and Prince I, the emperor's first cousin, 'a tall, dignified man with an intelligent countenance, though a somewhat unpleasant eye'.[17] The emperor granted them special and newly cut seals proclaiming 'Prince, Imperial Commissioner'. Everything, the new commissioners wrote soothingly to Elgin on 11 September, was a mere misunderstanding, and could be satisfactorily settled if the Allies would only retreat to Tientsin. Elgin retorted that he would advance to Tungchow, only twelve miles from the capital, with access both by land and by canal to Peking. Prince I angrily rebuked him for his rudeness and disobedience to an official of such exalted rank as himself, and reminded him that Seng-ko-lin-ch'in and his forces lay between the allies and Tungchow.

The pitch of the court still screamed from one end of the peace register to the other, where Tz'u-hsi pleaded for war. But Hsien-feng was ill and frightened, and he longed, as he had done when the Taiping rebels reached Chihli in 1853, to run away and skulk at Jehol, his summer palace and hunting park north of the impregnable Great Wall. Seng-ko-lin-ch'in advised it, probably because once the emperor was out of reach he could pursue a more consistent policy on the battlefield. But Tz'u-hsi, exasperated at Hsien-feng's cowardice, echoed the views of many officials, whose memorials began to besiege the sick and unsteady emperor and beg him to stand firm. Almost as Hsien-feng was packing his bags, he also gallantly announced that he would lead his armies in person, but that the battle would be staged north of the city, not south where the Allies were actually encamped. It was all a pretence: he merely wanted to slip over the Wall. Remonstrations poured in. On 12 September, the President of the Board of Civil Office, with forty others, informed the emperor that he should stay in Peking for the safety of the empire; twenty-six other officials urged him to remain if only to save face; a prominent censor, and seventy-four other mandarins put their names to a lengthy, well-argued and outspoken memorial, which criticized the Son of Heaven bitterly. 'Will you cast away the inheritance of your ancestors like a damaged shoe? What would history say of your Majesty for a thousand years to come?' Interestingly none advocated aggression, but all advised a strong defensive stand, comparing the menace favourably to the Taiping advance of 1853. The Taipings had made a bid for the Mandate of Heaven; the foreigners had not, for unlike the court (and unlike Tz'u-hsi) these officials had clearly noticed that 'the barbarians who have come far from across the ocean have hitherto shown that their object was only to trade ... not to take possession of the country, nor have they attempted any conquest of China'.[18]

Elgin ordered the armies to press on; as hoped, the Chinese capitulated once more. Although Elgin's stock of optimism might well have been exhausted by now, he was again happy. But when he reported to London that the Chinese had 'conceded unconditionally', he failed to give proper weight to their proposals that, while ratifications would be exchanged at Peking, Elgin and Gros would travel with a 'small armed guard' only, and leave their forces behind them. Elgin, who must have been aware that marching on the capital, however peacefully, might rock the weakened dynasty, proposed instead that the Allied armies should advance to Chang-chia-wan, four miles from Tungchow, and that he and Baron Gros should be escorted by one thousand men to Peking, where he would deliver Queen Victoria's letter to the Hsien-feng Emperor in person.

The commissioners struggled doggedly with Parkes and Wade but when, on 13 September, they yielded, Peking disagreed; the war party was given its head; Seng began mobilizing. On 18 September, Harry Parkes and Henry Loch, Lord Elgin's private secretary, rode off to Tungchow to make last-minute arrangements about transport and accommodation for the embassy in Peking. On their way back, as they passed through the site of the Allies' future camp at Chang-chiawan, they glimpsed the fluttering of Manchu banners and heard the movements of troops, the whinnying of horses and the creaking of gun-carriages concealed in the millet. One of the commissioners, Heng-ch'i, was taken aback at the appearance of Chinese soldiers, but when Parkes angrily demanded an explanation, Prince I and Mu-yin informed him curtly that until the added question of Queen Victoria's letter was settled 'there must be war'.[19]

Harry Parkes and Henry Loch spiked a white handkerchief on the lances of one of the Sikhs in their escort as a flag of truce and rode the gauntlet of jeering and turbulent soldiers who surrounded them. Hsien-feng's bloodthirsty decree had already been proclaimed and there was therefore a handsome price on the heads of the British party. A Chinese officer, seeing the makeshift flag, offered to take them to Seng-ko-lin-ch'in for a safeconduct. Seng, however, when they reached him, was in no mood for diplomatic niceties. Flung face down in the mud before him, the Englishmen were berated for causing so much trouble and war, and when Parkes requested a pass, Seng's 'only reply was a derisive laugh and a torrent of abuse'. Seng taunted them: 'Were they not content with attempting to impose conditions which it could have been derogatory for the dignity of the Emperor to accept?'[20] Ankles and wrists bound together, and arms tied behind their backs – the punishment for 'rebels' – Parkes and Loch were hustled into wooden carts, and sent to Peking. In the carts they found two more prisoners – both French. In all, at the orders of the proud Prince I, the Chinese took twenty-six British and thirteen French prisoners that day.

At the first large Chinese camp they reached, Parkes and Loch were forced to their knees, searched and stripped of their papers and ornaments. From the Chinese abuse Parkes realized – Loch could not speak the language – that because he had conducted the nego-tiations and had shown himself intimately acquainted with China's affairs, the Chinese overestimated his authority, and imagined that he ranked as high as their own negotiators and could therefore give orders to stop the advance and modify the terms of the peace. At one moment the Chinese seemed on the point of executing them, but Parkes and Loch were naturally more valuable to them as hostages, and they were therefore spared and bundled once more into carts which rattled on towards Peking. Bound from head to foot, they were tossed helplessly about the unsprung vehicles; each jolt of the uneven road hurled them against the wooden sides; the heat of the day beat on them like a fist; they were refused water, and the Chinese guards chaffed at the miseries. Loch wrote that had it lasted, they would have died of the journey. At Peking they were thrown into the stench-filled, unsavoury prisons of the Board of Punishments. There Parkes was seized by the hair and ears, and forced to the ground:

'State the name of your headman,' demanded his inquisitors.

'Which one do you mean,' replied Parkes, 'the Ambassador, General or Admiral?'

'You have no such functionaries. Do not presume to use such titles.'[21]

When Parkes gave their names in Chinese, he was ordered to give them in English. When the clerks could not transcribe them, he was angrily told to revert to Chinese. When Loch protested he could not understand his gaolers' questions, he was beaten. Finally both of them, loaded in chains, were led to separate gaols. In Loch's quarters 'about forty half-naked, savage, villainous-looking fellows as I ever saw in my life . . . criminals of all descriptions, murderers, thieves, etc.'[22] were imprisoned. Only half of the prisoners were chained to the wall, and the others were kind to Loch, making room for him to lie down, covering him with a vermin-ridden rug when he shivered, wiping the weals under his fetters carefully each day to prevent them festering from a deadly maggot indigenous to Chinese gaols.

At Changchiawan, meanwhile, a sharp battle broke out between Seng's army and the British and French, who fought all the more fiercely and determinedly when the disappearance of their men was discovered. Although the Chinese outnumbered them five to one, they handled their old-fashioned artillery so clumsily compared to the dexterous and well-equipped Allies that they were swiftly and decisively driven back towards Peking, to a bridge at Palichiao, a village only a few miles from the capital. There the struggle concentrated on the bridge, held valiantly by the Chinese, while behind the Allies, the town of Changchiawan was officially yielded up to loot, ransacked and destroyed. For seven hours the Chinese fought with the coolness and tenacity under fire at which Westerners always marvelled, but their outmoded gingals and matchlocks could do little against the French superior artillery. Chinese casualties were very high, and even the general in command of the action, Sheng-pao, had his jaw blown off. In revenge he ordered the execution of foreign prisoners. Two men were beheaded on the bridge: a French priest, the Abbé de Luc, and Captain Brabazon of the Royal

Artillery. Their bodies were flung into the canal, and never recovered.

The remaining prisoners taken on 18 September, including the correspondent of *The Times*, the head of a French scientific mission, and an attaché to Bruce's embassy, were first taken to the Yuan Ming Yuan, the main summer palace, where the Emperor and Tz'u-hsi were holding court, and then split into four groups and imprisoned. One of the captured Sikhs who survived the experience later reported that he and eleven others were tied up with ropes wetted to contract them further. If they spoke their mouths were stuffed with mud. For three days and three nights in the sweltering September weather, they were abandoned without food or water or shelter. The hands of Lieutenant Anderson, one of the prisoners, burst open from his bonds, exposing his wrists to the bone. When his fellow prisoners tried to approach him to help him, they were kicked away by the guards. The worms began to crawl in his wounds, and he died in delirium. The *Times* correspondent and the attaché also perished. In all thirteen men were 'barbarously murdered'.[23]

With the bridge at Palichiao in their hands, the Allies could march straight on Peking. Or so it appeared to the majority of Chinese, who, from the emperor down were in blind terror that the invaders were bent on seizing the Dragon Throne for themselves, whatever experienced officials said to the contrary. Hsien-feng refused to listen either to the men who urged him to stand fast because the foreign powers only wanted to trade or to the Imperial Clansmen who spoke out for continued war. On 22 September a higgledy-piggledy train of sedans, chairs, carts, baggage, animals and eunuchs scrambled out of the summer palace and headed for the hills and for the Great Wall, beyond which lay Hsien-feng's haven and goal, the palace of Jehol. Tz'u-hsi, shamefaced and furious at the emperor's cowardly flight, was forced to travel with the rest of his household, for she could not abandon her child and Hsien-feng would not leave him in Peking as hostage to the unruly barbarians. Her angry protests over the exodus to Jehol marked the end of her reign as favourite, for her company from then on only reminded the emperor of her outspoken contempt and of his own weakness.

A few days later Elgin was informed that 'His Majesty the Emperor is obliged by law to hunt in the autumn'.[24] The message came from Prince Kung, the emperor's younger half-brother, who had been left in charge of the capital and of the negotiations. In 1860 Prince Kung was twenty-seven years old, slight, almost effeminate, with a small face, an arresting glance and dramatically hooded eyes. His right cheek was 'blemished by cicatrices, close together, apparently the mark of two small boils'.[25] The missionary W. A. P. Martin described him, 'lank in figure, swart in complexion, and so nearsighted he appeared to squint, Prince Kung was not a handsome man'. But he was 'kindly and gracious in demeanour, and his rapid and energetic utterance made an impression of independent strength'.[26] His mother had brought up Hsien-feng when the latter's own mother had died, and the two boys had been very close as children, but Tao-kuang had nominated his less able son his successor. Prince Kung was the first statesman in China to grasp the essential in dealing with foreigners: that they abided by the limits of the treaties, once these had been agreed, and that by enforcing them, the Chinese could co-exist with the Western powers. At Tz'u-hsi's side, he was to become the key figure of the next decade and more of China's history, serving her and his country diligently and selflessly. His personal seal, his own signature, was inscribed 'No Private Heart'.[27]

In the Peking abandoned to Prince Kung, the Chinese, panic-stricken at the desertion of the Son of Heaven, fled like men on volcano slopes before engulfing lava. Unless they had travelled to the treaty ports or met an intrepid missionary, few of them had ever laid eyes on a 'big-nosed hairy one', and the accumulated folklore was ghoulish. Chinese officials had also abandoned their posts: 86,000 troops roamed wild in the streets, without orders and without pay. When Wen-hsiang, the gifted and loyal Manchu who had signed one of the memorials pleading with Hsien-feng to remain in Peking, went to see the soldiers on the city walls on 22 September, he 'discovered that for several days the garrison troops had not received their rations and that their weapons were entirely inadequate. Our general position was about to collapse. Matters were so urgent that ... the only thing I could do was to open up the storehouses and distribute the money and rice, leaving the memorial until later'.[28]

In the correspondence that passed icily to and fro between Lord Elgin and Prince Kung, the latter showed the British envoy at first all the Chinaman's traditional scorn. He referred to Elgin as a 'subject' and told him to mend his language. Until 5 October, the Allied army waited at Tungchow for supplies and ammunition, yet the disorder prevailing upon the Chinese was such that they did not take advantage of the Allies' delay. Prince Kung and Lord Elgin merely battled over the question of the prisoners. They were, the prince knew, trump hostages, and he was playing them for all he was worth. But Elgin refused to be drawn, and reiterated his threat: if the prisoners were not returned, he would destroy Peking. Prince Kung could not know that the menace was empty and that the English general, Sir Hope Grant, was aghast at the thought of breaching Peking's massive walls with his light guns.

On 29 September, Parkes and Loch were transferred, at Prince Kung's orders, to better quarters together. But he did not surrender them; and the other less important prisoners continued to suffer torments. As the court drew safely further and further from Peking, its bravado grew more resounding. From the fastnesses of the mountains, Hsien-feng grandly decreed: 'I command all my subjects to hunt them down like savage beasts. Let the villages be abandoned as these wretches draw near. Let all provisions be destroyed which they might secure. In this manner, their accursed race will perish of hunger like fish in a dried-up pond.'[29] Imperial Clansmen like Prince I and Su-shun wanted the hostages' deaths, because then war would be inevitable, and all would unite against the common enemy. Also, the Chinese continued to feel deeply injured because, as Prince Kung wrote to Lord Elgin, treaties negotiated 'in the presence of an armed force' led to a certain 'insecurity of peace'.[30] The indemnities were now so exorbitant that they almost cancelled out the revenue from foreign trade, which China had never wanted in the first place. Moreover there was no guarantee that, if the prisoners were returned, the Allies would be true to their word, ratify the treaties and depart peacefully.

By 7 October, Prince Kung had every reason to doubt it. For on the night of 6 October the French army outdistanced the British and stumbled on the Yuan Ming Yuan and the complex of faery palaces of the emperor of China. K'ang-hsi, the great Ch'ing emperor, had begun building the 'Round Bright Garden' in 1709; after riding one day, he had come across the ruins of a Ming prince's garden about eighteen miles from Peking. Since then all his successors had continued to adorn and increase the wonders and the numbers of the pavilions and palaces and temples of this enchanted garden. Scarlet and golden halls, miradors, follies and gazebos clustered among artificial hills and lakes in the Imperial Hunting Park, the Jade Fountain Park, and the Round Bright Garden, the Yuan Ming Yuan itself. Tranquil tracts of water were filled with fan-tailed goldfish with telescopic eyes, and covered with lotus and lily pads; a super-abundance of flowering shrubs and trees luxuriated in the gardens; antlered deer wandered through the grounds; ornamental ducks and rare birds nested on the lakeside. One of the Jesuits, Père Attiret, whom the Ch'ien-lung Emperor had employed in the eighteenth century to embellish his summer palaces, wrote in a letter home in 1743: 'Here is represented a natural rustique landscape, a kind of "solitude" rather than buildings constructed according to the principles of symmetry and equipoise. . . . Each one of these palaces seems to be made after some strange model, almost au hasard and not one piece seems to be made to match another.'[31] To contrive something so perfectly that it looked accidental was the aim and acme of Chinese art, reflecting the Taoist love of natural spontaneity, and yet the Confucian belief in man's ability to improve on nature.

When the French found themselves in this Eden in 1860, they became possessed of a joyous, wanton, omnivorous greed. Prince Kung and his mother, the widow of Tao-kuang, who were still living there, only just managed to escape in time to a nearby village. Fighting briefly with a few courageous eunuchs and killing two of them, the French plunged into the palaces: 'Officers and men seemed to have been seized with a temporary insanity: in body and soul they were absorbed in one pursuit, which was plunder, plunder.'[32]

The French general assured the British when they arrived the following morning that he had expressly forbidden looting. Yet as he led them through the golden, richly carved halls of the central buildings towards the emperor's own quarters, where jade and silver *cloisonné*, enamel, ornaments, paintings, embroideries and all manner of exquisitely worked bibelots had been left intact by the fleeing court, his officers calmly helped themselves. 'Gold objects and watches and small valuables were whipped up by these gentlemen with amazing velocity,' wrote one jaundiced Englishman, 'and as speedily disappeared into their capacious pockets.'[33] The English were restive with envy: 'The French camp was revelling in silks and *bijouteries*. . . . One French officer had a string of splendid pearls, each pearl being the size of a marble . . . others had pencil-cases set with diamonds; others watches and vases set with pearls.'[34]

But the next day the British were placated, for 'the General now made no objection to looting.'[35] Anything that could not be taken away was wilfully destroyed: even the British chaplain, the Rev. M'Ghee, accompanied by a friend whom he diplomatically left nameless, enjoyed himself hugely, and reported: ' "What is this?" said S, "Gold is it not?" taking up with some little difficulty a deity about two feet high. "Gold, my dear fellow, do you think gold is so plentiful in China that they have golden gods in a remote temple like this, where anyone might carry them off?" "It's precious heavy then," he said, "if it is not gold, let us smash him and see"; and down went the divinity, with a heavy thud on the marble floor, but no sign of a smash in him. "I'm sure it is gold" said S. "Bring it home then" said I, laughing.'[36]

Two days after the ransack of the Yuan Ming Yuan, Prince Kung released Parkes and Loch and other prisoners. The remaining survivors trickled into the Allied camp during the following week. Prince Kung tried to pass over the dead: 'A certain number were missing after the fight or have died of their wounds, or of sickness.'[37] Their bodies, disfigured by the quicklime in which the Chinese had buried them, were also surrendered. In the same dispatch, Prince Kung complained frostily of the looting of the Yuan Ming Yuan and refused to yield the southern gate of Peking to the Allies, as the pledge of good faith they had demanded. It must have been fear of further reprisals that moved Prince Kung to free Parkes and Loch, for Heng-ch'i, the ex-commissioner who visited the prisoners many times, told Parkes soon afterwards that Prince Kung, hearing through spies that the bloodthirsty clique in Jehol had prevailed and that an order for their decapitation was on the way, set them free a quarter of an hour before the decree arrived.

Lord Elgin insisted on the surrender of the gate, and China was hardly in a position to refuse. On 13 October it was duly conceded, to the relief of the Allied commanders; a date for ratification was fixed; the enormous indemnity was collected from the stricken country and paid to the conquerors. That might have sufficed, but Lord Elgin by this time confused diplomacy with the Old Testament: deeply distressed by the deaths and treatment of the prisoners taken under a flag of truce, he wanted 'to mark by a solemn act of retribution' the Allies' 'horror and indignation'.[38]

Razing the Yuan Ming Yuan to the ground was an excellent idea, given Elgin's premise. He had pledged himself not to destroy the city of Peking; if he pressed for the punishment of the men responsible, like Prince I and Seng-ko-lin-ch'in, he would most probably be offered scapegoats; but the destruction of the emperor's favourite dwelling place would strike at him directly and not at his innocent people; also, some of the prisoners had been incarcerated at the summer palace, and to destroy the scene of their sufferings would only be fitting.

When Elgin reported his reasons to the Foreign Secretary in London, he glossed over the wholesale looting that had taken place beforehand – which a conflagration would so effectively conceal – and did not even mention the official public auction that had taken place in the British camp. 'As almost all the valuables had already been taken from the place,' he said, 'the army would go there, not to pillage. . .'.[39] A trifle sanctimoniously, in view of the French behaviour, the politic Baron Gros refused to co-operate: 'In the eyes of Europe,' he wrote 'the glory will be ours in this business.'[40]

The British army was ordered to destroy the Yuan Ming Yuan, the emperor's summer palace. But there was some confusion, for the Yuan Ming Yuan was only one palace within a spacious complex of several gardens, and yet on 13 October the British soldiers were deployed throughout the area cradled by the Western Hills. Systematically they set fire to over two hundred pavilions, halls and temples, in the grounds of five palaces, which, to the Chinese, were distinct from the Yuan Ming Yuan. The Imperial Hunting Park and the Jade Fountain Park were utterly consumed, for the delicate woodwork burned easily and fiercely; the 'European' palaces designed by the Jesuits stood north of the Round Bright Garden. Built of stone and marble, they withstood the blaze more bravely, to leave, in crumbling drifts of masonry, signs of former splendour to later generations. Some marble pagodas and a few stone bridges survived, especially in a garden palace a little distance away called the Garden of Clear Rippling Waters, where Tz'u-hsi was later to build her own New Summer Palace.

The great fire spread through the lovely woods and shrubberies and buildings, and rose in a shroud of grey and black ashes to be carried by the westerly wind towards Peking, until, an omen of discord in heaven, it hung over the city, and settled in the hair and eyes and clothes of its inhabitants. Charles George Gordon, who had volunteered for the China expedition, was then a captain in the Royal Engineers. He wrote home: '[We] went out, and, after pillaging it, burned the whole place, destroying in a Vandal-like manner most valuable property which would not be replaced for four millions. We got upward of £48 a-piece prize money before we went out there; and although I have not as much as many, I have done well.

'The people are civil, but I think the grandees hate us, as they must after what we did to the Palace. You can scarcely imagine the beauty and magnificence of the places we burnt. It made one's heart sore to burn them.'[41]

As the pall of ashes settled on the city, the Russian envoy, Ignatiev, who had been buzzing noisomely around Peking for a year as an 'impartial observer', persuaded Prince Kung that the burning of the summer palaces signified that the French and English were not going to leave as they had promised and that China would therefore need the military support of Russia. Prince Kung, disorientated by the horrors of the last few days, gave in to the envoy and signed the Sino-Russian Treaty of Peking on 14 November 1860. In it he ceded the Amur lands in the north which the Tsarists had already seized, the whole of the Ussuri east of them on the borders of Korea, and the crucial Chinese port of Haishenwei, which had been already stocked with likely Russian inhabitants the year before and rechristened: Vladivostok.

Hsien-feng, who had reached Jehol on the same day as the Yuan Ming Yuan had been consumed in flames, beat his breast before his people and begged heaven's forgiveness for not taking his own life after bringing such shame upon his office and his ancestors. When the news reached Jehol that the summer palaces had also been destroyed, his anguish grew intolerable.

Prince Kung, having at last bade farewell to Elgin and Gros, wrote from Peking, that in his opinion. 'All the barbarians have the nature of brute beasts'.[42] Tz'u-hsi must have heartily endorsed his view. She was learning the ways of the foreigners who were to play such a part in the events of her future reign.

Chapter Five

UTTERLY CONTRARY
TO OUR WISHES

In 1860 at Jehol, Hsien-feng, twenty-nine years old, was dying. The news of China's consent to all the Powers' terms, of a fresh onslaught of the Taiping rebels into the countryside around Nanking, of the sack and destruction of his summer palaces and of his personal humiliation, inspired in him a despairing, prolonged debauch of women, drink and drugs – for pleasure and for relief of the pain of his illness. Scarcely able to stand through the palsy that swelled his leg, he plunged into lavish and spendthrift ceremonies, and was vilified in the capital for his squandering at the time of his country's need.

The palace at Jehol had been built by K'ang-hsi and Ch'ien-lung in their own dramatic and harsh northern landscape as an alternative summer retreat to the Yuan Ming Yuan. In the hills and forests around they hunted tiger, boar and deer, and afterwards returned to the pleasure-gardens of the walled palaces, scattered over the terrain in several pavilions and lakes on the same paradisical lines as the devastated summer palace.

Ironically, by 1860 the palace at Jehol mirrored the deterioration of the emperor and of the dynasty. It had not been inhabited for forty years, since Tao-kuang in his thrift had abolished the annual hunt of the Ch'ing emperors. Weeds grew on the marble terraces; the gold and vermilion paint was peeling. As Hsien-feng lay in the seedy and decaying halls, yielding himself up to illness and death, he let slip the reins of power further into the hands of his older Manchu kinsmen, Prince I, one of the commissioners the Anglo-French party met, Prince Cheng, and the most dominant personality of them all, the volatile, talented and unscrupulous Su-shun.

Factions within the court evaporated once they were safely out of the Allied armies' reach, and all endorsed a policy of war, accusing Prince Kung of betraying his country by appeasement. Though Tz'u-hsi was of the same mind, her stand over the emperor's flight had disgraced her; she was excluded, ignored, reduced to needle-work, gambling and tittle-tattle with the other court ladies. The eunuchs were her only informants, and she saw the emperor dist-antly, at court ceremonies.

Some of these took place in the lamaistic Buddhist temples, huge, fortified, towering, brickwork monasteries that clung to the crags of the Lion Valley in which Jehol was situated. There the esoteric and mystical rites of the lamas were performed. Although the Forbidden City at Peking also included a lamaistic temple where eunuchs officiated, it did not dominate the palace there as these massive warrens with their hundreds of *bonze* inmates did the palace at Jehol. The arcane, superstitious atmosphere might well have made a profound impression on Tz'u-hsi at this precarious moment of her life, laying the foundations for her later Buddhist credulity.

It was evident that her love affair with the emperor was irrevocably over. On her side it had always been opportunist, or at best, fatalist, even though, till the end of her days, she wept copiously and dutifully on the anniversary of his decease. But if she had little feeling for Hsien-feng in life, her pride was sorely hurt; and then, gossip reached the emperor that she flirted with the Manchu guards who had accompanied the court.

Jung-lu, twenty-four years old in 1860, was a vigorous soldier of the superior Plain White Banner, with an ancestry of fighters from the mountains behind him, who sidestepped the Chinese examination system to win high honours in the military field. He was tall, dashing and handsome, a real Tartar, 'the Alcibiades of China';[1] he had known Tz'u-hsi from her girlhood; there was even a rumour that they had been betrothed.

Although Tz'u-hsi's child was the only son, primogeniture was not Ch'ing law. The succession was conferred at the reigning emperor's discretion on anyone of the imperial line, as long as he was of the younger generation who alone could perform the prescribed rites at the ancestral tablets. Hsien-feng could, if he so desired, nominate as his heir apparent any of his brother's sons. But the child he had by Tz'u-hsi was nevertheless the most likely to succeed, and the Manchu princes, Hsien-feng's cousins, established possession of the boy, closed ranks around the sickening emperor. Tz'u-hsi in torment drew herself closer to Niuhuru, the gentle empress, and if their relationship had not been fast till now, she tightened it then and there, pointing out that their insecurity was mutual, for an imperial child might be 'adopted' by another wife or concubine of the emperor, as Hsien-feng himself had been by Prince Kung's mother, but not by anyone as distant as the wife of a cousin. The position of all the emperor's wives was therefore precarious, she continued, and their prospects were bleak, if not brief. Su-shun, the most acute of the emperor's coterie, noticed the alliance and its dangers, and tried to set the two women against one another. Later Tz'u-hsi railed in a decree: 'He actually demanded an audience with the Empresses separately, and his words, when addressing them, indicated a cunning desire to set one Empress against the other and sow seeds of discord.'[2]

Tz'u-hsi played the subtle instrument of court intrigue with a sure touch and she knew her youth, her helplessness, the wrong done to her as a mother and to Hsien-feng's official wives could win the sympathies of powerful men. She was moreover vivacious, charming, an accomplished student of the classics, and she used her faithful eunuchs and the guards, including Jung-lu with whom she coquetted, to keep her in touch with the capital.

Prince Kung, in charge of the caretaker government trying to maintain order in the tumultuous city, had formed the Peking Field Force, crack troops of military police, numbering up to twenty thousand men, who were equipped with modern armaments and drilled in western style. The young soldier Jung-lu was prominent among its officers. Also, courtiers, officials or concubines often fell out of favour and the state was not irreversible, for Tz'u-hsi was still the boy's mother, and above all, the covey of princes around the emperor's sickbed was generally loathed. China's domestic disintegration was blamed on them, and the defeat by the English and French was attributed to their arrogant negotiations. Most of all Su-shun, the youngest and ablest amongst them, was hated.

Now in his forties, a burly man built on a big frame, he was Prince I's younger brother, and had been in his youth 'a conspicuous figure in the capital, famous for his Mohawk tendencies, a wild blade, addicted to hawking and riotous living'.[3] The fever in his blood had abated in middle age, and he had risen through various boards of government rapidly, acquiring influence and power, until in 1859, he was appointed President of the Board of Revenue. There he inherited a history of bungled economic measures and galloping inflation. Su-shun took a characteristically hard line and arrested many bank officials on charges of simony and financial wrongdoings. Whereupon the Board of Revenue's buildings burned down. More arrests followed. The Board had probably been set alight by a petty official who feared that his embezzlements would be discovered in Su-shun's purges, but feeling nevertheless ran very high in Peking that Su-shun had ordered the arson himself to cover up his own crimes of peculation. By then also, the currency situation for the man in the street was almost beyond redress. As Su-shun was carried in his palanquin through Peking, handfuls of worthlessly inflated cash were thrown furiously in his face.

Rice had doubled in price since the emperor had fled, because transporting it to Jehol in the vast quantities that the court demanded created a shortage of all but the mustiest brand in Peking, and meant it could command higher prices everywhere. The inflation Su-shun's measures had failed to curtail was still rampant, paper money continued to drop in value and the wars had further run down the already failing economy. Fantastic stories of ever more sensational orgies, of macabre marriages of the bedridden emperor at Jehol streamed back to Peking and confirmed many of the mandarins' fears that the princes who surrounded Hsien-feng aggravated his decline in order to seize power for themselves. For almost everyone, Prince I and his clique were the inevitable scapegoats. Their fall, it was felt, was already overdue.

In March 1861 the French minister M. de Bourbulon, and the English minister Frederick Bruce, had installed themselves in the palaces the Chinese had set aside as their residences and had taken up their posts – posts which had cost so many lives. But their manners had greatly improved, their troops had scrupulously withdrawn from the capital, as promised in the treaties, and Prince Kung, who had emerged in Peking the *de facto* ruler of the empire, feeling it was now safe for Hsien-feng to return, urgently begged his brother to resume his Dragon Throne.

But the conservative Manchu spirit of injured pride and a desire for continued military resistance still possessed Hsien-feng, and he replied curtly that he was too ill to travel until the autumn. He had exacerbated his sure degeneration by debauch, perhaps consciously, because he could not face the ignominy of receiving barbarians in audience without the kowtow, or seeing at first hand the ruins of his favourite palaces. He refused to return, and decreed that Prince Kung should perform the temple sacrifices and ceremonies in his stead that summer. Prince Kung continued to plead, for without him he feared the throne might fall forfeit. As if to show agreement in heaven, a comet with a particularly brilliant curving tail appeared in the sky over Peking for the third time on 2 July. When sycophants told Hsien-feng it was a good omen, he had the honesty to rebuke them, and once again begged for heaven's forgiveness for his shortcomings. But the capital was already humming with the news of his imminent death, and during that hot summer weddings choked the streets, for, after an emperor died, no one could marry for twenty-seven months.

In Peking new ideas were in chrysalis. Prince Kung and key individuals of the official class like Wen-hsiang, who had a 'particularly astute and statesmanlike look about him',[4] were beginning to catch a glimmer that the West, though superior in arms, intended now to abide by the treaties, and that a policy of conciliation was the only way to rally the enfeebled country's forces. Foreign affairs were no longer a sideline of the Board of Rites, but handled by the newly-established Tsungli Yamen, a government bureau. Its members represented the more open-minded Chinese statesmen, and it controlled directly the equally new appointments of Superintendents of Trade in the treaty ports. There, Prince Kung and his advisers began to accept the idea of profitable co-existence.

The foreigner could be convenient: in the south the experiment of using foreign mercenaries against the Taiping rebels was beginning to bear fruit, and the customs, which during the disruption of Shanghai by the rebels in 1853 had been administered on behalf of the Chinese government by three representatives of England, France and America, had now been established with foreigners as staff in all the treaty ports. On a practical level, foreigners spoke the languages of the merchants and knew their manners and their goods, and could not therefore be manipulated as the Chinese had been; on a psychological level, dealing with foreigners as employees not conquerors reinforced the morale of the Middle Kingdom. It used their skills and paid them; they became subordinates, as the Jesuits had been under K'ang-hsi and Ch'ien-lung.

A dapper, blue-eyed, ambitious young Irishman, Robert Hart, who had picked up Chinese with effortless fluency, emerged in 1861 at the young age of twenty-six as Inspector-General, the head of the Chinese customs. His career as a servant of the Ch'ing, but also as a diplomatist between China and abroad, was to be long and idiosyncratic, and at its inception during that summer of 1861 Prince Kung and Wen-hsiang received him many times to discuss tariffs and dues. Prince Kung was applying himself doggedly, familiarizing himself with trade figures and arithmetic and calculations – subjects utterly spurned by Chinese scholarship. He excused himself to Hart: 'He [Mr Hart] must think him almost childish asking so many, and such apparently simple questions; but the truth was that, until lately, he was totally unacquainted ... with business matters generally, having had, until recent events compelled him to assume his present responsibilities, but little to attend to beyond amusing himself.'[5] Hart himself learned equally diligently how to approach the novel frontiers of Chinese diplomacy. 'Whenever I deal with people, and especially the Chinese,' he said, 'I always ask myself two questions: what idea that I do not want them to have will my remark suggest to them, and what answer will my remark allow them to make to me?'[6] His courtesy and shrewdness delighted Prince Kung: Wo-mun-ti Ha-ta, he called him, *Our* Hart.

When the monsters turned out less barbarous than their military vanguard had prefigured, the curiosity about the West that had slept so long suddenly shook itself awake. Prince Kung was surprised to hear that men who carried their heads under their arms, as illustrated in a learned scholar's work, did not exist; and with typical Chinese delight in the fine arts, he asked to see some English poetry. Thomas Wade, at the British Legation, translated and gave him 'Childe Harold's Farewell to his Page', and 'Auld Lang Syne' – an interesting comment on the taste of the English educated classes in 1861.[7]

On the powers' side also, antagonism was subsiding. The French and British had never intended to jeopardize the dynasty's authority to such a degree; and the squabbles that characterized all international co-operations meant that only a mutual policy of non-aggression could smooth them over. The Taipings by their brigandage and disorganization had ceased to be a creditable alternative. Also, they still held on the Yangstze certain of the treaty ports which had been granted in 1860, and their presence prevented the itching merchants from plying their trade on the river. Certainly, therefore, the foreigners' allegiance had altered. The Chinese themselves surprised everyone by their amiability, gentleness, courtesy, industry and charm – qualities of the race that the powers had signally failed to notice till then. As one English doctor attached to the Legation wrote, the factories of Canton were as typical of China as Wapping docks were of Western civilization.

In July 1861 Hsien-feng celebrated his thirtieth birthday. Tz'u-hsi was not invited to the ceremony. Immediately she sent distress signals to Prince Kung in Peking. A month later, as Hsien-feng's health grew worse and he had still not named his successor, Tz'u-hsi snatched up the son from whom she had been so cruelly parted, forced her way to the emperor's bedroom, and finding him lying on the imperial yellow satin sheets, showed him her child. 'The emperor being practically unconscious of what was taking place around him,' she described later, 'I took my son to his bedside and asked him what was going to be done about his successor to the throne. He made no reply to this, but, as had always been the case in emergencies, I was equal to the occasion, and I said to him "Here is your son"; on hearing which he immediately opened his eyes and said, "Of course he will succeed to the throne." I naturally felt relieved when this was settled for once and for all. These words were practically the last he spoke.'[8]

On 22 August the dropsical and unlamented Hsien-feng, Lord of Ten Thousand Years, 'mounted the fairy chariot and returned to the nine sources'. On the eve of his death he proclaimed Tsai-ch'un, Tz'u-hsi's son, heir apparent. Tz'u-hsi had worried that even that might be torn from her, as primogeniture was not a Ch'ing law. But her son's succession was now secure. All else however about Hsien-feng's going was as inglorious and confused as the manner of his living: for three months, while his corpse awaited in the resplendent catafalque the auspicious day of its journey to Peking and of its burial, a bitter struggle took place as the courtiers in their coarse white mourning clothes, with their heads unshaven in token of their grief, plotted and counterplotted and bowed politely at the emperor's widows.

The same day as Hsien-feng nominated Tz'u-hsi's son emperor, he established a board of eight Regents to administer the government during his minority: Prince I, Prince Cheng and of course Su-shun were included. None was of direct imperial lineage, and all the emperor's brothers were forgotten. But Hsien-feng's illness had been so acute he had not written the decree in his own hand, and its authenticity was doubted.

In China all documents, from imperial utterances down, were made valid by an official seal, not a personal signature. The emperor's twenty-five seals, enormous, beautifully carved and mounted, had their own special chamber in Peking, in the Hall of Blending of Great Creative Forces, where they were guarded by eunuchs; but in Jehol the procedure may have gone awry, for Tz'u-hsi – according to one story – bribed a eunuch to steal the Seal of Lawfully Transmitted Authority, and so render all the Board of Regents' documents worthless. She may even have asked the sixteen-year-old An Te-hai, who later became her favourite, for a further story claims that he stole away for her a decree of Hsien-feng's ordering that, if Tz'u-hsi gave any trouble, she should instantly be put to death. But an alternative, and more likely version, is that while Hsien-feng did create the Board of Regents from his chauvinist retainers, that he also entrusted his empress consort, Niuhuru, and Tz'u-hsi with seals, one to stamp the beginning, the other the close of each edict. The former's rank gave her a traditional right to authority; the latter, as the child's mother, as a high-ranking concubine, and through some deathbed relenting of the heart, was not passed over either. Hsien-feng may have intended the measure to curb the regents' powers, or merely to set up the board as a more orthodox regency, but Su-shun cavilled at the empresses' powers and battled with his brother and kinsmen to ignore the restraint. Their respect for the throne's word and for tradition made them hesitate, and when their first decrees appeared, from which the empresses' seals were absent, they yielded to the outcry and issued an edict raising both Niuhuru and Tz'u-hsi to the exalted rank of Empresses Dowager, the conventional honour bestowed on a departed emperor's senior wives, but one which gave the mettlesome young woman Tz'u-hsi further precedence over the eight seasoned regents. Though Su-shun complained, the first decree was smoothly sealed: the reign title Ch'i-hsiang, 'Well-Omened Happiness', was conferred on the emperor.

In Peking the Board of Regents, by excluding all Hsien-feng's brothers, violated historical precedent and therefore horrified the literati. Power, they felt, was being arrogated by inferiors, even if they were Imperial Clansmen. When, a month after his brother's death, Prince Kung, with Kuei-liang and Wen-hsiang, travelled to Jehol and met with blankness and hostility from the regents, they decided to give rein to the anger and venom accumulated in Peking over the last months. On 10 September Tung Yuan-chun, a censor, spoke out in audience before the regents with the customary frankness of that office and asked that power should be placed altogether in the hands of the empress, namely Niuhuru.[9] As this also violated both precedent and a dynastic law that women should never rule, he suggested that one or two of the imperial princes, brothers of the late emperor, should advise her. The Empresses Dowager – Tz'u-hsi took great care they should reply in one voice together – were overjoyed at the censor's suggestion. Tz'u-hsi knew, or rather hoped – correctly – that she could seize her chance later on, as Niuhuru was easily persuaded. The regents however naturally wanted to condemn the censor by imperial decree. As Tz'u-hsi later complained, 'Prince I and his colleagues adopted an insolent tone towards us and forgot their reverence due to our persons'.[10] The empresses refused to seal the regents' reprimand of the censor. They in turn refused to carry on the business of the government. With bad grace, the empresses had to comply.

From then on, as the day of the coffin's departure for Peking approached, rumours sped around the town that Su-shun, in charge of the regency's purse strings, was starving the empresses into submission. Prince Ch'un, the energetic twenty-one-year-old brother of Prince Kung and of the late emperor, had recently married Tz'u-hsi's younger sister, and Tz'u-hsi's position was therefore greatly strengthened. He arrived at Jehol to verify the suspicions and see the empresses, but they were not informed of his presence and he was insultingly kept waiting. Finally a eunuch smuggled him in, and together, in an atmosphere of quickening excitement, the empresses and Prince Ch'un laid plans for the day when the emperor should return to Peking.

On 5 October, the auspicious day, Hsien-feng's huge golden bier, borne aloft on the shoulders of one hundred and twenty-four attendants, set out down the wild passes from Jehol to the Great Wall. The stately cortège toiled its way through mud lashed up by heavy and persistent rains, preceded by the regents and the empresses with the boy emperor, whose duty it was to receive his father's coffin with proper sacrifice at the gates of the city.

The road was dangerous, the mountain gorges swarmed with bandits who could strike easily under cover of the terrain and the driving rain. Su-shun, following up behind, in the catafalque's escort, foresaw the dangers of inflamed public discontent, of the usefulness of the empresses as figureheads for the new regime, and decided to act. Bandits would provide a perfectly plausible excuse for murder. But Jung-lu, the handsome young warrior, anticipated Su-shun's possible plans, and galloping fast, joined the cavalcade with a swift-moving, well armed detachment of his new Peking Field Force, to press close to the threatened empresses' side. Jung-lu later, as an old man, testified in his valediction to Tz'u-hsi: 'When His Majesty Hsien-feng lay on his death bed, I had the honour to warn Your Majesty and the Empress Consort that the Princes Cheng and I were conspiring against the state. After the death of His Majesty those wicked Princes usurped the Regency and for many days Your Majesty was in danger so great that it may not be spoken of by any loyal subject.'[11] Flanked by Jung-lu's spirited troops, the empresses travelled on in safety. In an icy charade, messages passed to and fro: the empresses inquired politely of the regents the cortège's progress; Prince I replied all was well; they thanked him for his cares and awarded him a thousand taels from the Privy Purse.

On 1 November the emperor, the empresses and the regents (except for Su-shun who remained with the coffin) reached Peking, and their arrival gave Prince Kung the authority to follow up the plans they had laid, secretly and efficiently, during Prince Ch'un's visit to Jehol. It was a crisp, clear, winter's day as the procession of bearers and palanquins flowed through the streets of the capital over strewn imperial yellow sand, between screens of blue nankeen erected by soldiers to protect the Son of Heaven from the gaze of the *petit peuple*. Soldiers of the Peking Field Force, loyal to Prince Kung, stood serried on either side as Tz'u-hsi, her child the emperor on her lap, was carried in an imperial yellow quilted chair into the Imperial City. At the gates when Prince Kung met them and received the emperor, Prince I stepped between them to remonstrate, but Prince Kung haughtily indicated the troops and passed on to kowtow before his emperor and the emperor's mother. When they arrived within the Forbidden City, the regents, empresses and Prince Kung all convened in one of the throne-rooms. Prince Kung confronted them with a decree in the name of the child ruler. It stripped the regents of all their offices, blamed them – with some reason – for the recent troubles of China, and arrested them. In the immemorial fashion of the empire, the slate was wiped clean for their successors: 'Prince I . . . and his colleagues failed to deal satisfactorily with the peace negotiations, and sought to lessen their responsibility by their treacherous arrest of the British emissaries, thus involving China in charges of bad faith. In consequence of their acts, the Summer Palace was eventually sacked . . . and the Emperor was forced, greatly against his will, to seek refuge in Jehol.'[12] The deposed regents knelt quietly in the throne room and submitted without protest and with Confucian dignity as they were marched under guard to the 'Empty Chamber', the prison of the Imperial Clan Court. Meanwhile Prince Ch'un, with another brother of the late emperor, rode out swiftly from Peking to Su-shun's encampment around the catafalque. They surprised him in his tent: he was in bed with one of his concubines, in flagrant breach of the code of imperial mourning. They took him prisoner, and the cortège resumed its laborious journey home.

Memorials from all over China cemented the *coup*; two Grand Secretaries, representing civil and official support, wrote to recommend a new regency; Sheng-pao, the general whose face had been blasted at Palichiao and who had visited Jehol in September to inspect the Board of Regents personally, represented the military's solidarity. Their memorials criticized the regents for their gross historical impropriety – that in posing as 'councillors' they had in reality assumed supreme power, complained of the exclusion of the emperor's uncles, and begged that power should be vested in the empress. Tz'u-hsi again was not mentioned, but only Niuhuru, Hsien-feng's senior wife.[13]

The Imperial Clan Court was presided over by Prince Kung. It is therefore hardly surprising that Prince I, Prince Cheng and Su-shun were found guilty of 'subversion of the state', one of the 'ten abominations' second only to 'rebellion' as crime against the family, the sovereign, social relationships, and virtue – 'abominable in the eyes of Heaven and Earth, unpardonable and irredeemable'.[12] The punishment of the lingering death, the 'death of a thousand cuts' was recommended, but as a favour to their high rank, the sentence was commuted: 'Prince I and Prince Cheng are hereby permitted to commit suicide. . . .' In the Empty Chamber, the two princes stoically and uncomplainingly hanged themselves from a beam with the silken rope provided. 'As for Su-shun,' the decree continued, 'his treasonable guilt far exceeds that of his accomplices, and he fully deserves the punishment of dismemberment and the slicing process. . . . But we cannot make up our mind to impose this extreme penalty, and therefore, in token of our leniency, we sentence him to immediate decapitation.'[13]

Su-shun's immense fortune was confiscated, to transform the empresses overnight into enormously wealthy women. His riches were the first hoard on which Tz'u-hsi had laid her hands, and they bought her not only all the robes and theatricals she could ever want, but an efficient spy system as well. On 8 November Su-shun, Imperial Clansman and long a servant of his country, was led to the public execution ground in Peking. Spluttering his disobedient wrath, he was beheaded, like a common felon.

The next day a few more officials were stripped of office; but no proscription was carried out, so that the new era – for it was a new era – should begin in mercy. Only Su-shun's family continued to be hounded: three years later his sons were forbidden to hold office. One of the original Board of Regents, Ching-shou, was spared altogether. He was conveniently married to Prince Kung's sister.

By the time the new regency was officially announced, Tz'u-hsi had managed to worm her way in. The regency was called 'Listening Behind Screens to Reports on Government Affairs', because the two empresses were to conduct the business of government behind imperial yellow curtains, to symbolize that they themselves did not rule, but presided in the emperor's stead. Prince Kung was appointed I-cheng-wang (Adviser in the Administration of Government), the highest post in the empire, and excused the kowtow before the throne. Four of his tolerant, politic new party became Grand Councillors, including Wen-hsiang and Kuei-liang. All decrees were written solemnly in the first person of the child emperor, as if he himself had dictated them. Tz'u-hsi was given her first honorific titles, meaning Motherly and Auspicious, and her co-empress Niuhuru was called Tz'u-an, Motherly and Restful.[16] They were the first of sixteen titles Tz'u-hsi was to collect during her life, and they were worth 100,000 taels (about £30,000) each to her per annum.[17] Dutifully, without a hint of what was to come, the empresses jointly protested the honour: 'Our assumption of the Regency was utterly contrary to our wishes, but we have complied with the urgent request of our Princes and Ministers. . . . So soon as ever the Emperor shall have completed his education, we shall take no further part in the government. . . . Our sincere reluctance in assuming the direction of affairs must be manifest to all.'[18]

The direction of affairs had now taken a lighter and happier turn, and Tz'u-hsi launched her first regency on a tide of optimism, for in the south, Anking, one of the Taiping rebels' strongholds, had fallen in September; occupied Canton had been evacuated by foreign troops by 21 October; the policy of co-operation was maturing on all sides, for the powers had decided to concentrate on upholding a strong central government and to negotiate directly with Peking and not with the provincial authorities, and were therefore delighted with the emergence of the twenty-eight-year-old Prince Kung as a vigorous government leader. Furthermore, Chinese officialdom rallied to Prince Kung's standard, giving the period the flavour of a 'restoration' of a creaking dynasty. 'It is not a *coup d'état* or a revolution or a new age, but an Indian summer in which the historically inevitable process of decline is arrested for a time by the ability and effort of the whole gentry-bureaucracy.'[19] Prince Kung had renewed the Mandate of Heaven for the new Ch'ing emperor, and to solemnize the spirit of this Indian summer, his reign title was changed and the 'late flowering' of the dynasty was proclaimed with the strong, hopeful, convinced name T'ung-chih: Return to Order.

Prince Kung ordered the court historians to compile a book in which the historical precedents for such a regency were listed and discussed, and told the two empresses to pore over this and learn the legitimate sources of their authority. For Tz'u-hsi's claim to the throne, even in the surrogate capacity of regent, was shaky and imprecise. She had been asked to 'lower the curtain' at Niuhuru's side because the latter was 'rather illiterate' in Chinese and knew only how to read and write a little Manchu.[20]

Niuhuru, egged on by Tz'u-hsi, probably herself suggested to Prince Kung that the emperor's mother should join and help her. Niuhuru's inadequacies are a fair indication of how completely unimportant the empresses' abilities or calibre were considered to be and of how much their appointment was due to Prince Kung, who saw in them convenient and malleable figureheads who would not impede his policies. Tz'u-hsi was more intelligent and cultivated, so she could assist the more bovine Niuhuru. At this stage no one saw anything more in the twenty-six-year-old mother of the T'ung-chih Emperor than a pleasant, quite pretty, quite bright ex-concubine. She had stumbled on the highest power, as if on a pebble in her path.

Chapter Six

THE INCOMPATIBLES

'The rebels menace our heart. . . .' Prince Kung had written to his brother the Emperor Hsien-feng. 'The British are merely a threat to our limbs. First of all we must extirpate the rebels.'[1] Although the Imperialists had reconquered Anking, the Taiping rebellion was not spent, and victory in the trial of strength between the insurgents' bid for the Mandate of Heaven, and the Ch'ing's bid to hold it was still the crucial task facing Tz'u-hsi and Prince Kung. It was an immense undertaking: for while the Anglo-French war in the North was raging in 1860, the imperial forces in the south had been consequently weakened, and the Taipings had broken their stranglehold and erupted out of the Heavenly Capital, driving eastwards to the Yangstze's estuary and down the Grand Canal, capturing and recapturing many cities including the prosperous, mighty and fortified Soochow and Hangchow. A brave and brilliant commander now rode at the head of the banners of the Heavenly King's subjects: Li Hsiu-ch'eng, dubbed the Chung Wang, or Loyal Prince. Li, a poverty-stricken peasant from Kwangsi, had joined the rebellion in its earliest days, but his high purpose had not withered like his colleagues', for when he emerged as a forceful and gifted general, he showed mercies previously unknown in the Taiping campaign: he provided ten thousand coffins for the dead – even for the enemy dead – he lent money without interest, he distributed free rice to the hungry. But humane and appealing as the Loyal Prince was, daring as his attack had been throughout, his strategy was less sure. For he failed to pounce on Hunan, where Tseng Kuo-fan, the illustrious Chinese general, was able to raise his 'braves', and he failed to seize Shanghai in 1861, losing the master key to the complex kingdom of waterways, canals, islands and river towns that the Taipings had again carved out for themselves.

When in 1861 Tseng's Hunan braves had captured Anking, one of the first decrees of the new regency rejoiced, and Tseng Kuo-fan, a hard disciplinarian, was given supreme military command in all the provinces infested by the rebels: Chekiang and Kiangsi, Kiangsu and Anhwei (of which he was already viceroy). Tseng, by this time in his fifties, was the epitome – and in many ways the paragon – of the type of Han Chinese whom Tz'u-hsi patronized. In his youth he had lived wildly and drunkenly, and even experimented with opium. But with the steeliness that characterized him till his death, he had overcome the habits of excess and reformed. A scrupulous and self-critical scholar, 'with a black straggling beard and moustache, a careless dress and a very ancient hat',[2] he made a most unlikely commander-in-chief. But he typified a very new animal in the Ch'ing world: a scholar who took up the despised profession of a soldier, and a Han Chinese who acquired immense military power under the once-warrior Manchu race. When asked to appoint two subordinates of his choice, Tseng lit on men of his own stamp: younger and tougher, they too were Chinese scholar-soldiers. One was Tso Tsung-t'ang, a pug-faced, rough and ready Hunanese (like Tseng himself), simple in his appetites and dogged in his tactics, who now became governor of Chekiang; the other was Li Hung-chang, very tall and commanding, a man of exceptional ambition, who spoke in the broad brogue of his native Anhwei. At Tseng's recommendation, Li became, in July 1862, at the age of thirty-nine, governor of Kiangsu. Li's family had been killed by the Taiping rebels, so that his moral commitment to the Ch'ing cause was reinforced by his personal loss. The same year, a force of six thousand men – the Huai army – raised and trained by Li Hung-chang on the same lines as Tseng's Hunanese, was transported down the rebel-occupied river to Shanghai under the protection of gunboats lent by the British, now solidly aligned with the dynasty, and put in the field against the rebels.

Shanghai had however been held the year before against the onslaught of the Loyal Prince by a force of British and French troops, organized by the foreign community and the interested Chinese merchants. The irregular bunch of men was led by an American filibuster, Frederick Ward, only in his twenties, 'quick, nervous and animated in his movements', with 'thick raven hair hanging over his shoulders like an Indian's'.[3] Ward always led the vanguard into battle; he never armed himself with anything more lethal than a short rattan cane and he always wore a frock coat. His adoring men considered him invulnerable. At first he recruited drop-outs and riff-raff along the Shanghai waterfront, but the British protested that he was attracting deserters from the Royal Navy, and he was forced to raise an army of Chinese troops. The combined force, once trained and drilled and armed by Ward, was spirited and efficient, and kept the Taipings at bay around Shanghai. In March 1862 Tz'u-hsi sped a happy decree from Peking: in recognition of its exploits, Ward's force was resoundingly proclaimed 'The Ever-Victorious Army'.

As auxiliaries to the regular imperial forces under Tso Tsung-t'ang, Li Hung-chang and Tseng Kuo-fan, the Ever-Victorious Army, which never numbered more than four thousand men, was paid more than the other Chinese troops. Drilled and led by foreigners, the fast and resilient force became the chief instrument that held the waterways of the Taiping stronghold and loosened the rebels' grip. For Ward developed adventurous tactics of reconnaissance, followed up by a pincer use of steamships, artillery and pontoons, in order to constrict and confine the Taiping armies in the canals and rivers. Appalling bloodshed marked the advance of his army: in one battle alone, three thousand Taipings were slaughtered, and by the autumn of 1862 a radius thirty miles around Shanghai had been scoured clean of the uprising. But in September, at Tzeki, a small town near the port of Ningpo ninety miles south of Shanghai. Ward, exposing himself to fire as brazenly as ever, was hit full in the abdomen and instantly killed.

Ward's second-in-command, Henry Burgevine, a popular swaggering hot-headed soldier of fortune, took over. But Li Hung-chang feared that the Ever-Victorious Army, with injudicious leadership, might be turned against the imperial cause. He distrusted Burgevine, and by provoking him, engineered his stormy dismissal. Li might have been justifiably suspicious: Burgevine defected to the Taipings, with whom he hoped to find the glory that had eluded him on the Ch'ing side.

What had begun in necessity grew into policy: under Li Hung-chang, the barbarian was used, in time-honoured Chinese tradition, for Chinese ends. After a great deal of hesitation and discussion, the British gave permission for one of their nationals to lead the Ever-Victorious Army. Charles George Gordon was thirty years old when he took service under the Chinese in 1863. The blue-eyed, soft-spoken soldier who was to die so celebrated at Khartoum in 1885, was shy, temperamental, a devout Christian, given to bouts of righteous rage and severe depression. When he accepted the command of the Ever-Victorious Army, he wrote home to his mother: 'I am afraid that you will be much vexed . . . that I am now a mandarin . . . [but] I can say that, if I had not accepted the command, I believe the force would have been broken up and the rebellion gone on in its misery for years . . . You must not fret on this matter. I think I am doing good service. . . . I keep your likeness before me, and can assure you and my father that I will not be rash. . . .'[4] Gordon was morally convinced the Taiping uprising should be crushed, and believed, with other foreigners in China, in the regeneration of the Ch'ing. As a general he cut a poor figure in his men's eyes compared

to the glamorous Ward, for, with 'his quiet manners and disposition
... deeply religious sentiment ... Colonel Gordon presented few of
the characteristics usually associated with the common notion of the
dashing leader of an irregular force. Great pleasure in activity, a
self-sacrificing disposition, and a sense of duty have been evidently
the mainsprings of his conduct.'[5]

The army Gordon took over, already mutinous through lack of
firm leadership since Ward's death, rebelled at Gordon's ascetic
strictures against women, drink and loot. Nearly half the men –
1,700 out of 3,900 – deserted. 'Very disorderly lot,' commented
Gordon, 'Ward spoilt them.'[6] Imperturbably, he then enlisted two
thousand Taipings who had been taken prisoner, and brought the
force up to quota. His disregard for previous loyalties was quintess-
entially Chinese: General Chen, one of the most successful in the
campaign against the rebels, had defected from the Taipings and
bought his freedom and his imperial commission from Li Hung-
chang for a generous sum. One of Li's numerous ambitions was to
acquire great wealth – Chen's ransom laid the foundations, it was
rumoured, of his later fortune.

Gordon imitated Ward's tactics: he too went coolly into battle
armed with only a riding crop; he too, by occupying the waterways,
concentrated on squeezing the Taipings into their cities and then
laying merciless siege to them with heavy artillery and steamships.
Soon, the Ever-Victorious Army, in their British Empire-type dark
green jackets, knickerbockers and turbans, had cut a swathe to the
west of Soochow, the lovely city of gardens and villas and temples
that had been exceptionally prosperous until the rebels tore at it like
jackals, reducing its population by two-thirds to twenty-five
thousand. Forty thousand Taipings under the Loyal Prince defended
Soochow, both inside the ramparts and in the field before it, but
their communications were severed all around them, and on 4
December 1863, the city fell. Ten thousand imperial troops under
General Chen, and twenty-five thousand under Li Hung-chang's
brother also took part in the battle. The Ever-Victorious Army,
numbering three thousand odd, cannot have been as decisive a factor
in the fighting as the foreign public, spellbound before their newspapers at 'Chinese' Gordon's heroism, wanted to believe.

Yet Li Hung-chang still feared the existence of a mercenary army
in the south; and Gordon, after the fall of Soochow, foresaw the
swift eclipse of the Taiping rebellion. Only Nanking, defended by
the Loyal Prince, held out, so Gordon agreed with Li to disband the
force. He decided soon after, that 'The Chinese are a wonderful

people. . . . Li Hung-chang is the best man in the empire; has correct ideas of his position, and, for a Chinaman, the most liberal tendencies.'[7] Tz'u-hsi, on the advice of Li Hung-chang, now awarded Gordon the decoration he most coveted: the Yellow Riding Jacket, the highest order in the empire, equivalent to the Garter in Great Britain, together with ten thousand taels. The dutiful son wrote home: 'The country is clear of rebels, and the Imperialists are quite able to be left to themselves. I may say the Chinese government have conferred upon me the highest military rank and the yellow jacket, a distinction conferred on not more than twenty other mandarins in the empire and which constitutes the recipient as one of the emperor's bodyguard. I have declined money in any shape, and I think the Chinese government trust me more than any foreigner has ever been trusted. I have never cringed or yielded in any way to them, and they have respected me all the more.'[8]

Gordon left a memory with the influential Li Hung-chang that helped to form policy in Peking. He wrote, in a famous memorial to the throne in 1869: 'The memorialist . . . has had several years' experience in conducting business with foreigners, and is thoroughly familiar with their character. He has found that, no matter what they are engaged in, they act honourably without deceit or falsehood. . . . Their bearing . . . in military matters affords clear evidence of their straightforwardness. . . . There is the instance of the Englishman Gordon. . . . .'[9]

Li Hung-chang's comments chipped at Tz'u-hsi's conviction of foreign barbarity and falsehood, but did not destroy it completely. She did however have to acknowledge that by the spring of 1864 the Ever-Victorious Army had helped to obliterate the thousands of rebels who had disturbed the reign of her dead husband Hsien-feng. In a triumphant and gory litany, victory edicts streamed from Peking, lingering over the enemy dead, the sacked towns, the righteous revenge of the imperial fighters. Li Hung-chang held the Grand Canal, which cut the Taiping realm in half, and Tso Tsung-t'ang had taken Hangchow in March 1864. The resistance of Nanking, the Heavenly Capital, besieged now for seven years by Tseng's armies, was at last cracking. Within, the early Taipings' great ideas had been wiped out by the years of battle; the troops were riddled with opium; the treasury drained to purchase the drug and by the general corruption of the régime. The Heavenly King himself, Hung Hsiu-ch'uan, bedecked in finery, spouting visions, reached an apotheosis of dementia. When the Loyal Prince told him of the extreme danger to himself and to all his followers in Nanking,

Hung merely exhorted his people to trust in God. He refused to escape or even to defend himself. 'I have at my command an angelic host of a million strong: how then could 100,000 or so of these unholy Imperialists enter the city?'[10] . When the people begged for food, he told them to eat 'sweet dew' – grass. When he went up on the parapets to view the siege, he distributed pearls from his necklaces to his starving soldiers. They wept, for they could not eat them, and there was no food in the city left to buy. On 30 June, suddenly realizing the utter futility of his position, the Heavenly King poisoned himself. When the city fell on 19 July, Tseng reported to the throne: 'Not a single rebel surrendered. Many buried themselves alive rather than be taken.'[11] The mass suicide of the Taipings in their capital was not only a horrific comment on the ruthlessness and callousness of the imperial troops; it was also an extraordinary and terrifying tribute to the frustrated scholar who had pronounced himself the Heavenly King of the Heavenly Kingdom of Great Peace thirteen years before, whose body was now found, shrouded in imperial yellow, emblazoned with dragons, and lying in a sewer.

Li Hsiu-ch'eng, the Loyal Prince, was taken as he fled with Hung's son, his new master, to whom, with a last gesture of typical fine bravery, he had given his best horse. The Loyal Prince's copious and detailed account – he wrote fifty-five thousand words in eight days of captivity at Tseng Kuo-fan's request – is one of the great documents of the Taiping insurrection, and sets it apart from other unchronicled grass-roots revolts. Although the throne ordered that the Loyal Prince should be sent to Peking alive in a cage to be exhibited as a warning to the people, Tseng realized the dangerousness of his immense charm and popularity, and had him beheaded immediately.

A few last small bastions clung on until May 1865, but the Taiping rebellion was over. It had stripped and scarred the rich agricultural provinces so deeply that the weals, empty tracts of once-blossoming land still remained defoliated and depopulated years later in testimony to the upheaval. A contemporary described it:

The rebellion had even altered the face of the country; destroyed its communications; deflected its rivers; broken down its sea defences. During its continuance smiling fields were turned into desolated wildernesses; 'fenced cities into ruinous heaps'. The plains of Kiangnan, Kiangsi and Chekiang were strewn with human skeletons; their rivers polluted with floating carcasses; wild beasts descending from their fastnesses in the mountains roamed at large over the land, and made their dens in the ruins of deserted towns; the cry of the pheasant usurped the place of the hum of busy populations; no hands were left to till the soil, and noxious weeds covered the ground once tilled with patient industry.[12]

During the uprising six hundred walled cities had been occupied, sixteen provinces had been crossed, five provinces ravaged as the opposing armies clashed and clashed again. Upwards of twenty million people had been liquidated. It had been a holocaust, and its like was not seen again until the World Wars of the twentieth century.

The Taipings had alienated the inhabitants of the towns they seized through brutality and greed; they had failed to overcome the intense prejudice of the literati against the Christianity and heterodoxy with which their movement was tainted, and the entrenched Confucianist gentry, the pillars of Chinese society, had rallied *en masse* to 'restore' the Ch'ing. The Taipings had theorized about welfare and agrarian reform, but acted ineffectually upon their ideas, while the Ch'ing, on the other hand, threw themselves headlong into conventional 'benevolent' measures during the T'ung-chih Restoration. For after their ruthless suppression of the rebellion, the Manchus wooed the people sedulously. In spite of the huge expense of the campaign which had drained the treasury, the land tax was remitted by thirty per cent all over China, easing the pressure on the hard-hit peasantry.[13]

Yet Tz'u-hsi and the government at Peking could not easily win the unsettled people's love. More rebellions flared and were as mercilessly extinguished: the Nien-fei, or 'twisted turbans' had roved Shantung and other provinces in the centre of China since 1853; the Miao, the aborigine splinter group, many of whom had joined the Taipings, continued to gather, mainly in Kweichow; the Moslems were trying to secede in the weird and flower-filled crags and valleys of Shensi, Yunnan and Kansu, the 'Edge of the World' to the west. Seng-ko-lin-ch'in, Tseng Kuo-fan, Li Hung-chang and Tso Tsung-t'ang were all dispatched with their armies to stamp out each successive rising, and stamp them out they did. By 1873 the revolt was over. The Middle Kingdom was at last at peace.

It was, however, peace won at a bloody price: the valleys of the Taipings were laid waste, and so were the valleys of Yunnan, Kweichow, Shensi and Kansu. Their cities were ruined, blasted by battle, their populations scattered and destroyed. It was estimated that nine-tenths of Shensi's Moslems, and two thirds of Kansu's were annihilated – more than three million dead; in Yunnan – four to five million dead or fugitive; in Kweichow – nearly five million dead. The rehabilitation of the country was an overwhelming task, and although the government set about it bravely, their traditionally unbridled measures of suppression had scored deep and the wounds never healed. For one all-important characteristic of these upheavals was never respected: the Taipings, and Moslems, the Miao – though not the Nien-fei – were minority groups who wished to keep and develop their cultural, religious and social differences. But the Confucianist empire, while allowing some divergences, as with its very rulers the Manchus, believed so ethnocentrically in its own exalted virtue that it could not allow them to express themselves. Tz'u-hsi imbibed the strong-arm policy of the T'ung-chih Restoration which Prince Kung in particular shaped, and seeing it triumph over popular revolution, she therefore learned to remain unshaken herself when the dynasty was most shaken, and to trust in the force of arms completely when other more pleasant Confucian methods failed.

While rebellion was bloodily crushed in the traditional Chinese manner throughout the empire, the second great task of the Restoration – relations with the treaty powers – focused increasingly on Peking and the newly founded Tsungli Yamen, the Bureau of Foreign Affairs. When Hsien-feng was still alive, Prince Kung and others among the more far-sighted officials reported to him that 'We should act according to the treaties and not allow the foreigners to go even slightly beyond them. In our external expression we should be sincere and amicable but quietly try to keep them in line. Then within the next few years, even though occasionally they may make demands, still they will not suddenly cause us a great calamity.'[14] Feng Kuei-feng, a brilliant, lucid scholar who was at one time secretary to Li Hung-chang, amplified: 'The barbarians always appeal to reason. We should forthwith take their methods and apply them in return. According to reason, if a demand is acceptable, then we should try to accept it; according to reason if it is not acceptable, we should try to convince them on rational grounds.'[15]

Frederick Bruce, the first British minister and Elgin's younger brother, was succeeded in 1865 by Rutherford Alcock, an idealistic if pedantic diplomat, who had trained as a surgeon but had been prevented from practising by a wound that had crippled his right hand. They both agreed with the Chinese over enforcing the letter of the treaties on their nationals in China. The American minister, Anson Burlingame, was of the same mind: 'We are making an effort,' he wrote, 'to substitute fair diplomatic action for force.'[16]

This 'fair diplomatic action' took place in the halls of the Tsungli

Yamen, stifling hot in summer, bitter chill in winter, and approached, comically enough, through the kitchens where the diplomats saw their refreshments being prepared in conditions of immense squalor. There the mandarins like Prince Kung could not entirely break their immemorial habit of prevarication, and joked and smoked, producing their pipes from the fur lining of their boots, marvelling at some curiosity in the foreigners' dress, offering them sweetmeats and tea. 'The Prince of Kung was very serious and fidgety. He twisted, doubled, and dodged like a hare,' wrote one young Englishman at the legation. 'At last when Sir Rutherford had him, as he thought, fairly in a corner, I saw a gleam of hope and joy come over the Prince's face. He had caught sight of . . . my eyeglass. In a moment he had pounced upon it, and there was an end of all business. The whole pack of babies were playing with it, and our Chief, who was furious, saw his sermons scattered to the wind.'[17]

Nevertheless Chinese and foreigners struggled together to keep the treaties peacefully, and although lengthy negotiations hampered every move, there was co-operation – a co-operation so marked it gave rise to mutterings and anger among the merchants, who still chafed at the restrictions on residence inland, and at the payment of Chinese transit taxes, or *likin*. But the diplomats and the politicians held firm for a time, because from their point of view, relations and trade with China could only improve if China was domestically united and strong, and they wished to husband her strength, not dissipate it by continual harassment.

In their anxiety to support the new government of the Ch'ing they played into the hands of the Chinese, who were again acting upon the ancient saw 'Use the barbarians to control the barbarians.' Although the Tsungli Yamen officials in the 1860s came to realize, to their astonishment, that the purpose of the British and other powers was trade and equal status, not supreme rule, they still could not do otherwise than try to absorb the foreigner into the existing Confucian framework, as the Manchus themselves had been absorbed and sinicized. The use of foreign soldiers in the south, and the employment of foreign staff in the customs did not differ from the earlier emperors' use of Jesuits at court to read the stars, design buildings, make clocks and teach mathematics. One race was being suborned to serve the other.

Intent on their Confucian vision of an agricultural, frugal society, Tz'u-hsi and ministers like Prince Kung rejected the idea of strengthening the country by increasing trade and industry, as the West would have liked and would have taught. Throughout the decade they refused more advanced advice to build telegraphs and railways, mines and mills, the organs of the modern world, insisting, correctly, that such innovations would attack the very fibre of traditional Chinese society. But in so doing, they rendered the Restoration's efforts at self-strengthening piecemeal and inchoate.

For when the Chinese took stock of the defeat of 1860, they were convinced of the superiority of the West in little else but firepower, and military improvement therefore became a paramount concern. As Feng Kuei-feng wrote: 'Now let us order one half of them [scholars] to apply themselves to the pursuit of manufacturing weapons and instruments and imitating foreign crafts. . . . The intelligence and wisdom of the Chinese are necessarily superior to those of the various barbarians, only formerly we have not made use of them.'[18]

The Chinese did explore foreign military skills. Tseng Kuo-fan established the Kiangnan arsenal and ship-yard to forge weapons and build warships at Shanghai; Tso Tsung-t'ang followed with another at Foochow, and in 1867 two French engineers were employed as designers. Horatio Nelson Lay, the first Inspector-General of the Chinese Imperial Maritime Customs, the self-same Lay who had so belligerently negotiated the Treaty of Tientsin in 1858, returned to England on sick leave with £250,000 of Chinese money and a brief to buy a flotilla of steamships with ammunition and crews for the Chinese government. Lay engaged a captain in the Royal Navy, Sherard Osborn, and with his usual high-handed arrogance, promised him supreme command of the fleet, subject only to his, Lay's, orders. Lay had neither the authority to guarantee such a position, nor could the Chinese possibly allow a foreigner the final word over the nucleus of their modern navy. Therefore, when Osborn and the fleet arrived in China in 1863, a stormy and unhappy quarrel blew up. Lay and Osborn refused to give ground, and the ships were finally sent back. It was a tragic fiasco – it cost the Chinese the navy that they struggled fruitlessly twenty more years to establish.

'We shall learn', said the percipient Wen-hsiang to W.A.P. Martin, the missionary, 'all the good we can from you people of the West.'[19] Fastidiously the Chinese tapped foreign skills. Martin himself became, as Robert Hart had done, a Chinese civil servant, and taught English at the T'ung Wen Kuan, the College of Languages in Peking which was expanded in 1867 to embrace sciences – engineering, mathematics – hitherto scorned by the literati as fit only for clerks. Martin also translated manuals of international law into Chinese, and in 1864 Prince Kung told Tz'u-hsi: 'There are occasional passages which are useful. For instance as with the case this year of the Danish ship captured by Prussia outside of Tientsin, your ministers used some sentences from this book.... The Prussian minister immediately acknowledged his mistake.'[20] At the Kiangnan Arsenal, John Fryer, an impoverished English teacher who was lured east by dreams of fair Cathay, began translating works on every scientific topic for his Chinese employers. In the customs, foreigners of every nationality worked for the Chinese, although ironically the revenue they so scrupulously collected often only repaid the indemnities their own countries' demands upon China incurred. In 1872 students were sent to American universities. But above all else, the most startling change of heart during Prince Kung's era of influence was the decision in 1866 to send a Chinese mandarin to Europe. P'in-chun, a man of no particular distinction – 'a shocking twaddle', according to one English diplomat – was nevertheless the first unofficial Chinese envoy abroad.[21] The following year the Tsungli Yamen broke sharply with tradition and appointed the retired American minister Anson Burlingame their ambassador. Even though Burlingame was 'a master of saying beautiful and empty things'[22] and though he painted a flamboyant picture of the Chinese people thirsting for the Christian message, though he died, his mission uncompleted, in Russia, he set, as an official Chinese emissary, an altogether revolutionary precedent.

The spring tide of cordiality between China and the foreigners in her cities and on her shores rose in 1869 when the Treaty of Tientsin was judiciously and thoroughly revised. The Yamen had previously written to high-standing officials in the provinces for advice. In his reply, celebrated for its shrewd understanding of the foreign powers' position, Li Hung-chang stressed passionately how important China's internal strength was to secure foreign respect and therefore malleability. He also pointed out that the powers could not be bent on conquest, for 'with the exception of Russia, foreign countries are all too distant from China, and the acquisition of its territory would be nothing but an embarrassment'.[23]

Sir Rutherford Alcock, the British minister, genuinely wanted to clarify the trading regulations so that merchants could no longer take advantage of obscurities, or of the complications of the tariffs system; he also wanted to set China on a path of legal reform which would render extraterritoriality unnecessary. His sympathies lay with the Chinese against the heavy pressure groups of panting merchants and burning missionaries, and the Alcock Convention of

1869, arrived at after much debate, tea and sweetmeats at the Tsungli Yamen, therefore smoothed some of the more obvious inequalities in the previous treaties. Above all, the Convention was remarkable and pleasing to the Chinese for its courtesy. For the first time, an agreement with China was phrased in such a way that their dignity was not insulted: 'Great Britain on the one part agrees . . . ; China on the other part agrees. . . .'[24] The Tsungli Yamen breathed happily over China's first diplomatic achievement, if not victory, and Tz'u-hsi, Niuhuru, her co-empress, Prince Kung and the presidents of the government boards all stamped their seals upon it in sign of their approval.

But in England the China merchants clamoured that it was a pathetic surrender to Chinese interests, that Alcock was a blunderer and a dupe, that his Convention contained none of the concessions needed, desperately needed to lay hands on the immense wealth within their grasp in China. They whipped up England's thriving industrialists and middle classes into a white heat of indignation. Alcock had feared the merchants, but he had counted on his government. It failed him. Though the Foreign Secretary expressed his regret in the matter, in 1870, Prince Kung and the Tsungli Yamen were informed that Great Britain rejected the Alcock Convention. It cannot have seemed otherwise to the Chinese but that any agreement which treated China with decency was unacceptable to foreign powers; and it fanned the xenophobia only briefly submerged in Tz'u-hsi's heart.

Tz'u-hsi and the ministers of the Restoration assumed that China's centuries of civilization would withstand the shock waves of the new culture and ethics of the West, and that they could pick and choose the best for China's purposes, and need not dismantle or alter basic institutions. Only Li Hung-chang glimpsed the colossal divergence between Confucian society, with its stratified hierarchy, its anti-commercial, anti-military values, and the aggressive philosophy of the West. But even Li trusted to orthodox Confucianism as the perfect module in which all differences could be incorporated, not seeing that merchants, soldiers and industries were incompatible with the peasant-based, scholar-run, family- and emperor-worshipping society of China, and it did not have the elasticity to absorb the change.

It would have been possible to remain deaf, for a time, to the tremors in the structure, even in spite of the failure of the Alcock Convention and the subsequent hardening of anti-foreign opinion, of the breaches of extra-territoriality and other abuses, had it not been for the Christian missionaries. The missionaries exposed the impossibility of syncretism between East and West and laid bare the wound that the twenty-year battle until 1860 had inflicted – a wound which would not be healed by diplomats' good wishes at the capital or nibbles at Western technology.

The ministers in Peking had tried to rein in the merchants and restrain the missionaries, but, with some justice, the Christian element retorted: 'Christianity may be revolutionary in customs and opinion, but it is not seditious. . . . *But the very presence* of Anglo-Saxons in the East is revolutionary, and therefore we are warranted in arguing that if Christianity is to be banished because of its tendency to produce changes, the British and American governments ought to recall every Anglo-Saxon in China. . . . If the despotic Governments of the East are to be left unimpaired, if nothing must be done which is at all likely to interfere with the ideas on which they were founded, then we have no right to bring to China the laws of the commerce of Christendom, and force the Chinese to accept them.'[25]

The French feats of arms in China had won them a protectorate over the missions. For unlike the English and the Americans, the French had only a small trading interest. In 1860, when the Chinese had granted protection and freedom to Chinese and foreigners to practice, profess and preach Christianity, they had also undertaken to restore all confiscated mission property and to allow missionaries to buy land and build as they wished. In their zeal, missionaries declared that long-standing Chinese temples were former Church property and requisitioned them; given permission to build, they chose conspicuous and hallowed sites on purpose. In Canton, the French bishop turned down several key positions in favour of demolishing the well-loved governor's own *yamen* and erecting his church there. The priests paid no attention to the superstitions of the people whom they were about to convert to more temperate beliefs, and when they built, played havoc with the *feng shui*'s sensibilities. The Franciscans even tried to collect rent arrears for the last three hundred years. In Szechuan between 1863 and 1869, 260,000 taels – an enormous sum – was collected as 'redress' or damages.[26] Missionaries made converts by tally, offering free food and shelter, and therefore attracting vagabonds and ne'er-do-wells and bandits. These 'rice' Christians would hardly have mattered if the missionaries had not often helped a Chinese, in return for conversion, to go scot-free for some crime by claiming in the magistrates' court that the issue was religious, and that the charge therefore contravened the treaty agreements to protect Christians. Even if the priests had avoided bribing troublemakers, they still took advantage of the local officials' duty to safeguard foreigners and Christians, and often deadlocked their attempts to bring wrongdoers, if they were converts, to justice. The Chinese educated classes found Christianity a shallow and muddled philosophy, and despised it especially as Protestants and Catholics squabbled and vied so fiercely with each other, and yet professed the same religion based on love, fellowship and humility.[27] Li Hung-chang told Martin: 'The missionaries are good men, I know, but your code of morals is defective ... it lays too much stress on charity, and too little on justice.'[28]

Christians made enemies of the gentry and officials as well. Hard-pressed to keep order already, a local magistrate resented the priests who claimed equal, if not greater authority than himself, who usurped the official's traditional rôle as a moral example, and as the provider of succour for the needy and the poor, and who, in particular, hamstrung his judicial proceedings. Torn between incensed literati who retreated into yet more inflexible Confucianism, the pleas of the people to punish or at least curtail the Christians' activities, and the orders from Peking to keep the treaty and not incur further reprisals, the average official fell back into frustrated inertia, and liked the Christians no better for his enforced impotence and the gathering crisis around him.

When inflammatory anti-Christian literature infiltrated into their area, the literati therefore did little to stop it. As it was illegal, and as the moral climate was traditionally set by them, their silence was tantamount to encouragement. 'A Record of Facts to Ward Off Heterodoxy', the most famous and most salacious of the anti-Christian tracts, which continued to flourish in many forms throughout the century, was at first written anonymously by 'the most heartbroken man in the world', a propagandist of some apparent education. It appeared in 1861 in Hunan, a bastion of traditional philosophy, and heralded a spate of placards and pamphlets throughout the decade and later which cemented Taoist, Buddhist and Confucianist interests against the single common enemy with a passion that would eventually explode into the Boxer Uprising. Christianity, said the tract, and other religions later based on it, used magic and the cabbala to charm converts and drive them mad, to inspire them to smash their ancestral tablets and violate shrines; Christians boiled the corpses of their priests to extract an ointment used in baptism; they prepared children for sodomy by stretching their anuses as infants; they used the flesh of new born babies and the eyes and hearts of the dead for medicines, for alchemy, and even for photography; their success at alchemy accounted for the riches with which they seduced Chinese converts; they drank the menstrual blood of women – hence their pungent and horrid smell; their priests acted as spies for their country.[29] Amongst all the slanders and fantasy, the 'most heartbroken man in the world' interspersed enough accurate description of Christian beliefs to give his document validity. Certainly it encapsulated a powerful emotion, for throughout the 1860s, ugly incidents broke out all over the empire: in Kweichow and Szechuan, in Taiwan, in Fukien, church property was plundered and burnt, and missionaries were stoned and sometimes murdered. Chinese hatred was such that a church in southern Kwangtung was razed for a second time even after the villagers had paid for its previous restoration out of their own hard-pressed pockets.

Sometimes the consuls struck back with immediate, independent gunboat action, scaring the Chinese to their knees. But to force redress and restitution at the blunt end of a gun was a myopic and superficial solution to the growing problem. In one such action in Taiwan, thirty-four people were killed and wounded in a riot caused by the British consul's revenge for the destruction of some church property. The French were often even hastier, and vengefully dispatched punitive expeditions to troublespots. In 1869 a French minister slipped up the Yangstze with four gunboats, and exacted indemnities and apologies on the spot from the local officials. Immediately the merchants and missionaries rose to shout to the diplomats that it was pointless wrangling with the Tsungli Yamen, and that might prevailed much quicker. They failed to perceive how dangerously such actions stoked the people's hatred.

In the humid summer of 1870 an epidemic swept through the convent of the Sisters of St Vincent de Paul at Tientsin, carrying off thirty to forty babies in the nuns' care. The situation was already tense for, after the Treaty of Tientsin in 1860, the French and British troops had been quartered in the city for nearly three years. The memories of their occupation were not pleasant. The French cathedral, carefully placed on the site of a temple, a far more imposing building than the congregation warranted, had been consecrated with much pomp in June 1869. The French consulate was as offendingly situated – in the grounds of a destroyed imperial villa.

In stupid, blind kindliness, the nuns were so keen to save the souls of un-baptized children that they offered cash rewards for orphans brought to them, particularly if moribund, for then their unravished souls went straight to heaven. The toll in the convent was therefore abnormally high, and ugly tales of black magic practised on the children grew so fast and furiously that, when a series of kidnappings broke out in Tientsin early in the summer of 1870, the nuns were immediately implicated. Then a Chinese confessed, under torture, that he had had relations with a doorman who worked in the Catholic compound, and that he had sold him stolen children for the nuns. A group of Chinese marched to the cemetery, and disinterring the bodies of the baby victims of the epidemic, sent the wild angry story racing through the town. The officials immediately demanded a search of the convent in order to quieten the turbulent crowds. But the French consul, Henri Fontanier, a defender of the true faith, rudely accused the Chinese magistrate of stirring up the trouble himself. Ch'ung-hou, Superintendent of Trade in the three northern ports, called on Fontanier personally, and soothingly persuaded him to allow the search which would obviously clear the nuns of all suspicion. On 21 June three Chinese mandarins arrived at the convent to carry out the inspection. Fontanier, when he heard the news, rushed, two pistols in his belt, and brandishing a sword to Ch'ung-hou's office. He shouted abuse at him, screamed that the inspection had been sprung on him unknowingly, swiped madly at the furniture and crockery in the *yamen*, hitting the official's desk. Then he shot at him with his pistol, but fortunately missed. Enraged, Fontanier plunged into the crowd that had gathered outside – an indignant, curious, but orderly crowd, of householders and townspeople, not rabble. The consulate chancellor who was with him carved a passage with his sword. One of the Chinese officials moved forward to stop him, Fontanier thought he was attacking him, shot wildly and killed one of his retinue. His chancellor followed suit and fired twice.

The crowd went berserk, fell upon the consul and the chancellor, and tore them limb from limb. Surging into the cathedral, they set fire to it, and then swelled on through the town until they reached the nunnery. The orphanage was assaulted and set alight, and ten nuns were seized, stripped and obscenely mutilated and murdered. Two priests, seven foreigners, and a number of Chinese converts were caught up in the horror and butchered.

The magnitude of the disaster was not lost on Prince Kung or on Tz'u-hsi. All they had fought for since 1860 had been shattered. By 22 August, five French, one American and three British gunboats loomed off the coast; further south, at Chefoo, six more patrolled. The Chinese, well schooled now in foreign revenge, acted swiftly.

Tz'u-hsi summoned Li Hung-chang to Peking immediately, and in spite of the people's increasing detestation of the foreigner urged him continually to adopt a conciliating tone and so avoid further bloodshed and war. Nevertheless the edict Tz'u-hsi issued from the throne stated the case fairly: 'The disorder arose partly because of the suspicion in the hearts of the people that the rabble who use tricks to steal children were in direct contact with the Roman Catholics, and partly also because of the conduct of the French consul, M. Fontanier.'[30]

Tseng Kuo-fan, the viceroy of the area, and therefore nominally responsible, was much too valuable a piece to play and lose. Ironically, the viceroy in Tseng's former seat at Nanking, a Moham-medan who had been sympathetic to the Christians, was murdered in the wave of violence that followed the Tientsin massacre, and although the assassination of a viceroy in his *yamen* was a hideous affair, the empress breathed a sigh of relief and spirited Tseng back to his old post. Li Hung-chang, obeying Prince Kung and Tz'u-hsi's command, pacified the Christians with the execution of eighteen men, sentenced twenty-five to hard labour, paid 280,000 taels indemnity for the loss of life, 212,500 for the damage to property, and dispatched Ch'ung-hou to France to apologize to the French government in person. Li patched up the horror skilfully and humbly, and in view of earlier precedents, the Chinese got off lightly. However the real reason China was saved from another 1860 was not Li's craft, but the Franco-Prussian war of 1870, which, striking at Paris itself, turned French eyes away from troubles in the distant East.

The heartfelt if not entirely coherent efforts of Confucian states-men to come to terms with the West were consumed in the same flames that reduced the cathedral and convent of Tientsin to rubble. For the following year, when the Tsungli Yamen drew up a list of missionary abuses and proposed remedies, feasible and otherwise, to the situation that had flared into the massacre, the treaty powers rejected them all summarily. The T'ung-chih Restoration had ultimately failed to bind Chinese and Western interests by a policy of mutual compromise; and its stand on traditional Chinese values revealed the irreconcilable differences between Eastern and Western beliefs and ambitions.

Tz'u-hsi, all eyes and ears as the regent, sighed angrily about the problems caused by the missionaries when she received Tseng Kuo-fan in 1870 after the massacre. 'It would be a fine thing', she said, 'if we could secure ourselves properly against invasion. These missionary complications are perpetually creating trouble for us.'[31] Soon, she would take for granted the words of her minister to Paris and London, Tseng Chi–tse, Tseng's son, when she gave him audience in 1878: 'Chinese ministers and people usually hate foreigners, as goes without saying, but we must plan gradually to make ourselves strong before anything can be done.'[32]

Chapter Seven

GLORIOUS SUCCESSION

During the years of the T'ung-chih Restoration, Tz'u-hsi saw Prince Kung each day at the dawn audience in her council chambers. He was her mentor, her example, the statesman from whom she learnt the methods and skills and procedures of government, who shaped her outlook and her policies. Yet the strict etiquette of the Forbidden City prevented them from meeting informally to eat together or walk in the gardens and discuss an affair of state. Their meetings were distant and formal, but they probably wished them to be. Prince Kung was not an easy man, but proud and short-tempered with a tendency to scorn and flippancy; Tz'u-hsi, conscious of her debt to him, stood on her dignity, and was offended he did not take her as seriously as she took herself. Their original alliance had not been based on friendship, but on necessity, for it was Su-shun's ambitions that had made each recognize in the other a quality that could be useful. Although Tz'u-hsi had adopted Prince Kung's eldest daughter, Jung-shou, in 1862 at the age of eight, as a mark of her friendship towards the child's father, there continued to exist, behind the subtleties of *comme-il-faut*, a certain discomfiture between the regent and her chief counsellor.

Prince Kung was remarkable because he adapted to foreigners' presence on Chinese soil, because he grasped that the line of least resistance was, in their case, a strong one. But he was not a man of revolutionary vision and his limitations, his reliance on traditional Confucian doctrine, coloured Tz'u-hsi's later actions. During the first five years of the Restoration, from 1861 to 1865, as she took lessons obediently in history and the classics, as she improved her calligraphy, she kept her faculties sharp, and so witnessed the pitiless crushing of many rebellions, and the co-operative policy with foreign powers in action. The former was despotism's time-tested method, but Prince Kung's endorsement fed Tz'u-hsi's natural warlikeness, and did not help to open her eyes to the possibility that men and women of different persuasions could live together in harmony; the co-operative policy burgeoned, but died with the massacre at Tientsin. Prince Kung's shortcomings mirrored those of China's guiding philosophy, and as Tz'u-hsi observed him and agreed with his counsels, her faith in conformism was enhanced and her dependence on violent means of obtaining it increased.

In 1852 Hsien-feng had given his brother Prince Kung a palace of fabled beauty and opulence to the west of the Forbidden City. Earlier it had belonged to the favourite of Ch'ien-lung, Ho-shen, his chief adviser, who by unbridled graft and corruption had become the richest man in China. With consummate craftsmen's skills he had furnished and decorated his palace in sumptuous style. Prince Kung held the highest authority of any minister in the empire, and he never took pains to disguise it. His manners were 'short'[1] and before he came to power had already landed him in trouble: in 1855, when his mother died, Hsien-feng, who had been brought up by her, stripped Prince Kung of all his posts for his unseemly absence of mourning.

When, in 1864, a few months after the inspiring collapse of Nanking and the Taiping rebellion, Tz'u-hsi celebrated her thirtieth birthday and was given two more honorific titles, Tuan-yu (Orthodox and Heaven-blessed) and the 100,000 taels that accompanied each of them, she felt a corresponding rush of confidence in her own powers and began to abandon the docile behaviour of a pupil. In April 1865, in audience with Prince Kung, she suddenly began shrieking for help, and staging a terrible rage, had Prince Kung hustled from her presence. He had moved near the throne to attack her, she claimed and gave orders that he should be instantly discharged of all his duties. Her accusations were ridiculously vague: rebellion, presumption and nepotism.

Tz'u-hsi, chafing under Prince Kung's domination, had now unsheathed her claws, and declared that while Prince Kung had placed her on the throne, she could use her power to topple him. Giving him a week to digest the development, she then announced, with gracious magnanimity: 'The position which he has occupied in special relationship to the Throne is unparalleled, therefore we expect much from him, and, when he erred, the punishment which we were compelled to inflict upon him was necessarily severe.' With some relish, she continued: 'He has now repented him of the evil and acknowledged his sins. For our part we had no prejudice in this matter, and were animated only by a strict impartiality; it was inconceivable that we should desire to treat harshly a councillor of such tried ability, or to deprive ourselves of the valuable assistance of the Prince. We therefore restore him to the Grand Council, but in order that his authority may be reduced, we do not propose to reinstate him in his position as "Adviser to the Government".'[2]

In 1865, when she issued that decree, Tz'u-hsi's personality suddenly took on form and substance, as the face of a friend detaches itself from rows of phantoms in a group photograph. She had declared her interest, and relegated the most powerful man in the country to a post – an important post – but one which no longer singled him out. She further stemmed his powers: striking one brother down, she raised another up. Prince Ch'un, seven years younger than Prince Kung, significantly married to Tz'u-hsi's younger sister, was an agreeable but narrow Manchu, less positive or far-sighted than his brother. He was now appointed supervisor of the boy emperor T'ung-chih's education – an office of prestige and influence. It was the first instance of a method Tz'u-hsi practised till the end of her life, for she always tried to balance a reactionary against a progressive in her councils – a method that usually dissolved both sides' policy.

At this stage Tz'u-hsi only established that it was to her, not to Prince Kung, certainly not to Niuhuru, her co-regent, that questions of policy were to be directed. But she did not depart from the description of this, her first regency: 'Listening behind Screens to Government Affairs'. She had all the facts at her fingertips, as she listened to her councillors' debates from behind the yellow curtain, and she probed them with streams of questions, listened to their answers, responses and ideas, and tried to nudge them towards a decision. But she rarely suggested a solution herself. Later, when the decrees had been drafted, she and Niuhuru signed them together. During the T'ung-chih Restoration, Tz'u-hsi did not block the forward movement of the co-operative policy, or disagree with Prince Kung and the others' insistence on self-strengthening by adopting certain Western methods. She was open-minded, concerned and compliant. What she effected was a marked but subtle shift of psychological emphasis which made her ministers look to her as a personality as well as a figurehead.

In private she flung herself into the pleasures and extravagances of palace life with ebullient happiness. Her morals were widely debated, for Jung-lu, whom she had known as a young girl, and who had escorted her and her child with a posse of his Peking Field Force cavalry back from the mountains of Manchuria, was the intimate of her young widowhood. 'Your slave', recalled Jung-lu as an old man, 'received many marks of the imperial favour and rose to be Minister of the Household; I was thus constantly in attendance on Your Majesty.'[3] Torrid tales were breathed in the theatres and streets of the capital. Certainly the stifling luxury of the palace with its

Accompanied by Li Lien-ying and other eunuchs, Tz'u-hsi sets out on her favourite wanderings through the palace gardens

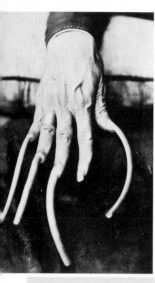

The hand, and the 'lily' foot, of the leisured classes in China

The house of a Confucian official: his wives and daughters stand apart, but his eldest son has the place of honour at his side

Above: A company of Manchu bannermen, employed as guards for the British consul in Canton

Left: Prince Kung, China's most statesmanlike adviser of the period

Above: On 21 August 1860, the British and French troops scaled the fortifications of the north Taku forts, slaughtering over a thousand Chinese

Left: The Kuang-hsu Emperor, 'of Glorious Succession', on his charger

大清國當今慈禧端佑康頤昭豫莊誠壽恭欽獻崇熙皇太后

Tz'u-hsi paid the strictest attention to appearances, but her vanities were rooted in respectable Confucian teachings

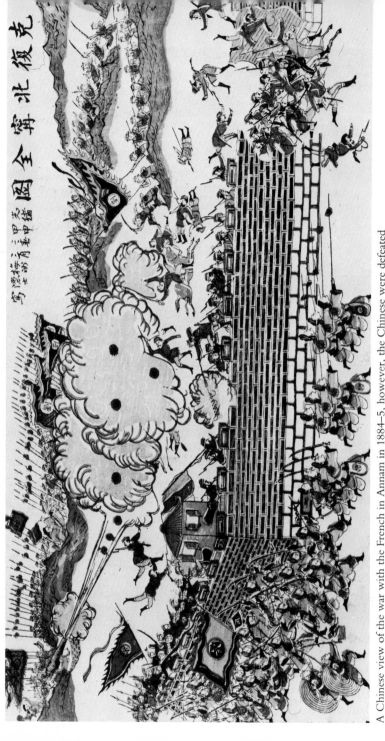

克復北寧全圖

光緒十年甲申孟春粵東寫照

A Chinese view of the war with the French in Annam in 1884–5, however, the Chinese were defeated

Tz'u-hsi as Kuan-yin, Goddess of mercy, with the Chief Eunuch as an attendant divinity

The only gun inside the legations: 'Our Betsy', or 'The International'

After her return to Peking in 1902 Tz'u-hsi stooped to conquer the wives of foreign diplomats and their adopted Chinese orphans

thousands of emasculated inmates must have made Tz'u-hsi long for diversion; certainly she was young and full of vitality. Although Jung-lu never took an examination, although politically he was unimaginative and often undecided, he rose to the highest positions in the country under Tz'u-hsi. Altogether he epitomized a type Tz'u-hsi always favoured, for, in spite of the Chinese flavour of her upbringing, the Manchu *mensch*, the quick-draw who rode at full gallop at the head of his men had, especially as she grew older and more sheltered, an irresistible glamour for her, often leading her later to listen to the advice of robber chieftains and ex-bandits.

On the flanks therefore of the Manchu statesmen in Peking, a new type of official – the Chinese soldier – was beginning to interest her. The bureaucracy had been shattered by the Taiping rebellion, and energetic and martial men had rushed in. Tz'u-hsi was attracted by them: her decrees to Tseng Kuo-fan, to Li Hung-chang and Tso Tsung-t'ang ring out her enthusiasm for their exploits. In an audience with Tseng in 1870 she discussed the Tientsin massacre, but showed searching concern for his personal safety and health. Her style of giving audience was brusque and ingenuous:

Tz'u-hsi: Have you quite lost the sight of your right eye?
Tseng Kuo-fan: Yes, it is quite blind; but I can still see with the left.
Tz'u-hsi: Have you entirely recovered from your other maladies?
Tseng: Yes, I think I can say that I have.
Tz'u-hsi: You appear to kneel, and to rise from that posture quite briskly and freely as if your physique were still pretty good?
Tseng: No, it is not what it used to be.[4]

Although Tz'u-hsi's colleague Niuhuru was present at Tseng's audience, he mentions her only in passing and it emerges clearly from his account that Niuhuru had continued to pale into the background, and that, placid and indolent by nature, she was delighted to let her quicker-witted, more ambitious friend and colleague read and collate the piles of dry memorials each week and take all political initiative.

When, three years later, Tseng Kuo-fan died at his post in Nanking, his eminent place in China's affairs was taken by Li Hung-chang, who had fought under him in the Taiping rebellion. Tz'u-hsi was disturbed by Li's crude Anhwei accent, and by his familiar offhand manners, but she found a real comrade and a trusted adviser in him, for with his business acumen he was almost unique among Chinese at the time in seeing the virtues of Western industrial development, and was able to divine Tz'u-hsi's fatal flaw, her love of money, of acquisitions, of wealth, of a material show of allegiance, of squirrelling useless hoards. Li, who had been poor himself also, was equally keen: his commercial instincts prodded China into modern times, for, in the 1870s and 1880s he built railways and telegraphs, opened mines and started a fleet of merchant ships, all of which helped to line his own pockets and to win his way into Tz'u-hsi's good graces. In 1865 she appointed him acting viceroy of Liang-kiang; in 1867 viceroy of Hunan and Hupeh; in 1871 she summoned him to her side after the Tientsin massacre, and gave him the key viceroyalty of Chihli, the metropolitan province, a post which by further generosity to the throne and his own decided, if devious, gifts, Li Hung-chang kept for twenty-five years until he was seventy-three, breaking with the tradition of rotating officials every few years throughout China. As viceroy of Chihli, Li moved the provincial capital from the small closed town of Pao-ting to the treaty port of Tientsin, an indication of how well he understood that China's relations with foreign powers were the central issue of his time. Li became the statesman on whom Tz'u-hsi relied in foreign affairs, sending him to negotiate treaties with Japan, Russia, France and Great Britain throughout his long life. The 'colossal' diplomat, with his 'very small, bright and scrutinizing eyes' who was 'the exaggeration of the Mongol type', and had 'a certain beauty and lordly demeanour'[5] was famous in Europe, and although his abilities were respected, his venality was notorious, and hardly increased the foreign powers' confidence in China's regeneration. As early as 1864 Robert Hart had awarded Li 50,000 taels to reconcile him with Gordon after a quarrel over the executions of some Taiping princes at Soochow, and by 1870 Li's corruption and nepotism were common knowledge. Hart wrote spitefully home at the time of the Tientsin massacre in 1870: 'Li Hung-chang has been sent to Tientsin; it is thought he will at all events deal energetically with the question, but, as rumour has it, his hand itches, and, if his palm has been greased, he will fail to advance the question very much towards settlement.'[6] Li was also blunt and suspicious, and suspected in others the same grubbing characteristics he knew in himself. In 1872 John Thomson, the photographer, was presented to him and Li was shown photographs possibly for the first time in his life. Instead of marvelling at the invention, Li demanded crossly what 'rewards' Thomson expected, and when given an album of his pictures, he 'rapidly turned the leaves pettishly over, and remarked: 'The book is not full; how is it I do not get more? Are you cheating me?'[7]

Li Hung-chang's presents to Tz'u-hsi, and others like his, were the produce of the provinces under the officials' control, and therefore ground from the labour of the Chinese people, who already paid several taxes and heavy tribute to Peking in rice, in order to keep the Dragon Court in accustomed magnificence. The Restoration's reform programme never touched the canker of graft which was eating into every branch and ramification of the Chinese bureaucracy. Rank itself was sold to raise revenue: it was estimated that thirty-six per cent of the lower gentry after 1854 had bought their status. In 1883, according to K'ang Yu-wei, the great reformer of the nineties, Tz'u-hsi needed funds and began selling the rank of magistrate for two or three thousand taels, of prefect for four to five thousand and of circuit intendant for seven or eight thousand.[8] Rank did not entail office, but made the holder eligible for office. Provincial officials, paid a meagre salary, traditionally raised money elsewhere at their own discretion, and in troubled and rebellious times, often degenerated to cheating and bribery, favours and oppression. At Peking the Forbidden City became more and more extravagant under Tz'u-hsi and the maladministration of the eunuchs she spoiled. One estimate reckoned the annual cost of upkeep at £6,500,000.[9] Gifts to the throne had always been customary before an audience was granted, but under Tz'u-hsi they became almost statutory. In the sixties and early seventies Tz'u-hsi had only just begun to tap this rich vein of profit; twenty years later, she was pumping it dry. Of the great men under Tz'u-hsi only Li Hung-chang was as grasping, or as wealthy, as she was, for the Chinese system, which trusted its 'men of ability' to be honest and true, was sometimes rewarded: Tseng Kuo-fan, Wen-hsiang, Tso Tsung-t'ang and many later viceroys all repaid that trust by living and dying in Confucian simplicity.

In 1865, Tz'u-hsi's important thirtieth year, her son the emperor was nine years old. T'ung-chih was a good-looking, clear-complexioned little boy, but in many ways he disappointed his mother. For he was bored by his studies, by the hours of arid indoctrination in the classics, by the laborious lessons in calligraphy and the Chinese language, by learning Manchu as well. In spite of the flower of Chinese academe to teach him, he made little progress. Weng T'ung-ho, one of his most important tutors, continually bewailed in his diary the emperor's lack of concentration, his diversionary tactics, and the way the child 'played and laughed while I was teaching him'.[10] T'ung-chih had inherited his mother's wilfulness, but also his father's 'wandering spirit'. Niuhuru, Tz'u-hsi's colleague, reassured the child in her mild and unaffected way that she completely agreed that his studies were desiccated and dull, though necessary for an emperor. But Tz'u-hsi wanted her son to excel, and therefore drove him on and into the arms and affections of the tender and gentle Niuhuru.

For political as well as maternal reasons, Tz'u-hsi was fiercely attached to T'ung-chih her son. Having had him stolen from her once before at Jehol in 1860, she knew the pain and precariousness of losing him, and she now found him so handsome, so dutiful, the way he brought her, when he was only ten, the first persimmons to ripen that year before eating them himself.[11] Also, they shared one particular love which bound them close: they were both addicted to theatricals. Tz'u-hsi relished the highly romantic tales of star-crossed lovers, the edifying stories of filial piety, the religious masques based on Buddhist lore. They had fun, mother and son, dressed up in the magnificent costumes and parading to the clash and tinkle of the court musicians, but it was extravagant fun, and it increased the influence of the eunuchs, the actors, over the young emperor. In 1866 the censors wrote sternly: at a time of great national distress and poverty, when every penny was needed for the army, and for relief measures in the rebel areas, the court was dallying at the theatre. Significantly they also reminded Tz'u-hsi and Niuhuru that 'there should not be about the Throne any young eunuchs of attractive appearance, creatures who make it their aim to establish influence over the emperor'.[12] The empress, in a decree, agreed wholeheartedly. But nothing was changed. T'ung-chih remained the only man in the Forbidden City of six thousand people, stifled during his growing years by women and eunuchs, alternately cosseted, pampered, scolded and adorned by his master-ful and overpowering mother. When the early Ch'ing emperors had been children, they had been educated to shoot and to hunt, and had spent their summers at Jehol, wheeling and careering in the moun-tains on their sure-footed, shaggy Mongol ponies, and dozens of brothers and cousins had played with and learnt lessons beside them. But the Manchu strain had weakened and the emperor's family had shrunk: T'ung-chih was the first Ch'ing emperor to grow up alone, without siblings and almost without cousins of his own age for company. In such an orchidaceous atmosphere it was hardly sur-prising that he was self-willed, petulant, spoilt and effeminate.

Tz'u-hsi indulged the eunuchs and paid no heed to the danger of their influence over her son, because they were her only constant companions. An Te-hai, the Chief Eunuch, who may have helped her machinations at Jehol in 1861, was her favourite during the

1860s, the head of her household, her emasculated cicisbeo. Born in 1844, he was, by all repute, tall and handsome, well-educated and accomplished, and sang and danced beautifully. He was not a eunuch at all, the gossips whispered. But the inspections at the palace were strict, and Tz'u-hsi, a young widow, could relax psychologically, flirting and enjoying the company of the attractive eunuch who could not menace her.

Forgetting the censure of three years earlier, Tz'u-hsi sent An Te-hai in 1869 to Nanking in the south on a special mission to the factories where the silks and brocades were woven for the court's use. She had ordered a new design, and she wanted An te-hai to inspect its progress. Secretly, she may have asked him to raise more funds on her behalf. Eunuchs were however forbidden to leave Peking, and yet An Te-hai sailed down the Grand Canal, the superb feat of ancient engineering which links Tungchow near the capital with Hangchow, the southern port eight hundred miles away. Flying dragon and phoenix flags as emblems of his imperial mission, the Chief Eunuch travelled in a procession of junks, including two imperial dragon barges, and behaved with such authority and ceremony that local officials, nonplussed and awestruck, met all his requests and even brought him tribute. When his birthday fell, as he was passing through Shantung, he hired girl musicians to play on the poop, and, dressed in dragon robes, to the sound of their pipes and cymbals, he received the congratulations of his retinue.

In the face of Prince Kung's exasperation when he read the report of the Governor of Shantung, describing the illegal presumption and folly of her Chief Eunuch, Tz'u-hsi was helpless. An Te-hai's execution was ordered, and Tz'u-hsi herself was forced to seal the death warrant of her favourite. She hoped to run a messenger to him in time, before the order reached the governor, and effect his escape. But he was incarcerated, and even if he had escaped, a palace eunuch could hardly have found cover. On 12 September 1869, An Te-hai was beheaded and his companions strangled.

Prince Kung may have plotted beforehand to remove An Te-hai and his pernicious influence; or he may have ordered the execution after the governor's report, but secretly, without Tz'u-hsi's knowledge. Many versions of the story say that Prince Kung forced the gentle and obliging Niuhuru to take an independent decision for once, and that their action marked the beginning of the split between the two women. But it is much more likely that Prince Kung abruptly and angrily confronted Tz'u-hsi with the consequences of her own violation of dynastic laws, and forced her to have a hand in her friend's death. Yet her resignation and penitence must have been complete, for Ting Pao-chen, the governor of Shantung, retained his post; he was promoted to viceroy of Szechuan in 1876 where he remained, honoured and respected, until his death ten years later.

Although for some years after her favourite's death Tz'u-hsi's revels were more restrained, the damage had already been done to her son. The first Ch'ing emperor with no summer palace at all as refuge, no uplifting expanses of parkland and lake, T'ung-chih grew impatient with his confinement within the Purple Forbidden City, and soon found the eunuchs in his entourage willing to introduce him to the spectacles and pleasures of the city of Peking outside. Stealing out incognito, T'ung-chih drank and caroused and smoked and watched dancing girls in the bars and restaurants of the capital, frequented the many theatres and street shows, with their painted catamites and transvestite actors. He was only fifteen, but he was Hsien-feng's son, and he had, it seemed, inherited all his father's ambisexual leanings and taste for debauchery.

Tz'u-hsi fostered his downfall, for then he neglected his main duties as emperor and left the government to her. Or so it is alleged. But his nightly escapades may have been concealed from her, or proud of his maturity, and blind to its dangers, she may have enjoyed vicariously the glamorous and adult and exciting tales of her child. Psychologically also, her hold on her beloved only son became stronger, when the only women he knew were harlots and dancers and forbidden lily-footed Chinese.

In 1872 T'ung-chih reached the age of sixteen, old enough to marry, and therefore, as Tz'u-hsi had done nearly twenty years before, the daughters of Manchu officials answered the imperial summons and appeared at the palace. Unlike his father Hsien-feng, T'ung-chih, expert of the brothels of Peking, was present to choose his bride. Alute, eighteen-year-old daughter of Ch'ung-ch'i, a Mongol official of the old stamp, great-grand-daughter of Prince Cheng (who was sentenced to suicide in 1861) was fitted by her high breeding to become T'ung-chih's empress, while her appointment would also heal the discord between the throne and her powerful Mongol clan. Also, T'ung-chih was enchanted by her looks. As his jealous mother complained later, 'We made a mistake in selecting a wife for him. How could we tell that her beauty was false? She was so very beautiful, but she hated us.'[13] Three other concubines were chosen for the young emperor – one of them was, surprisingly, Alute's own aunt. Some writers have claimed Tz'u-hsi's choice of empress was a different girl, and that Alute was Niuhuru's favourite, and that the rivalry between the two empresses for T'ung-chih's affections was therefore exacerbated. But Tz'u-hsi's dislike of Alute arose very simply: the innocent young girl threatened to supplant her, not only in her son's heart, but also in political power. While T'ung-chih lived, Tz'u-hsi, his mother, was comparatively secure in her authority over him. But should he die, leaving a family, Alute would become Empress Dowager with direct influence, even though Tz'u-hsi, as an Empress Dowager of a senior generation, and grandmother of an emperor, would hold higher rank.

On the night of 15 October 1872, at 11.30 pm, the hour appointed by the court astrologers, Alute left her father's house to live in the Forbidden City. Her furniture – a bed, a mirror, two wardrobes, chairs and eight marriage chests – had symbolically preceded her. Her path was strewn with yellow sand, and the streets lined with soldiers of the eight Manchu Banners, who had forbidden everyone to watch her progress, had closed all shutters and doors and erected screens. Prince Kung and the president of the Board of Revenue, as mediators of the marriage, walked at the procession's head. Silent musicians, yellow plumes waving in their hats, followed in serried ranks; then came hundreds of attendants in scarlet robes bearing painted lanterns on slender wands, or huge festal ceremonial umbrellas embroidered with *feng* birds, symbol of the bride; then the Seal and Book of the new empress; then horses caparisoned in golden harnesses and saddles; then sundry gifts, incense burners, golden ewers, lavishly upholstered chairs; then gaily coloured banners of all description, including some on which the dragon and the phoenix were intertwined in union. As this gorgeous train stepped softly and solemnly through the darkened city, the inhabitants of Peking peeped through holes they pushed through the precautionary blue screens to see the empress's golden-yellow palanquin, carried aloft by sixteen bearers, surrounded by eunuchs in imperial-yellow robes and by the imperial guard, pressing close, superbly mounted, with leopard's tails dangling from their lances.[14]

Five days after the emperor and Alute were married, Tz'u-hsi and Niuhuru ordered the astrologers to name a time auspicious for T'ung-chih's official assumption of his imperial powers. The stars pointed to 23 February 1873, and on that day, the T'ung-chih Emperor, aged seventeen, the moral advice and exhortations of his mother ringing in his ears, took up his throne.

Immediately afterwards, the Tsungli Yamen received a collective note from the foreign ministers in Peking requesting an audience with the new emperor. In 1861 Hsien-feng had lain inaccessibly at

Jehol; until now, the Yamen had always offered T'ung-chih's minority as an excuse. The Chinese tried, halfheartedly, to stall – Wen-hsiang was ill and could not attend to business, they said. On 5 March the ministers sent another note, and finally, Prince Kung communicated that the young emperor, hearing that the foreign representatives had implored an audience, had graciously consented. The etiquette was thoroughly rehearsed, though to the horror of the Chinese the ministers and their interpreters giggled and joked as they went over it. On the 19 June 1873, a fine Sunday in Peking, at 5 am, the ambassador of Japan, and the ministers of Great Britain, France, Russia, America and the Netherlands gathered together and, after tea with Prince Kung, entered at 9 am the Tzu Kuang Ko, Pavilion of Violet Light, a large raised building where the emperor sat upon his throne. Although they did not have to prostrate themselves before the Son of Heaven, but only incline their heads, the pavilion in which the foreign emissaries were received was not one of the many imposing Halls of Audience in the Forbidden City itself, but a smaller one in the Sea Palaces to the west, where, normally, military examinations were held and the envoys of tributary nations given audience. Also, this momentous occasion, won at the cost of so much bloodshed and sweat, lasted under half an hour. The emperor, who looked about fourteen to the assembled ministers, spoke inaudibly in Manchu to the kneeling Prince Kung, who then translated his words into Chinese. Nothing of any importance was said, but the all-important principle had been upheld.

The Chinese saved face. The *Peking Gazette*, not an official publication but a bulletin of government matters, reported that the ministers had not performed the kowtow, but had nevertheless trembled from limb to limb and been struck dumb in terror at the awesome majesty of the emperor: 'The ministers have admitted that divine virtue certainly emanated from the Emperor, hence the fear and trembling they felt even when they did not look upon His Majesty.'[15] Tz'u-hsi must have chuckled at the interpretation.

Neither T'ung-chih's new responsibilities, nor his alleged love of Alute could reform his proclivities. Kuei-ch'ing, one of his tutors, criticized his behaviour and his carelessness publicly, named eunuchs and members of the household who were his drinking companions, and was cashiered from all his posts for his pains. Much to her delight, T'ung-chih's mother was therefore left the care of politics and government, and was able to conspire for the one desire of her covetous and sybarite nature: the reconstruction of the ruined summer palace, the Yuan Ming Yuan. T'ung-chih understandably also longed for a retreat from the opressively hot summers of Peking, and wanted to restore the symbol of his dynasty's pride and might. Tz'u-hsi, now that her son had officially assumed the throne, was to retire, and in emulation of his august predecessors K'ang-hsi and Ch'ien-lung, T'ung-chih was willing to present her with a garden palace on her fortieth birthday, which would fall in 1874. Accordingly Prince Kung gave his sovereign twenty thousand taels towards the rebuilding, and other mandarins followed his example.

When the British had burned down the Yuan Ming Yuan in 1860, they had in their haste left some buildings standing, and if the Chinese had been able to face the shame immediately afterwards and carry out a detailed survey, they would have been able to salvage much more. Twelve years of neglect, of wind and weather, of scavengers and thieves had however successfully wrecked the palaces and the gardens. Nevertheless some exquisite pagodas still stood, and some marble and stone buildings and bridges remained. In 1873 workmen moved into the grounds and began repairs and reconstructions. But a censor wrote indignantly that the country could not afford such irresponsible waste when the land was still ravaged by the recently crushed Taiping rebellion, when the Miao and Moslem uprisings had not yet been suppressed, when the Chinese people needed every tael, candareen or cash to relieve its hunger and its sufferings. The censor was rebuked for obstructing the emperor's filial action toward his mother, but a year later, after a great deal of expense, the contractors were charged with cheating over the timber supplies, and Prince Kung, Prince Ch'un, his brother, and Wen-hsiang, the statesman, begged the emperor in a written petition to call an end to the repairs, to avoid the corrupting company of his favourite eunuchs, to supervise the conduct of the court more closely, and above all to pay attention to good advice, like theirs, when given. They also exhorted him to take healthy exercise in the open air. When his memorial was presented to the emperor, Wen-hsiang 'nearly died of weeping'.[16]

The emperor was enraged, and flying into a temper which recalled his mother's, charged Prince Kung with using language lacking in proper respect, ever since he, T'ung-chih, had begun to rule. He degraded Prince Kung one rank, and abolished the hereditary title he had granted him on the day of his marriage to Alute. But T'ung-chih, even in his anger, could not spare Prince Kung from the Grand Council, and in spite of Tz'u-hsi's remonstrations against the minister who had again dared to defy her desires, T'ung-chih reinstated him on 11 September 1874, and ordered that the reconstruction of the Yuan Ming Yuan be abandoned. Tz'u-hsi repined in frustration, and cast about for other more stealthy and more effective means of obtaining the garden palace that she coveted.

The emperor's uncles had urged him to get plenty of outdoor exercise because the adolescent boy's nightly dissipations were beginning to take a toll on his health. He was drinking and smoking in excess – and may even have tried opium quite frequently; he is rumoured to have caught venereal disease, from the dancers or from the transvestites of the Willow Lanes and Flower Streets of the city. When the planet Venus passed across the face of the sun that year, the superstitious Chinese feared for the life of the Son of Heaven.

In December 1874, T'ung-chih's weakened frame was 'visited by the heavenly flowers'. The Chinese did practice a form of inoculation against smallpox by taking a scab off a victim and inserting it up the nostril of a child to inhale. It was not an entirely efficient method, and whether or not it had been tried with T'ung-chih is not known. As he lay feverish, Prince Ch'un, his uncle, made the ancestral sacrifices at the Temple of Heaven, recalling an earlier year when Hsien-feng had lain ill at Jehol and Prince Kung had officiated for him in the capital. From his sickbed, the emperor decreed: 'I beg the two Empresses to have pity on my state and allow me to take care of myself . . . . In looking after the affairs of state for a time, the Empresses will crown their great goodness towards me and I will show them everlasting gratitude.'[17] Tz'u-hsi was, officially, Regent once more.

On 23 December, the spots had dried out and the fever had abated. In the rejoicing that followed the recovery, T'ung-chih bestowed gifts and titles on his officials, including the forgiven Prince Kung. But the celebrations were premature: in January, his fever returned. In his valediction T'ung-chih thanked the Dowager Empresses for 'their greatest possible tenderness in the care of our person', and on 12 January 1875, he died. His face was turned towards the south and he was arrayed in the robes of longevity for his journey to the grave. He was only nineteen, and although he had been emperor since 1861, he had ruled for under two years.

A court official, Yün Yü-ting, accused Tz'u-hsi in his memoirs of precipitating the emperor's relapse. The loving Alute, he said, was visiting T'ung-chih on his sickbed, and, complaining of Tz'u-hsi's interfering and domineering ways, was happily looking forward to the day T'ung-chih would be well again and they could live and rule together. Tz'u-hsi, warned by eavesdropping eunuchs, entered the room in stockinged feet, and hearing Alute's criticisms, flew into a rage and rampaged through the room, seized the young girl by the hair and hit her, shouting that by making love to the emperor she would bring on his illness again. She ordered the eunuchs to take her away and beat her. T'ung-chih, barely over the worst of the pox, suffered such a terrible nervous *crise* that the fever returned and killed him.

Tz'u-hsi did have, in spite of her fondness for decorum and mystique, an uncontrollable temper. One official described a fit he once witnessed: '[Her eyes] poured out straight rays; her cheekbones were sharp and the veins on her forehead projected; she showed her teeth as if she was suffering from lockjaw.'[18] Tz'u-hsi certainly feared and probably hated Alute, who threatened her influence; she was a widow at the threshold of middle age, and the sight of a love affair might well have enraged her with frustrated envy. But the charge that Tz'u-hsi deliberately corrupted her son, provoked his collapse and rejoiced in his death is unconvincing. Later, she is reported to have exlaimed: 'I thought I could be happy with my son as the Emperor T'ung-chih, but unfortunately he died before he was twenty years of age. Since that time I have been a changed woman, as all happiness was over as far as I was concerned when he died.'[19]

On the day of her son's demise, losing no time, 'always equal to emergencies', Tz'u-hsi instantly called a meeting of the Grand Council, the Imperial Clan, the ministers of the household and T'ung-chih's secretaries and tutors. While the icy wind blew down sand-storms from the deserts of Mongolia into the Forbidden City, fanning the braziers in the courtyards, and flaring into orange sparks in the flames, soldiers from Li Hung-chang's army stationed in Chihli surrounded the palace at Tz'u-hsi's orders, and officials hurried to her summons in sedans or on horseback or on foot depending on the privileges of their rank. In the Palace where the Heart is Nourished, a large columned hall to the west in the Forbidden City, with ebony carved columns and a gold and scarlet coffered ceiling, Tz'u-hsi sat on the Dragon Throne, Niuhuru amiably at her side. T'ung-chih had left no heir, and an emperor had to be chosen.

The assembled ministers must have glimpsed some plan crystallizing in Tz'u-hsi's ambitious mind, for Alute, the emperor's consort, was not present, but mourning by her husband's bier at her mother-in-law's orders. According to some sources, Alute was pregnant. If her child were a boy, he was the clear successor to the throne. But at the opening of the proceedings Tz'u-hsi stated implacably that the empire was in far too dangerous a state to conceal the death of T'ung-chih, for rebellions had only recently been crushed, and upheavals still shuddered through the country. Tz'u-hsi spoke with the authority vested in her by her son when he lay ill and feverish, and with the traditional right of the Empress Dowager, mother to an emperor, and the ministers at her feet were swept along by her decisiveness and resolution.

She suggested three candidates, members of the Imperial Clan, whose fathers were all three present in the hall. P'u-lun, two months old, grandson of the Emperor Tao-kuang's eldest son, was first in line, but Tz'u-hsi dismissed him peremptorily, reminding his father that he himself was only a foster-son, adopted from a junior branch of the imperial family. She knew of no precedent, she said, for the son of an adopted son to mount the Dragon Throne. Prince Kung produced an example from the Ming dynasty. Tz'u-hsi flashed back: 'His reign was a period of disaster; he was for a time in captivity under the Mongols.'[20]

The next in line was Prince Kung's own eldest son, Tsai-cheng, Tz'u-hsi rejected him as sharply, claiming that she could not spare Prince Kung as a minister – no father could, in a Confucian society, kowtow to his own son, and as all subjects had to kowtow to the Son of Heaven, the living father of an emperor had to retire into private life. Tz'u-hsi then announced that her own choice fell upon Tsai-t'ien, son of Prince Ch'un, a little boy of three, for would it not be an excellent idea, she asked the company, if the government remained in the hands of the empresses where T'ung-chih had placed it?

Tz'u-hsi was willing to spare Prince Ch'un, this boy's father, from her council chambers because he was, it was true, less experienced and less able than Prince Kung. Also, he was ill and weak at the time. Above all, however, he was her brother-in-law, the husband of her sister, and the little child she wanted to succeed to the throne was her own flesh and blood, of the Yehe Nara clan, and her own nephew. Her choice was not pure nepotism: Prince Kung's son was eighteen years old and would therefore, if chosen, assume powers as emperor immediately, forcing Tz'u-hsi into retirement.

P'u-lun had been summarily dismissed; yet he was the only nominee who did not violate the laws of ancestor-worship. Only a male heir, a natural or adopted son, could make the ancestral sacrifices at the graves of his father and his ancestors. Brothers or cousins could not, because they were of the same generation. Both Prince Kung's son and Prince Ch'un's were T'ung-chih's first cousins, and therefore debarred by religious law from officiating at

T'ung-chih's grave, and from adoption as his son and heir. But Tz'u-hsi, who could always manipulate tradition and precedent when she chose, could equally proceed happily by rule of thumb when she wanted, and crash the barriers of prejudice. Her unscrupulous decision that her nephew should be emperor, her cavalier disregard for her son's unattended spirit and for the worship of his grave would scandalize the solid Confucian ancestor-worshipping bloc who were the dynasty's mainstay, but she did not care.

At the foot of the throne, as the wind sighed outside and the lanterns flickered and guttered in the hall, the councillors hesitated before Tz'u-hsi's breach of tradition. But it was an open vote, and only ten men dared defy her wishes: seven voted for P'u-lun, the only justifiable candidate, three for Prince Kung's son. But fifteen declared for Tsai-t'ien, Tz'u-hsi's choice. When Prince Ch'un heard that his child was to be emperor, adopted as Tz'u-hsi's son, he trembled from limb to limb and, weeping, fell into a faint.

Tz'u-hsi immediately gave word that the child should be brought that night to the Forbidden City. A detachment of guards, led by Jung-lu, her ever-faithful soldier, marched through the streets in the dark to the house of Prince Ch'un. There, they gathered up the sleeping child, and brought him back to the palace where he was to spend his life. The soldiers' feet and their horses' hooves were muffled in straw and sacking, so that the news of the emperor's death and the appointment of his successor would not break unofficially on the city and provoke the riots and disorder that often accompanied a change of ruler. When the baby, a thin and unhealthy three-year-old, arrived wailing at the Palace at 3 am, he was presented to his aunt, his new foster-mother, dressed in dragon robes and taken to the bier of his dead cousin to kowtow. Strangely, the dragon robes fitted him – they had either belonged to T'ung-chih when he was a baby, or Tz'u-hsi had known the succession was a foregone conclusion and that she would carry the Council. Later she described that night: 'When the Emperor Kuang-hsu was brought to me as a baby three years old, he was a very sickly child and could hardly walk, he was so thin and weak. . . . You know his father was Prince Ch'un and his mother was my sister, so of course he was almost the same as my own son, In fact, I adopted him as such. . . .'[21]

On 25 February 1875, the child formally assumed the Dragon throne, and was proclaimed the Kuang-hsu Emperor, Emperor 'of Glorious Succession'. Tz'u-hsi gave her word, as she had done before, that 'so soon as the Emperor shall have completed his education, we shall immediately hand over to him the affairs of government'.[22] But she knew, as did China, that she was set for another decade at least.

Tz'u-hsi also decreed, in her own name and that of Niuhuru, that they were absolutely compelled to select Tsai-t'ien for the throne, and that he should become heir by adoption to his uncle Hsien-feng, 'but that, so soon as he should have begotten a son, the T'ung-chih Emperor would at once be provided with an heir' to minister at his grave.[23] But at his most precocious, the new child emperor could hardly conceive an heir for another eleven years, and so Tz'u-hsi's promise did not quieten the indignant literati who were deeply shocked at the blasphemous neglect of T'ung-chih's ancestral rites. The empire buzzed with the *coup*; in some of the downtown meeting places and tea houses, gossips suggested that the new emperor was Tz'u-hsi's own son, by Jung-lu, or by a false eunuch, and had been born clandestinely in her sister's house and passed off as the latter's child.

Four years later, when T'ung-chih's mausoleum was at last finished and the auspicious day for his burial arrived, an ex-censor called Wu K'o-tu accompanied the cortège, and staying behind in a Taoist monastery, wrote a memorial to the throne: 'Once went a man to his death, and he could not walk erect. A bystander said to him, "Are you afraid, sir?" He replied, "I am." "If you are afraid, why not turn back?" He replied, "My fear is a private weakness; my death is a public duty."' 'This is the condition,' wrote Wu K'o-tu, 'in which I find myself today. "When a bird is dying its song is sad. When a man is dying his words are good."'[24] Wu took poison and died. His extreme and antique gesture of protest against the irregular succession of Tz'u-hsi's nephew reverberated throughout China. But Tz'u-hsi, though alarmed at the gathering anger at her tactics, could do nothing to placate her critics except repeat her earnest promise to provide an heir for T'ung-chih as soon as she could.

Tz'u-hsi had hoped to toss Alute a new title – the Empress Chia-shun – as a palliative for her exclusion from the arrangements for the succession. But the neglected, humiliated girl continued to despair at her mother-in-law's treatment, and could find no one to support her. Even her own father Ch'ung-ch'i, a diehard patrician loyalist who had been created a duke on his daughter's marriage, feared cravenly for his own position should his contrary and rebellious daughter continue to grate on the Empress Dowager's nerves. Later, Ch'ung-ch'i proved how deep-rooted was his disregard for death and belief in the honourableness of suicide: he hanged himself in 1900, and his son and others of his family followed suit. On 27

March 1875, seventy-four days after her young husband's death, Alute proved herself her proud aristocratic father's daughter and poisoned herself with an overdose of opium. Ch'ung-ch'i may even have smuggled the drug in to her, for he very much wanted to please Tz'u-hsi; certainly, he took the news of Alute's death like a man and remained at his post in the court.

The reports that Alute was pregnant do not however seem likely. Rivalry and factionalism were always so inflammable at court, that had she been, one party or another would have adopted her cause, and her unborn baby and heir, if only for their own interests. Also, as early as January, Tz'u-hsi promised the angry literati that the irregularity would be adjusted by appointing Kuang-hsu's firstborn his heir. It was understandably too dangerous to await the birth before appointing a successor on the throne, but the matter of a ritual heir was less urgent, and therefore, if Alute had been pregnant, Tz'u-hsi, in January, need only have asked the literati to wait and see – unless she had already had designs on Alute's life. But if she had had, her decree promise would have betrayed her intentions, or at least pointed to them later.

Other speculations are dubious: that Tz'u-hsi ordered Alute to commit suicide because her presence was repugnant to her – Tz'u-hsi's behaviour was usually a little more oblique; that she taunted the girl with examples of dutiful wives who followed their husbands to the grave – she was surely too shrewd not to see the irony in that; that Alute was simply grief-stricken and starved herself to death. What is certain is that the young wife of T'ung-chih passed away unmourned, that Tz'u-hsi did not even bother to weep crocodile tears, for, at the *mezzo del cammin*, she had arrived at a turning where even a pretence of helpless femininity was no longer part of her craft.

Alute had been chosen as T'ung-chih's empress partly to heal past enmities in the court; she had died broken on the wheel of further dynastic intrigue. Officially her death was due to long and serious illness, and when a censor wrote to the Throne in 1876 that as a wife who had committed suttee after her husband's death, she should be posthumously honoured, Tz'u-hsi rebuked him curtly for writing a memorial based only on 'rumour'.[25]

Chapter Eight

THE CENTRE
CANNOT HOLD

At the meridian of Tz'u-hsi's second Regency of 1875–89, Weng T'ung-ho, Grand Councillor and tutor of the new child Kuang-hsu Emperor, lamented: 'In the morning an order is issued; in the evening it is changed. Unavoidably outsiders will laugh. But there is nothing that can be done about it.'[1]

Tz'u-hsi was a conscientious and applied despot, but she had no policy. Every incident, every misadventure during this, the minority of her nephew, the heyday of her rule, was met *ad hoc*, without consistent method, not because she and her ministers were gifted with flexibility and cunning, but because until the question was menacingly on top of them they had not yet adopted a line of conduct. Consequently China's fortunes slithered headlong down and the satellites that swam in China's orbit became magnetized by other powers to swim in theirs. Countries like Korea, the Ryukyu Islands, Annam and Burma, who had brought tribute to Peking during T'ung-chih's reign, came less regularly and soon came not at all, and China's outer defences were therefore weakened and her psychological standing diminished. The sheer size and antiquity of the Eastern giant, which previously had signified her might, now seemed only to emphasize her creaking unwieldiness.

From the isolated heart of the Forbidden City, Tz'u-hsi tangled with Tsarist Russia to the north, Great Britain's Indian Empire to the west, the French in Indo-China to the south, the rising Sun of Japan to the east.

In 1868, the brilliant and far-sighted Meiji Emperor had succeeded to the Japanese throne and had set in motion a full-scale revolution of reform in which sentiments of national pride and expansion played an important part. In 1871 some sailors from the Ryukyu Islands were murdered in Formosa by aborigines, and the Japanese seized on the incident as a pretext to press China about this archipelago that stretches in a bracelet between Formosa's northern and Japan's southern tips, a country which had always paid tribute to China as suzerain. When the Japanese demanded reparation from the Chinese for 'their' sailors, the Tsungli Yamen absent-mindedly retorted: 'We can't be responsible for the actions of savages beyond the pale of civilization.'[2] The Japanese therefore moved into Formosa to avenge themselves. The Chinese, recovering their senses, realized that they had not only let the Japanese calmly supplant them in Ryukyu but had also relinquished their authority over the vitally important island of Formosa. But China could not take on the burstingly new power of Japan, and so she paid up for her bungling diplomacy: an indemnity of 500,000 taels. In 1877 the traditional envoy from Ryukyu tried to bring tribute to the Son of Heaven in Peking, but the greatly embarrassed Yamen sent him home, and the following year, the Ryukyu Islands were officially surrendered to Japan.

In 1875 a young British interpreter, A.R. Margary, was murdered 'south of the cloud' in Yunnan, the province in the south-west recently ravaged by the Moslem rebellion and still turbulent. He was accompanying an expedition to reconnoitre trade routes from Burma into the mountains of Yunnan, Kweichow, and Szechuan, which the British quite rightly suspected to be rich in minerals and ore. Margary was probably ambushed and murdered by bandits, but the patient and deliberate optimism that had characterized foreign affairs in the sixties had evaporated and the courteous Rutherford Alcock had been replaced by Sir Thomas Wade, famous in China since he had interpreted beside Harry Parkes in 1860. Again, Wade saw in the affair a providential pretext for forcing China's hand over a new treaty, and was determined to extract full poundage from the incident. After much display of temper, Wade met Li Hung-chang, then viceroy of Chihli, whom Tz'u-hsi had ordered to take charge, and together they negotiated the uninspired, unhelpful Convention of Chefoo, by which several more ports were opened to trade, including Wuhu on the Yangstze where Tz'u-hsi had spent her childhood. More significantly, Li agreed that Great Britain could send another expedition from India through Burma, to delineate the Burmese-Chinese frontier. In this way he implied China's admission that Burma, which only the year before had sent tribute to Peking, had been unofficially annexed by Britain, 'as stealthily as silkworms nibbling at mulberry leaves'.

In 1871, at the height of the Moslem rebellion, Russia moved into the far westerly wildernesses of Sinkiang, a region called Ili after the river, to protect it on behalf of China and prevent it from seceding as an independent Moslem state. In 1878, when Tso Tsung-t'ang, one of Tz'u-hsi's great Chinese commanders, had finished sweeping away the uprising like so much shattered crockery, the Chinese asked their charitable Russian neighbours for the return of Ili, and sent Ch'ung-hou to St Petersburg to negotiate. Ch'ung-hou was the

Manchu who had been in charge at the time of the Tientsin massacre, and who had since travelled in Europe to present China's apology to the emperor of the French in person. In St Petersburg, this meek, well-meaning official granted Russia half the area – the richer half – extensive privileges of trading, military control of strategic passes in the mountains, and a refund of five million roubles as the expenses of occupation. On his return to Peking, an order for his instant decapitation awaited him.

From the lowest ranking official to the viceroys, all shouted for war. Tso Tsung-t'ang, always game for a fight, still had sixty thousand troops standing in the area; Chang Chih-tung, a Chinese scholar who reached eminence later, wrote angrily to the Throne: 'The enormous outlay of millions of taels, spent year after year in the manufacture of munitions of war, has been incurred with the view to preparing for just such a crisis as now exists. . . .'[3] The hour was so critical that even Gordon, now serving in India, was invited to Peking by Robert Hart to offer advice. Disgusted with the state of the rundown empire, Gordon gave peremptory orders: 'If you will make war, burn suburbs of Peking, remove the archives and emperor from Peking, put them in centre of country, and fight (a guerrilla war) for five years; Russia will not be able to hurt you.'[4] Needless to say, the Chinese did not act upon them. Hart himself commented on this, Gordon's last visit to China: 'Much as I like and respect him, I must say he is "not all there". Whether it is softening of the brain – I don't know, but he seems to be alternately arrogant and slavish, vain and humble, in his senses and out of them. It's a great pity.'[5]

In the face of mass rage Li Hung-chang persisted in his dove-like policy, and prevailed. Queen Victoria herself had sent a telegram begging for Ch'ung-hou's life, and the bewildered official was spared. Tseng Chi-tse, son of Tseng Kuo-fan, as accomplished, but more urbane than his self-critical father, was sent to St Petersburg to resolve the Ili affair by diplomatic means. Tseng Chi-tse talked the Russians into yielding somewhat over the question of land and trade – but at a price. The treaty was signed in February 1881: nine million roubles was paid by China for its own territories. Yet, at court in Peking, the return of Ili was considered a supreme victory for Chinese prestige, for no land had been sequestered.

In April that year Niuhuru mysteriously died. She was forty-four, and had been Tz'u-hsi's co-empress and friend since the day they were chosen together as concubines for the Hsien-feng Emperor. Now Tz'u-hsi found herself alone in charge of the empire, and alone, did even less to arrest the critical and dramatic erosion of China's frontiers and sovereignty.

In the south, the French had wrested Cochin China (South Vietnam) from Spain in 1862 and were now drawn, as hungrily as the British, towards trade in the south-western provinces of China, for which they needed control of the navigable Red River in Tongking (North Vietnam). After several swash-buckling and patriotic adventurers had failed to capture the region, France made the king of Annam (Vietnam) accept a treaty in 1874 which gave the French privileges of overlordship such as China traditionally enjoyed. Yet the king, finding it hard to break his allegiance to old masters, continued to send tribute to Peking, much to France's irritation, in 1876 and in 1880, while his lands were torn by French soldiers of fortune fighting Chinese bandits under the ex-Taiping rebel, Liu Yung-fu, leader of the Black Flags, whom the Chinese covertly hoped to use to repel the French.

Liu's Black Flags held the province valiantly, but, when the king of Annam died, the French negotiated another treaty with his successor. Its avowal was bald: 'Annam recognizes and accepts the protectorate of France. . . .'[6] The Chinese delivered an ultimatum; the French attacked in response and by March 1884, major cities had fallen. In Peking, when Tz'u-hsi heard the news, she flew into raging belligerence: 'She has single-mindedly advocated war,' wrote one official. 'She summoned the members of the Grand Council to court and decreed to them: "The Hsien-feng Emperor regarded the war of 1860 with great remorse, but he died with an ambition unfulfilled. Now we ought to wipe out the humiliation for the former Emperor." However, all the officials alike shirked their duties, and none could be tolerated in office. So she changed the members of the government.'[7] In a sweeping coup, Tz'u-hsi furiously dismissed the entire Grand Council and four members of the Tsungli Yamen. Amongst others the tutor Weng T'ung-ho was sacked, and more crucially, Tz'u-hsi's longstanding colleague and adviser Prince Kung, whose cunning offices had put her on the throne twenty-three years before. The ministers' policy of war with France had failed: their posts were forfeit. But the edict in which Tz'u-hsi thrust Prince Kung aside reveals her at her most shabby: 'Prince Kung, at the outset of his career,' she pronounced, 'was wont to render us most zealous assistance but this attitude became modified as time went by, to one of self-confident and callous contentment with the sweets of office, and of late he has become unduly inflated with pride of place, displaying nepotism and slothful inefficiency. . . .' The charges were trumpery, and Prince Kung, 'permitted to retire into private life and attend to the care of his health',[8] set himself in bitterness and disillusion to cultivate the lovely garden of his palace in Peking. He was fifty-one, very young to retire in a country of elder statesmen, but he was the only man Tz'u-hsi had ever feared and she snatched greedily at the chance to expel him from the government. She had great powers, but not greatness enough to stomach the threat of equal gifts or ambitions beside her. Awed sycophants replaced the deposed councillors: Prince Ch'ing, member of the Imperial Clan, was remarkable only because he survived twenty-seven years undisturbed on the Tsungli Yamen during Tz'u-hsi's most ferocious time; Prince Ch'un, whose early energy had dwindled to subservience to his forceful sister-in-law, was recalled from retirement although, as father of the emperor, he was forbidden by tradition to hold office under his son. But Tz'u-hsi merely waved away the protests of the literati in order to secure his compliance in her council chambers.

Prince Ch'un obediently echoed Tz'u-hsi's continued thirst for war with France over Annam, but Li Hung-chang frustrated the aggressives in Peking by negotiating with the French at Tientsin in May. Always an appeaser, Li yielded unequivocally to the French demands: Annam was French. Tz'u-hsi, infuriated by the further humiliation, backed by the clamorous provincial officials, purposefully delayed the orders for the evacuation of Tongking as had been agreed between Li Hung-chang and the French. (The agreement had, it was true, been ambiguous as to dates.[9]) French troops therefore advanced into China as they thought had been arranged, met with fierce resistance from a Chinese garrison in Kwangsi and were decimated.

The French fleet, under Admiral Courbet, sailed into Foochow harbour. A state of peace, however shaky, existed in theory, so the French gunboats moored unmolested in the Chinese port; friendly exchanges took place for a few weeks; in Peking, the court, breathing war, was hampered by its generals, and by Li Hung-chang in particular, who simply did not obey and send the reinforcements Tz'u-hsi ordered to the troublespot.

On 22 August 1884 the French opened fire with all guns without warning or declaration of war on the Chinese junks and numerous ships riding at anchor beside them, set them ablaze and sank them within minutes. They then swivelled their guns on the famous Foochow arsenal, pride of the T'ung-chih Restoration's self-strengthening policy, and built with French advice, reduced it to rubble, and killed and wounded six hundred and sixty-nine men. The French termed their action 'a state of reprisals' and refused to call it war. For seven months the Chinese fought bravely, and sometimes successfully, on the sea and in Formosa, but the French naval blockade of the straits between Formosa and Fukien strangled their supplies, while growing difficulties in the north with Japan over Korea made even the warlike Tz'u-hsi wish to shift the struggle northwards and have done with the troublesome French. In the spring of 1885 China ceded Annam unceremoniously to France, as she had agreed during the now disgraced Li Hung-chang's negotiations months before. Robert Hart conducted the diplomacy on behalf of the Chinese, for, although a foreigner, his unimpeachability could not be called into question. After protracted war, long sufferings, ignominiously capricious decision-making from Tz'u-hsi and her councillors and a tragic death toll among her people, all China had obtained was the abolition of the original indemnity to France.

While the ministers of the Tsungli Yamen tussled with Sir Thomas Wade's temper in 1875–6, the expansionist Japanese sent a naval force to Korea to prise open the Hermit Kingdom. Again, as over Ryukyu, the Japanese had taken China's measure: although Korea was China's most strategic vassal, the point of access to the Bay of Pechili and therefore to Peking itself, the Chinese issued no protest. In 1882 the United States of America concluded a trade treaty with Korea; this implied the country's equality among the nations and independence of its suzerain China. By 1883, while China was distracted with the French war over Annam, the Western-style reforms which Japan urged on Korea and then financed to her own profit had ignited a fiery conflict between the pro-Japanese and anti-Japanese factions in the country.

Li Hung-chang, recognizing the very serious threat, sent in his hardbitten Huai army, created during his campaign against the Taipings, to quell the riots. As early as 1874 Li, usually a leading politician of conciliation, had shrewdly analyzed the situation for Tz'u-hsi his ruler: 'Although the various powers are strong, they are still seventy thousand *li* away from us, whereas Japan is as near as in the courtyard, as on the threshold, and is prying into our emptiness and solitude. Undoubtedly she will become China's permanent and great anxiety.'[10] Tz'u-hsi, although she wanted to fight on against the French, saw the strength of Li Hung-chang's argument: the remote territories like Burma, the Ryukyu islands, and even Ili and Annam could be yielded up for though their loss weakened China's defences, it did not shatter them. Korea on the other hand was the thumb to China's hand. Tz'u-hsi therefore consented to the resolution of the Sino-French war in order to concentrate defences in the north.

With the force Li sent into Korea went Yuan Shih-k'ai, a twenty-three-year-old stocky Chinese, ambitious and courageous. When the pro-Japanese faction attempted a coup in December 1884, at a ceremonial banquet, Yuan Shih-k'ai, Chief of Staff at the garrison, took the king of Korea and his consort hostage after a fierce struggle in the very courtyards of the palace, and silenced the Japanese and their Korean disciples. His prompt and confident military riposte averted then the fall of Korea to Japan, and for this Tz'u-hsi rewarded him generously: at the age of twenty-six, anachronistically young in China, Yuan was made Chinese Resident in Seoul. By the treaty Li Hung-chang concluded with Japan in 1885 both countries agreed to withdraw their troops to allow a third power to organize reforms in Korea, and to intervene only with military assistance after notifying the other. In 1890 Korean envoys again kowtowed like vassals before the Dragon Throne, as if nothing had changed.

As China's satellites drifted from her orbit, Tz'u-hsi presided at the very heart of affairs, from the Dragon Throne itself. All commands issued from her, the emperor's surrogate, and all reports of further loss returned to her, for throughout the vast empire ran a complex of institutions which devolved upon the Throne, where she sat in all majesty each morning. Each day the Grand Council met at dawn, when the Chinese believe the mind to be clearest, and its members deliberated with Tz'u-hsi both their own advice and the memorials sent in by officials from the provinces and from the six principal boards of government in Peking. The Grand Council was a flexible, vigorous unit of men – rarely more than five – hand-picked by Tz'u-hsi as her most trusted confidants. Granted its own seal in 1732, it had superseded the Grand Secretariat as the supreme decision-making organ. In theory, because its position was comparatively volatile in the hierarchy of government, the cumbersome procedure of promotion could be side-stepped. In practice, under Tz'u-hsi members of the Imperial Clan found their way by birth and not by talent into its ranks.

The choice of councillors was therefore the heart of Tz'u-hsi's power, and of all Ch'ing rulers before her: she depended upon them, and upon the censorate, a courageous body of men in the capital and in the provinces who enjoyed a certain freedom of speech to rebuke the throne and report the people's whisperings and wishes; and upon the provincial officials who voiced informal opinion in the memorials they sent down the *yen-lu*, (pathway of words). From their information Tz'u-hsi could accomplish the throne's rôle as 'a passive arbiter rather than active inaugurator.'[11] Tz'u-hsi was a prisoner of the throne's mystery and majesty; they were not. But their crucial rôle did not diminish the ruler's despotic powers: Tz'u-hsi saw all important memorials, and even ones of less consequence. The chancery of memorials sorted them and drafted conventional replies to routine matters, which she then endorsed in the vermilion ink exclusive to the emperor of China's use; and she always read the relevant literature before any pivotal decision was taken, turning down the corner of the scroll to mark it for presentation to the Grand Council at the following morning's audience. When the matter had been debated, the councillors returned to their office in the Forbidden City, where the staff was kept select and small for speed, efficiency and discretion, and drafted an imperial edict or decree, the *ssu-lun* (silken cords) of the Throne's words. If Tz'u-hsi approved the draft, she sealed it, and then, if urgent, it was swept off by fast-moving couriers on relay horses to its destination, or after the 1880s, by cable; if less urgent, it was printed in the *Peking Gazette*, and disseminated throughout the country by the usual postal runners.

Tz'u-hsi united all legislative, executive and judicial powers in her person during the Kuang-hsu Emperor's minority, but she adhered devotedly to the Confucian theory of government by men of ability, because her officials were her only links to the world outside her palaces. She never however built up a system of private correspondence – not that is known anyway – as the illustrious K'ang-hsi had done, scrawling impetuous messages of good-will or anger on private decrees to his officials. Nor did she break taboos and travel through China like K'ang-hsi in great progresses to inspect her subjects' welfare at first hand. Because her position as an empress on the Dragon Throne was irregular, she proceeded with the greatest caution in order not to antagonize public opinion. As the mother of the T'ung-chih Emperor, her authority had been legitimate through the laws of filial piety; but Kuang-hsu, as T'ung-chih's first cousin, violated the ancestral laws of ritual; the suicide of Wu K'o-tu that had personified so much literati feeling still echoed through China, and her adoption of Kuang-hsu as her son had been a ruse transparent to all. Even if it had not been, the rule of a woman was strictly forbidden, hence Prince Kung's order for a book of precedents in

1861 to legitimize it, hence the importance of his exalted position in the T'ung-chih Regency. After Nuhuru's death in 1881, Tz'u-hsi ruled alone, and she was therefore most scrupulous to observe the forms by 'lowering the screen' at audiences, by issuing decrees in the first person of the emperor, and by flattening, as much as she could her personality into a hieratic effigy of the good, wise and benevolent Confucian ruler, blotting out excrescences or idiosyncracies, sifting, with a carefully engineered appearance of disinterestedness, the finest blend from the advice offered before the Throne.

It was a struggle; occasionally fierce and reckless censors would voice the rumours about Tz'u-hsi's morals and she would once again feel the sharp and unpleasant lash of the insecurity of her position. She attempted therefore to win the love of the people, and continually, during the business of government, weighed out how far she could override the opinions expressed in the memorials without losing credit and respect; how far she could overrule the wishes of mighty independent viceroys like Li Hung-chang when they contradicted the mass of the mandarinate (as over the war with France), and yet not lose their vital support; how far she could follow, under the guise of yielding to outside pressure, her own instincts and desires. It was because she was so adept at this precarious equilibrium, because she could thread her way through so much divergent advice and come up with a synthesis that was, usually, ironcast in convention and authenticated by the hallowed Confucian classics or by the historical precedents she had so trippingly upon the tongue, that the litany of crushing defeats and of signal political failures was never attributed to her inadequacy, and did not topple her from her illegitimate eminence on the Dragon Throne.

Tz'u-hsi epitomized many vices seeping incurably throughout China. The most damaging tenet however in the store of conventional wisdom which made her, despite all her drawbacks, the most acceptable ruler in China, was her continued incomprehension of the equality of nations. Because no country in her eyes could equal, let alone diminish, China, she was blind to the reality of foreign powers' encroachments until it was too late, and her subsequent warlike thunderings and indignation appealed to the many scholar-officials and members of the gentry who also did not choose to see that times and circumstances had changed. The rigid orthodoxy of her world view, combined with her very real powers of life and death, dismissal and appointment, also helped to silence opposition even when she flagrantly flouted these same traditions, as she so often did when it suited her.

Her vices were often Confucian virtues, to which she added a new gloss. She trusted the doctrine of rule by men of ability, but her tastes drew her to swashbuckling, ruffianly types, reformed (or not quite reformed) bandits and adventurers who were as often Chinese as Manchu. Jung-lu was the paragon in her eyes, but she gathered others to her side. During the war with France over Annam she made it a condition of the treaty that the Black Flags under the ex-Taiping Liu Yung-fu should not be disowned by the Chinese government. Another outlaw, originally leader of a band in Kwangsi, Feng Tzu-ts'ai had been rewarded for his exploits against the Taipings with a Yellow Hunting Jacket, like Gordon in 1864, and was summoned to Peking for audience with Tz'u-hsi in 1879. She sent him back to Kwangsi to supervise the defence of the border, and in 1884 he fought valiantly in the campaign against the French. That year, Tso Tsung-t'ang, blind in one eye but toughened by decades of hard campaigning, was given supreme control of all the forces in the empire, including – although he was Chinese – the Manchu Bannermen.

Tz'u-hsi was driven to muster outlaws because the ideal Confucian scholar society had cast out the military man. But she sought in the conquered race the martial spirit that had brought her Manchu ancestors to victory. She trusted men who had endured battle because her devouring appetite for popular theatre had filled her with longings for the mysterious heroism of war. In psychological terms, the men in her life – her incompetent father, her dissolute husband, her weakling son and the thousands of eunuchs who now surrounded her – made her yearn for the virile, valorous and strong. Her favourite heroine in Chinese legend and literature – and Tz'u-hsi was well read – was the Chinese Joan of Arc, Mu-lan, who led troops into battle disguised in her father's armour.

The empress's reliance on brilliant and loyal men meant that the provincial viceroys and governors with complete authority over their semi-autonomous districts sometimes contradicted the Throne or refused obedience, as Li Hung-chang had done during the war with France. Yet while Tz'u-hsi understood how the great viceroys could undermine her, she fostered independent action and administration by officials. Some strong-willed, frugal and disciplined officials therefore rose in the provinces: Chang Chih-tung, a Chinese scholar, who combined old-fashioned pugnacious and rabid Confucianism with reforming zeal, became viceroy of

Kwangtung and Kwangsi in 1884, after he curried favour with Tz'u-hsi by denouncing Wu K'o-tu's suicide on ideological grounds. In the two Kwangs, he built steamships and an arsenal and promoted industry; the conservatives were astounded when his newfangled notions increased the provinces' revenue. In Szechuan, the viceroy who, as Governor of Shantung, had executed Tz'u-hsi's favourite eunuch An Te-hai a decade before, re-organized the collection of taxes on salt, the *gabelle*, a government monopoly that had virtually collapsed since the rule of Tao-kuang. Li Hung-chang, viceroy of Chihli, saw China's first railway built north of Tientsin in his province in 1881. The same year the first telegraph wires appeared between Shanghai and Tientsin, Li's viceregal capital. Li Hung-chang's business acumen overcame in his case Confucian prejudice. But in the rest of China it was a different matter, and mines, industries, and railways continued to develop extremely slowly. The Chinese sensed, for instance, that railways could be instruments of foreign imperialism as much as of domestic wealth, and they saw their suspicions corroborated in other empires' dominions. So in 1876, when the very first railroad was laid in China, by the British and without permission, it was bought out by the Chinese and uprooted.

Curiously, the Irishman Robert Hart, the dressy, cautious, meticulous Inspector-General, was one of Tz'u-hsi's most unquestioning admirers and loyal supporters. Nearly twenty-five years in China had made him legendary. He was a martinet chief, and as regular in his habits as clockwork; he relaxed with metaphysical philosophy or the full-blooded music of a brass band, which he had trained some Chinese to play. 'They come, I know why they all come,' he said of his many visitors, 'It is just to get a sight of the two curios of Peking, the I-G and his queer musicians!'[12]

Li Hung-chang, jealous of the rise of others, assured of his own independence and army in Chihli, urged Tz'u-hsi to rein in other governors in their provinces and to continue the centralization policy of the sixties. Although he did not impinge on the standing of men like Chang Chih-tung, he had his way. The destruction of the Foochow arsenal in the south by the French in 1884 and the simultaneous outbreak in Korea helped to switch the military emphasis from the south, cradle of Tseng Kuo-fan's old Hunan army, to the north, where his former rival Li Hung-chiang, as viceroy of Chihli, had marshalled his own Huai army. The fortifications began of Port Arthur and of Weihaiwei, commanding together the Bay of Pechili, and in 1885 Tz'u-hsi became convinced, after numerous memorials to the throne, that a navy was needed for defence. Accordingly an Admiralty Board was set up, grandiose sums were earmarked for vessels and munitions of war. Prince Ch'un was appointed controller of the new board, while Li Hung-chang and Tseng Chi-tse advised him on policy. At last, China seemed on the way to becoming a military power commensurate with her size.

But there were not enough able men to shore the Ch'ing's long, slow collapse. Li Hung-chang complained in 1881: 'The stupidity and confusion of our scholar officials, and the lack of men of ability in the court are really ridiculous.'[13] The recent shocks to China's nerves had paralysed all new talent, it seemed: most of Tz'u-hsi's soldier-braves were Taiping veterans and therefore pretty long in the tooth, and few had filled the places of the dead. 1876 saw the death of Wen-hsiang, the lucid and pleasant-mannered statesman of the T'ung-chih Restoration. Five years before, in 1871, the dedicated Tseng Kuo-fan had also passed on, mourning in his diary, 'The dead leaves of disappointed hopes fill alll the landscape, and I see no prospect of settling my affairs. Thirty years have passed since I took my degree, and I have attained the highest rank; yet have I learned nothing, and my character still lacks true solidity. What shame should be mine at having reached thus uselessly old age.'[14]

In audience with Tseng Chi-tse, before his departure as Chinese minister to Great Britain and France, Tz'u-hsi regretted his father's death: 'It is also bad luck for the nation that before long Tseng Kuo-fan departed from the world. Now there are many great officials in various places who are cowardly.' Tseng replied by citing many 'loyal and sincere ministers' including Li Hung-chang, but Tz'u-hsi sighed: 'All of them are good but all are old troopers. The new ones all fail to equal them in ability and have not kept abreast of new ideas.'[15] One of the Chinese officials whom Tseng praised during his audience, Kuo Sung-tao, had himself railed against the pusillanimity and empty-headedness of Tz'u-hsi's counsellors, particularly during the war with France: 'Of all the officials in and outside the capital, there is not a single one who is versed in foreign affairs. All they do is cautiously watch the intention of the court and show their zeal for war.'[16]

Yet although Kuo Sung-tao pinpointed many of the hindrances against which Tz'u-hsi vainly struggled, Kuo's views were otherwise too progressive for her, for he had been China's first minister to Great Britain and France, and had been deeply influenced and impressed by Western institutions. In Tz'u-hsi's conventional eyes he was dangerous and heterodox, and on his return from Europe, in 1878, he recognized her distrust, did not seek office and was not offered it. Tz'u-hsi was therefore instrumental in the stagnation of talent.

Kuo had also nailed another of the obstacles she fought to overcome. Her dependence on the information she received from outside the Forbidden City's high embattled walls was complete; in spite of her absolute powers, she was at the mercy of any official who chose to distort events and keep the truth from her. Kuo wrote: 'The condition of the Chinese official and the people is that they are too distant from each other; in addition, both are trying to cover the eyes and ears of the court in order to facilitate the pursuance of their selfish purposes. For this reason the people's ideas are frequently and miserably suppressed and never reach the emperor.'[17]

Each step of the communication system was hazardous. At court, the accurate report of a piece of bad news could unleash the ruler's fury on the teller. After 1900, for instance, when some newspapers were published in the foreign settlements of the treaty ports, Tz'u-hsi asked one of her ladies-in-waiting to read them aloud. When she heard that a prominent 'rebel' had returned clandestinely to China, she flew into such an apoplexy that the lady-in-waiting resolved to censor her reading more carefully in future. This must have happened all the time. In the provinces, only officials above the third rank had the right to memorialize the throne direct, and any report an inferior might wish to make had to grind through the established, often sluggish, channels. Tz'u-hsi's natural bossiness and her peremptory rages hardly encouraged outspoken criticism, and indeed it is often startling how frank her officials were. The same year as she drove Prince Kung and his colleagues from the Grand Council, she decided she was bored of hearing officials' reiterated jingoistic views, even though they coincided with her own. A child, she could have stopped her ears; a despot, she whined: 'The court listens eagerly to the opinions of all and seeks the truth about conditions. It had been hoped that there would be real benefits derived from employing the opinions of many men in the administration of government. You officials should each purify your hearts and trembling obey the repeated imperial commands to reveal your loyal counsels. But you must not irresponsibly offer personal opinions.'[18] Such rebukes were sleight of hand: for the time being, everything that grated on Tz'u-hsi was 'personal opinion', and the pathway of words was closed.

Tz'u-hsi suffocated advice on which China could have built; in turn, the prejudices of the immensely influential local gentry and literati often made it impossible for the local official to enforce an imperial edict, although disobedience was a capital crime. Tz'u-hsi's repeated instructions about missionaries, Christianity and the protection of foreigners in China were enlightened and tolerant, as the treaties exacted. In many provinces they were simply ignored, and the local magistrate often did little with his recalcitrant subjects, but relied on distance from the capital and carefully worded memorials to gloss over his omission. Li Hung-chang explained to the great Japanese statesman and reformer Ito Hirobumi in 1895: 'My country is hampered by traditions and customs: one can hardly do what one wants. China also has people who understand modern affairs; but there are too many provinces, with strong sectionalism, just like your country in the feudal period, when one was checked and hindered by others and had no full authority for anything.'[19]

There were startingly few officials, too: at the turn of the century, they numbered only forty thousand: one man in ten thousand to deal with every question, legal, financial, personal and public that cropped up in the community for which he was responsible. The theory of rotating officials every two or three years, in order to prevent them establishing private, and therefore corrupt, interests, meant that a new magistrate, *taotai* or governor, often fell into the grip of his clerk and runner underlings, who knew the area well. A notoriously grasping, villainous group, completely uneducated, there were seven hundred thousand of them by the end of the century, outnumbering their masters nearly eighteen to one. They also seized, it was estimated, thirty per cent of the annual provincial revenue through extortion and fraud.[20] Above all the officials depended on the goodwill of their peers in the district: the local gentry who were dogmatic and conservative.

Shortage of competent and honest men, but above all shortage of funds and of the means to generate them bedevilled Tz'u-hsi's government. In the sixties it had been necessary and philanthropic to remit the land tax as much as thirty per cent over China because the peasants had suffered so terribly at the hands of rebels and imperial soldiers in wave after wave of bloodshed;[21] ten years, twenty years later, relief was just as imperative, for the summer of 1876 brought ruin to half of China. In the south floods devastated Kwangtung and Fukien and spread through Chekiang and central Kiangsi and Hunan; locusts devoured the crops in Kiangsu and in part of Chihli; a drought inflicted famine in 1876, in 1877, and in 1878 on the populations of Shansi, Shensi and Shantung, a famine in which millions – from seven to twenty millions, it has never been reckoned precisely – lost their lives. Timothy Richard, a Welsh Baptist working in China, wrote on 30 January 1878 in Shansi: 'Passed two men apparently just dead. One had good clothes on, but had died of hunger. A few *li* further on there was a man of about forty walking in front of us, with unsteady steps like a drunken man. A puff of wind blew him over to rise no more.'[22] Parents exchanged their children, Richard reported, because they could not bear to watch their own die, or to eat them.

Although Tz'u-hsi and Niuhuru contributed generously from their Privy Purse to the relief of the suffering, the luxury of the court remained unrestrained even in the face of the imminent bankruptcy of China. Foreign trade, for instance, which the interested countries had solemnly promised would benefit China, had been neglected by the Chinese, and exports therefore lagged perilously behind imports. Even the tea trade, which China had virtually monopolized in 1867, had literally been stolen by British-run India. In 1848 the East India Company, frustrated by a stubbornly unco-operative China, had hired a famous plant-hunter, Robert Fortune, to steal the tea plant and bring it to the West. Although not indigenous to India, tea grew there splendidly, and by 1905, China supplied only twenty-nine per cent of the world's consumption.[23]

Tz'u-hsi's second regency saw her into her middle age. It was a period of transition: her son had died; she was, she claimed, 'a changed woman'.[24] She discarded the coquetry and helplessness she had formerly used to manipulate her courtiers, and withdrew into matriarchal dignity, playing on the Chinese veneration of old age and of composure. Li Lien-ying, her constant companion and Chief Eunuch, gave her the chaffing and respectful name of Old Buddha. It became her favourite sobriquet. Others called her Venerable Ancestor, which she liked almost as much. She was casting away childish things.

Cast away amongst other playthings was Jung-lu, epitome of her hero image, who had ridden to her rescue in 1861, and had brought the infant Kuang-hsu Emperor under guard to the Forbidden City in 1875. Three years afterwards, in 1878, Jung-lu was granted 'sick leave', and the following spring, retired from all his posts. Weng T'ung-ho, the emperor's tutor, wrote in his diary that Jung-lu was suffering in his leg, on which a foreign surgeon had operated. But Weng was a crafty courtier and often preferred seemliness to accuracy. Other writers averred that Prince Kung was Jung-lu's ruin, for the latter had boasted of his influence over Tz'u-hsi and annoyed the great statesman who was then still in power. Yet others wrote that Jung-lu criticized Tz'u-hsi for consorting with eunuchs. But in the teahouses it was noised that Jung-lu had been discovered *in flagrante* with a lady of the palace. In Tz'u-hsi's official decree, he was charged with corruption; and in his last memorial to Tz'u-hsi as an old man in 1903 he only commented laconically: 'While acting as Captain-General of the Peking Gendarmerie I incurred Your Majesty's displeasure; therefore, for seven years, I awaited.'[25]

Jung-lu was a virile soldier of forty-three; Tz'u-hsi, who may have been his lover, was a year older. Gossip about the profligacy, extravagance and Borgian propensities of her court flowered evilly throughout China, and Tz'u-hsi may well have needed to strengthen her position by dismissing the lover rumour most conspicuously attributed to her. If Jung-lu was caught red-handed, she may have acted like a middle-aged and discarded leman; or, after nearly thirty years of stiflingly effeminate court life, her Confucian instincts of propriety may well have been truly outraged. By the time she recalled Jung-lu to office in 1887, her mask of irreproachable matriarch was fixed, and she had successfully created an image of herself, as an old and venerated dowager, much too staid and fastidious for voluptuous dalliance.

In 1880, when Tz'u-hsi was forty-five, she fell seriously ill, and was confined to her bed for almost a year. Weng T'ung-ho in his diary describes a liver disease, but Tz'u-hsi recovered to enjoy robust health for the rest of her long life and as Chinese medicine could not have eradicated her greed, it seems probable that her liverish complaint was nervous.

The gentle Niuhuru, her co-regent, ruled alone while Tz'u-hsi was ill, and the most important event of this time, the struggle with Russia over Ili, was settled by a treaty which was considered a diplomatic triumph for China. Tz'u-hsi, lying sick in her gorgeous apartments, did not feel in the least consoled by China's jubilance in her hour of absence. All her feelings of tenacity, all the grit she showed in times of crisis, overcame her nauseous condition. She rose from her bed, and by 17 April, Niuhuru had 'choked on spit' and died.

Rivalry had increased between the two women over the Emperor Kuang-hsu's affections, for the child showed signs, as T'ung-chih had done, of preferring the indulgent Niuhuru to his forceful and ambitious adoptive mother. Tz'u-hsi, failing bitterly once more to win the love of a boy, became impatient with him, and although he was good at his books, unlike her own son, she so terrified the thin, unhealthy Kuang-hsu by her exhortations that he threw himself into the arms of his tutor Weng T'ung-ho whenever she approached, as if 'facing lions and tigers'.[26] Jealousy between the two women may also have been increased by memories of their mutual husband, for the popular story that quickly circulated the capital and spread through China until it was accepted as gospel in the south was that Niuhuru, gossiping about the old days with Tz'u-hsi, revealed that Hsien-feng had entrusted her with a document. In it the emperor ordered that if she gave any trouble, Tz'u-hsi was to be instantly decapitated. Niuhuru fetched the decree to show Tz'u-hsi, and laughing at the changed times, tore it up before her. That very afternoon, a eunuch presented Niuhuru, as she gazed into a goldfish pool in the gardens of the Forbidden City, with some milk cakes as a gift from Tz'u-hsi. Niuhuru took a mouthful. By the evening she was dead.

For six years after Niuhuru's death, Tz'u-hsi enjoyed alone the supreme rule of the Middle Kingdom, and the habit of power became so ingrained that when the year of Kuang-hsu's majority – 1887 – approached, and he should formally assume the government, she flinched bitterly at the thought of her necessary retirement. Prince Ch'un, ready for peace at any price, observed the signs, stressed the youthfulness of the emperor, the great undertaking of the empire, and begged Tz'u-hsi to remain in power. After refusing the crown many times in a flutter of modesty and self-effacement, Tz'u-hsi was prevailed upon to accept. The young emperor announced: 'When I heard the edict [of my majority] I trembled as though I were in mid-ocean, not knowing where the land is. But her Imperial Majesty will continue to advise me for a few years in important matters of state ... Under the guidance of her Imperial Majesty care will be devoted to everything.'[27]

As Tz'u-hsi clung on beyond her time, her suspicions increased. Nepotistic as she was, she had always avoided conferring high office on her two brothers, but concentrated on exalting her family through its women, less of a threat to her power than its men. She felt Prince Ch'un, the father of the Kuang-hsu Emperor, menaced her, and when the Prince, who had never been very vigorous, fell seriously ill again in 1887 and his son Kuang-hsu visited him as required by filial piety in his palace in Peking, Tz'u-hsi always went too. She feared that alone together they might plot her removal. Her uneasiness was so acute that the following year, to assure her of the modesty of his ambitions, Prince Ch'un presented his palace to the throne as a symbol of his naked submission. In 1889, an eminent ex-censor memorialized that Prince Ch'un, as father of the emperor, should be paid exceptional honour, and raised to the rank of Imperial Father, following a precedent recommended by no lesser authority than Ch'ien-lung. But such rank conferred greater power on Prince Ch'un, and Tz'u-hsi countered sharply: 'Years ago ... the Prince ... expressed a fear that the very example which has now been cited by the present memorialist might be used by sycophants and other evil persons to advance improper proposals on his behalf. For this reason he handed· in a secret memorial in advance, with a request that, when the emperor should attain his majority, no change whatsoever should be made in his own rank and titles.'[28] Prince Ch'un's 'secret memorial' of 1875 was attached. Many felt it had been conveniently backdated.

The only panacea Tz'u-hsi could envisage to diminish the eventually inevitable loss of her absolute powers was a garden pleasance such as the K'ang-hsi and Ch'ien-lung Emperors had bestowed on their mothers, Empresses Dowager like herself. Tz'u-hsi had never forgotten the gentle, countrified landscapes of the vanished summer palaces: and when her longings became irrepressible, the egregious Prince Ch'un collaborated. He must have feared that his son Kuang-hsu might never rule in deed if Tz'u-hsi remained at his elbow in the Forbidden City, for he allowed Tz'u-hsi to milk the funds of the Admiralty Board of which he was president, and to divert huge sums, allotted for the construction of warships and desperately needed sea-defences into her Privy Purse, towards the restoration of the summer palace. In the name of the emperor, Tz'u-hsi decreed in 1888:

We then remembered that in the neighbourhood of the Western Park there was a palace ... that many of the buildings were still in fair condition and only required some restoration to make them fit for use as a place of solace and delight.... We conceived the idea of restoring the Ch'ing I Yuan [Garden of Clear Rippling Waters], conferring upon it the new name of I Ho Yuan [Garden (Park) for the Cultivation of Harmonious Old Age].

Tz'u-hsi, after demurring, replied, unblushingly:

I am.... aware that the Emperor's desire to restore the palace in the west springs from his laudable concern for my welfare, and for that reason I cannot bear to meet his well-meaning petition with a blunt refusal. Moreover the costs of the construction have all been provided for out of the surplus funds accumulated as a result of rigid economies in the past. The funds under the control of the Board of Revenue will not be touched, and no harm will be done the national finances.[29]

The Board of Revenue did remain inviolate, but important funds, estimated at thirty thousand teals, were defrauded from the Board of Admiralty.[30]

By 1889, when the reconstruction of the I Ho Yuan was well advanced and the Kuang-hsu Emperor was nineteen *sui*, tradition made it too embarrassing for Tz'u-hsi to remain any longer in control. In imitation of the illustrious Ch'ien-lung Emperor, she therefore 'abdicated' and symbolically moved her apartments in the Forbidden City to Ning Shou Kung (the Palace of Kindly and Tranquil Old Age) as Ch'ien-lung had also done when he abdicated after sixty years' rule in favour of his grandson Chia-ch'ing in 1795. Like him also, Tz'u-hsi retained far-reaching powers to 'instruct' the emperor, to dismiss and appoint officials of the two highest ranks, and to examine all state papers. But even if she had wanted, she could not have abjured all authority. For now, after long years of habit, her legitimacy was more secure, as Kuang-hsu's mother by adoption, as an empress who had 'lowered the curtain' – twice – and as senior member of the imperial family, she was entitled by Confucian tradition and by precedent to the highest respect and obedience.

Tz'u-hsi made one more move to ensure her continuing influence: on 26 February 1889, a week before she officially 'rolled up the curtain', Kuang-hsu was married. His own choice of empress, a spirited, independent-minded fourteen-year-old of the Tatala clan, was thrust aside – for Tz'u-hsi remembered Alute with a shudder – to become the Pearl Concubine, while her sixteen-year-old, fatter, slower sister became the Lustrous Concubine. Kung-hsu was forced to take as empress a sunken-chested, buck-toothed, long-faced girl, who at twenty-two was three years his senior. But she was Tz'u-hsi's niece, the daughter of Tz'u-hsi's incompetent brother Kuei-hsiang, and therefore Kuang-hsu's first cousin. To make sure that if her niece Lung-yü's services as spy were inadequate she would have other intelligence, Tz'u-hsi blocked the access between the emperor's apartments and those of the empress and the concubines. If Kuang-hsu summoned one of them to his bed, she had to pass over Tz'u-hsi's verandas, and Tz'u-hsi, lying wakefully in her bed at night, could hear the footsteps creak on the polished wooden boards.

Chapter Nine

CULTIVATE YOUR PERSON

The Kuang-hsu Emperor was slightly built, about five feet four inches tall, with a habitually melancholy expression, large mournful and shining dark eyes, a sensitive mouth and a long, prominent chin. His fingers were exceptionally tapering, his chest narrow, and his ill-health chronic. In 1898 a doctor examined him and diagnosed a lung condition of already twelve years' standing: two years before he formally assumed the Throne in 1889, he was already suffering from bronchitis, emphysema, or even tuberculosis. His chest troubles weakened his voice, which was 'light and thin like the hum of a mosquito. Those not in the habit of hearing him could not understand what he said, the sound was so fine.'[1] In 1889, when he was nineteen, he looked much younger. He was languid and often listless, but he sometimes liked a prank: he once announced, 'The Empress Dowager', in the throne room so everybody fell to the ground long before Tz'u-hsi appeared; another time he deeply offended Tz'u-hsi by saluting and clicking his heels together in Western fashion before the altar at the annual temple sacrifices.

Since the age of three he had lived as if orphaned in the palace with Tz'u-hsi and thousands of eunuchs and maids for company. The experience could not have done other than deeply warp his nature and his life-long attitude to the draconian woman who had placed him on the throne. Kuang-hsu's parents colluded with Tz'u-hsi over his lonely childhood and education: his mother acquiesced wholly in her dominating sister's 'adoption' of her son; his father, Prince Ch'un, was pitiably complaisant. He not only allowed Tz'u-hsi to drain the Board of Admiralty for her summer palace's construction, but he also permitted, in 1884, the Chief Eunuch Li Lien-ying to accompany him when he sailed out as head of the Admiralty to inspect the fleet and the new strongholds of Port Arthur, Weihaiwei and Taku that guarded the entrance to Peking. Li Hung-chang was also present and also condoned the open breach with tradition and law as Li Lien-ying, a palace servant, stood beside a prince of the blood and China's most senior statesman, and was accorded equal honour. Mandarin opinion exploded in outrage, but Prince Ch'un never remonstrated, and indeed, so moved was he by the events of the day and the impressiveness of China's new defences, that he composed a number of poems in commemoration.

In 1891, two years after Kuang-hsu's majority, his father Prince Ch'un died. He was only fifty, but his health, which his son had obviously inherited, had always been poor. When Tz'u-hsi heard her soothsayers declare six years later that a giant gingko tree near the Prince's grave had the power to perpetuate his direct line on the throne, she gave orders to cut it down. In the stump a nest of snakes was writhing – symbol of the Chinese Dragon. Tz'u-hsi then felt her years of suspicion of Prince Ch'un had been well-founded.[2]

Ineffectual and unhelpful as Prince Ch'un had been, his death left Kuang-hsu even more alone and thrust him more closely towards his only allies: his concubines and his tutor Weng T'ung-ho, who was sixty-one, 'prepossessing, courteous and scholarly',[3] a prac-tised statesman, and a gifted painter, who had always comforted him when, as a child, Kuang-hsu had burst into terrible tantrums or started at the thunderstorms that frightened him. Weng had been dismissed from his post on the Grand Council in Tz'u-hsi's purge of 1884, but he had retained his position as the emperor's tutor, had grown into his fast friend and mentor. After 1894 his comparative progressiveness and interest in reform counteracted the oppressive unenlightenment and ignorance of the court. Weng described to him the inventions and technical advances of the West, and Kuang-hsu was utterly gripped by their novelty and excitement. A shop in Peking belonging to a Dane imported mechanical toys – mainly clockwork – for the children of the legations' staff. Kuang-hsu was brought some, and was enchanted. His apartments were filled with clocks of every description, and his favourite pastime became – much to Tz'u-hsi's irritated apprehension – taking them to pieces, (including hers), and then trying to reassemble them. He even bor-rowed a bicycle from an Englishman at the T'ung-wen Kuan (College of Languages) but his queue got tangled in the wheel, or so they giggled in the legations.

Kuang-hsu's fascination with the West was not mere dilet-tantism: he also devoured books of practical wisdom. The T'ung-wen Kuan, established since the T'ung-chih Restoration, sent him volumes of astronomy, zoology, geology, physiology, law and political philosophy. It was rumoured among agog foreigners in Peking that he was even reading the New Testament. He began learning English with two of the American missionary W.A.P. Martin's pupils from the T'ung-wen Kuan, but he made little headway, and ten years later, when many vicissitudes had admittedly interrupted his studies, his pronunciation of the few words he knew was atrocious.

His avidity for Western knowledge was inspired and fostered by Weng T'ung-ho, but it was also spurred on by the Pearl Concubine and her sister, who, for Manchu women, had been unusually well educated under the tutelage of an eminent scholar, Wen T'ing-shih, and both thirsted for information and teaching. Lung-yü, the narrow-faced pedantic empress, took note and informed Tz'u-hsi, her aunt. The similarities between the Pearl Concubine's curiosity, intelligence, youth and charms, and Tz'u-hsi's own when she too had been a concubine and had influenced Hsien-feng, awoke all Tz'u-hsi's envy and fear. She ordered Lung-yü to keep a closer watch, and in 1894, when she heard that the official she had recommended for a post had been passed over in favour of the Pearl Concubine's nominee, she charged both sisters with accepting bribes for giving audience – not of course a fault she ever committed – and ordered them to be stripped of their ranks and titles and beaten by eunuchs as a lesson. Even the emperor could do nothing to save his favourite and her sister from the bamboo rod.

The Kuang-hsu Emperor did not however need such spiteful reminders that Tz'u-hsi's authority still menaced him. In the winter, for four months of the year, Tz'u-hsi's new garden palace was snowbound, and so she lived next door to him in the Forbidden City. For the eight months of fine weather, Kuang-hsu could not neglect her either: every week, at least once, and sometimes twice, he was borne on the two-and-a-half-hour journey to the I Ho Yuan to make his filial obeisance, remind her of his compliance, and inform her of all his actions and decisions during her years of retirement. Afterwards, he returned to the Forbidden City, and to his struggle to govern the empire along traditional lines and yet infuse it with the modern spirit he read about and longed to develop for the benefit of his people.

In these years of her retirement, from 1889 to 1898, the daily activities of the Empress Dowager Tz'u-hsi were still conducted along exact ceremonious lines. Ceremony was the cornerstone of the Confucian state: its intricacy and formality masked a man to make him a sublime official, disguised the humanity of the emperor to cloak him in divine glory. T z'u-hsi, through a calculated embrace of tradition and through a personal love of pomp and ritual, perfected this technique of solomnizing herself. Her rigid and unoriginal spirit concealed itself behind a panoply of majestic insignia that awed everybody into submission and reverence, where her own personality, stripped of mystique, would not have done. Her household, under the enigmatic Chief Eunuch Li Lien-ying, cost that staggering sum of £6,500,000 per annum,[4] because Tz'u-hsi knew that the magnificence of her court was a mainspring of her authority and continued power.

Tz'u-hsi's day began early during her term of office, and it continued to do so during her retirement. Usually she slept only fitfully, often leaving her bed at 2 am to wander wide awake around the bizarre crags of the rockery behind her apartments at the Forbidden City, or round the gardens of her summer palace, where weeping willows, gnarled juniper trees and feathery cassias and bamboo groves gave her the illusion she had returned once more to the wild and lovely southern countryside of her youth. If her sleep was sound, it was the unpleasant duty of one of her retinue to wake her at 6 am, for she always grumbled angrily when aroused. She slept in silk pyjamas, on a ten foot long *k'ang*, the brick bed of north China under which a fire is lit in winter to coddle the sleeper. Her head rested on pillows filled with rose petals or tea leaves, perforated so the aroma should escape and fill the room; her coverlet was filled with down, and the bed hangings were of white crêpe and apricot satin, woven with a design of *feng* birds and lucky symbols, with scent bags suspended from ribbons amongst them. A portrait of Queen Victoria stood by her bed, and over a dozen clocks, some by James Cox of London – for Tz'u-hsi did share some tastes with her nephew – ticked in the room, but in spite of her insomniac tendencies did not keep her awake. A serving-maid lay close by her at night on another bed, and six eunuchs stood guard at her door.

Once she was awake, maids brought bronze basins of hot water and towels, wet and dry, to wash her face and hands; even the lavatory of an empress was primitive, and its contents served later as manure. She was uncharacteristically earthy about such things, and would clap her hands suddenly at a garden party and ask her guests – always women of course – if they wanted to pee.

Her breakfast was light: she drank a bowl of hot milk sweetened with honey and almonds, and ate some lotus-root porridge, Gruesomely – and probably untruthfully – Princess Te-ling, her lady-in-waiting in 1903–4, reported that Tz'u-hsi's morning drink was mother's milk and that she kept a Manchu, not a Chinese, specially in the Forbidden City to provide it. Every ten days Tz'u-hsi also swallowed some crushed pearls which she believed to be an elixir. After breakfast, her ladies prepared her water pipe, and she took a few calming and deep draughts. She may have tried opium, but she never showed any sign of addiction: no emaciation, or enfeeblement of survival instincts or loss of energy, so her use of the drug, if any, was certainly intermittent.

Widows were forbidden to wear make-up, but the Empress Dowager explained that in her position she had to use it in spite of custom. She first sprayed her face with a mixture of glycerine and honeysuckle of her own concoction, and then, as her dark complexion was not admired in China, she wore a pinkish powder and rouged her bottom lip and cheeks to disguise it; she scented herself generously with musk (probably just as well as there was no dry cleaning in China – foreigners always complained of the frowziness of most eminent Chinese); she sweetened her breath with betel-nuts she kept in a purse at her side, along with a jewelled face-mirror and a precious fan. She was personally very fastidious: after patting one of her pet Pekingese, she wiped her hands on a handkerchief, and before eating, she always pinned a napkin to her breast with a golden brooch.

Scrupulous in her attention to detail, she now had the grey streaks in her once raven hair blotted out with black dye. It stained the scalp as well, and in later years she was delighted when a dye from Paris which left her skin white was procured for her. Her toilette took at least an hour, and she also changed many times during the course of the day. She was 'fussy and particular as a young girl'.[5] Once, when the eunuch who usually did her hair fell ill, she inspired such terror in his replacement that his hand shook as he combed, and he tweaked out two long black hairs. 'Put them back, put them back at once.' shrieked Tz'u-hsi. She was only placated when her devoted Li Lien-ying suggested the culprit should be beaten to death. Unfortunately, Te-ling, who witnessed the incident, does not record its outcome.[6]

Sumptuary laws governed the customs of all officials and courtiers: when the emperor, or Tz'u-hsi, felt the cold, it was decreed that autumn dress would now be worn. Accordingly everybody discarded the gauze apparel of summer, sometimes silk-lined or lightly wadded, for the fur-lined robes of winter. Tz'u-hsi's wardrobes overflowed with hundreds of dresses, every inch worked or woven in the tiniest stitches or invisible knots. Her shoes, too, her Manchu slippers with the central raised heel, were embroidered and beaded and decorated and sewn for her in their hundreds, by a dozen old ladies who lived and worked in a corner of the Summer Palace. Her elaborate vanities were however rooted in respectable orthodox teachings. For to neglect the body bestowed by one's parents was to show them disrespect and lack of affection; a salient Confucian maxim was 'Cultivate your person'.

In her full parure, with ladies and eunuchs beside her in their scarlet and azure and gold emblazoned robes, under her huge tasselled state parasols with twelve court musicians always in attendance, she must have presented a breathtaking sight of oriental splendour as she made her progress through the gardens of her palace. Yet she was, by her fifties, an unattractive woman: her skin had always been sallow, her ears a little large, but her chin had now tripled, her lips had narrowed, her teeth had begun to fall out, which showed when she crowed with mirth as she often did, and her whole face, which had always been on the heavy side, was now positively mulish. Slight and rounded in her thirties, she was by her fifties squat and dumpy. But she carried herself erect, and she had kept the imperious and child-like curiosity that had made her so lively a young woman.

In retirement she pursued her pleasures with as great a concentration as she had given her former powers. During the winter months she was carried in her sedan across the Forbidden City to the Sea Palaces, a cluster of pavilions on three artificial lakes to the west. When Marco Polo saw the 'Green Mountain' above the North Sea, he wrote, seven hundred years before Tz'u-hsi felt the same, 'The Great Khan has caused this beautiful prospect to be formed for the comfort and solace and delectation of his heart'.[7] Dominated by the White Dagoba, a Tibetan-style temple shaped like a bell, which was built by the first Ch'ing Emperor in 1652 to honour the Dalai Lama, the hill was an Eden of marvellous trees: the white-barked Peking pine, the sterner thuya and darker cypress, juniper and camellias and japonica and berry-laden jujube trees, paint-trees, maidenhair, magnolia and ailanthus grew among boulders and rockeries seeming strewn at random, between prettily perched pavilions and arbours. As in the destroyed Yuan Ming Yuan, the pavilions, or sometimes only an angle of one or a view of another, were evocatively named after passages of the classics. The Peak with the Wonderful Cloud Wreath, the Hall of Sweet Dew, the Hall of Sparkling Brightness, the Green Bowers, the Building of Felicitous Skies all clung among the outcrops of crag on the steep incline up to the White Dagoba. A house shaped like a fan was called Delay of Southern Fragrance, another which curled along the shores of the lake was called the Pavilion of Distant Sails. This group on the North Sea, bright with scarlet and gold and ebony, with long cool colonnades of filigree carved wood, resplendently coffered ceilings, and roofs as frilly and scaly as the imperial dragon itself, or accordion-pleated and surmounted by a gleaming globe, or shaped like saddles or pyramids, represented 'the finest Chinese rococo'.[8] There, Tz'u-hsi loved to paint during these her days of leisure, looking at the Five Dragons, delicate azure-tiled gazebos mirrored in the waters of the lake, watching the silver-grey herons who nested in the banks, and listening to the doves as they flew overhead, whistles tied to their tails so that they sang as they passed, and to the wind-bells hanging from the temples' eaves.

The garden of this North Sea was intensely cherished and cultivated by Tz'u-hsi both before she built the summer palace and afterwards. The love of nature with which she was born had been nourished by her study of the nature-revering classics since her arrival at court, and she now feasted on its sights and sounds and scents, for all her sensuousness concentrated on inanimate matter. She reorganized the ancient rockery, she kept the buildings in mint condition, she was never bored with being carried in her chair by eight bearers, or walking very fast, eunuchs at both elbows, up the sharp hill to find a vantage point over the vista. The Bridge of the Golden Sea Monster and the Jade Rainbow which divided the Middle Sea from the North Sea had always been open to the public, for otherwise a great detour was required to cross Peking. But Tz'u-hsi's favourite spot was on that bridge, and so she closed it to the people. In the springtime, standing as her eunuch gardeners plunged waist-deep in the mire to plant the lotus roots, or in winter, watching her courtiers skate on one blade only, pushing with the other foot, she experienced unaccustomed tranquillity. When she was sad she consoled herself contemplating from the bridge the lotus opening in the light of the morning, and breathing the perfume they exhaled. 'It is a miracle – the miracle of life,' she said. 'One feels very close to all living things at such a time.'[9]

She also painted at the I Ho Yuan, the summer palace. Her teacher, Lady Miao, said: 'We were both young when she began. Shortly after she was taken into the palace, she began the study of books, and partly as a diversion, but largely out of her love for art, she took up the brush. She studied the old masters as they have been reproduced by woodcuts in books, and from the paintings that have been preserved in the palace collection, and soon she exhibited rare talent.'[10] Her brush was eloquent and free and her paintings of nature tremendously attractive. She had eighteen artists who were expected to attend her in groups of six on a ten-day rota, but who often played truant, so exorbitant was the eunuchs' squeeze if they appeared at court. Lady Miao elicited unusual kindliness from Tz'u-hsi: she was the only Chinese woman ever allowed to live in the Manchu court. When she arrived, her feet had been bound, and Tz'u-hsi, who had always deplored the custom, employed the best doctors to restore their shape and health as much as was possible.

Long before Tz'u-hsi had begun cheating her own country to build herself a summer palace, she had conceived the despot's mania for everlasting monuments and had assembled, on a lovely island in the South Sea called the Ying T'ai, the Ocean Terrace, a gay and ornamental sequence of buildings, which stood on marble terraces dropping sheer into the water, with canals spanned by pretty bridges between them. The names Tz'u-hsi gave her constructions reveal her preoccupations: the Cultivate Elegance Hall, the Side Chamber of Quiet Rest, the Study of Reflection on Remote Matters, the Study of Singleness of Heart. She was pursuing an ideal of peace that through her own fault eluded her and would continue to do so. A certain loneliness can also be glimpsed in the names: an emphasis on dignity without friends. But the most imposing edifice she ordered, the two-storied kernel of a majestic compound, facing out onto a garden scattered with sundials and elegant bronze and stone guardian animals, was significantly called the Hall of Good Luck, disclosing Tz'u-hsi's growing superstition.

The Chinese among whom she had been brought up in the south were ridden with superstitious ceremonies and taboos; astrologers and fortune-tellers, claivoyants and augurers were consulted on every occasion. Tz'u-hsi was susceptible to such fancies of supernatural ordinance, for while her political terms of reference were Confucian, her personal life retreated increasingly into the more primitive folk religions she had witnessed as a child: nature-worshipping Taoism and divinatory Buddhism. She was also attracted to Buddhism because the Buddhist pantheon included women, and prominent amongst them the Goddess of Mercy, Kuan-yin, with whom Tz'u-hsi felt a very special affinity. Women could become Buddhist priests and the religion did not discriminate against them as the sexist rules of ancestor-worship in Confucianism did. Also, her loneliness as a despot drove her to rely on 'fate' and 'luck'. Ridden with suspicion and fears, she felt she had little where else to turn.

From 1884 onwards, once she had secured the agreeable Prince Ch'un's co-operation over her summer palace, it was on the I Ho Yuan that she lavished her country's funds. Her restoration and rebuilding there also confirms her growing belief in the ceremonial and occult side of Buddhism – she never of course showed any signs of adopting Buddhist ideas of self-denial. On the lovely Mountain of Ten Thousand Years, which rose above the serene K'un Ming Lake, there grew the flowering shrubs and trees so eagerly purloined from China by botanists and now common in Europe: laburnum and forsythia, azaleas and rhododendrons, roses of every species, gardenias, jasmine and lilies, blossoming and fruit-bearing trees. Flights of marble stairs and tunnels carved in the rock led up the hill through dozens of gazebos and temples where Tz'u-hsi strolled to enjoy the view, while sampling a basket of sweetmeats. On the peak, Buddha's Summer Incense Tower, octagonal and heavily restored by Tz'u-hsi, rose skywards; beneath it stood the largest building in the complex, the Ten Thousand Buddhas' Hall, of green and yellow glazed bricks, each one a miniature replica of the god. Both had escaped the destruction of 1860. From there Tz'u-hsi looked down on the waters, called after the T'ang Emperors' lake at their famous palace of Ch'ang-an in Shensi, and at the central floating island, which was linked to the mainland by a graceful seventeen-arched marble bridge that had also escaped the Allied soldiers. On the shores of the lake clustered vividly enamelled pavilions and residences Tz'u-hsi had commissioned; there also the Jade Girdle Bridge, which had survived 1860, rose in a camel's back over a feeder canal to meet its own reflection in a circle; the two-tiered paddle steamer, a folly of solid marble where Tz'u-hsi picnicked, seemed to float on the water. It was the only boat built with the navy funds she had appropriated.

The craftsmen and builders cheated the imperial household wantonly: when, thirty years later, the English tutor of the last emperor of China was appointed supervisor of the summer palace, he asked the traditional palace contractors for an estimate for some restoration. When he heard it, he took his custom elsewhere, for less than a seventh of their price.[11] Under Tz'u-hsi, the eunuchs took their cuts, and she had been a recluse from the market place so long she no longer had any sense of the value of money.

As Tz'u-hsi wandered through the I Ho Yuan, she was always accompanied by ladies and eunuchs. The eunuchs, utterly dispossessed in Chinese society, were the one group, however contemptible, Tz'u-hsi could trust to obey her completely; by a mixture of indulgence and tyranny, she had won the whole-hearted allegiance of her household, while Li Lien-ying, the Chief Eunuch, was her friend and intimate, always at her side. He was a tall, sagging man, 'very ugly . . . and his face was full of wrinkles but he had beautiful manners'.[12] He had become a eunuch after puberty, and his nickname Pi-hsiao Li ('Cobbler's Wax' Li) referred to a boyhood apprenticeship to a shoemaker. It was rumoured that, tempted by the riches and favours of the imperial court, Li had castrated himself with his cobbler's knife. Tz'u-hsi entrusted him with all the financial arrangements of the palace and of her audiences, and extortion and bribery progressed from strength to strength under his administration. It was known that the easiest access to Tz'u-hsi was through his pocket, and when he died in 1911 he was reputedly one of the richest men in China, with a fortune worth two million sterling in pawnshops and property in the city. Tz'u-hsi decorated Li with the peacock's feather and the ruby button of the second rank, although eunuchs were not allowed to hold higher rank than the fourth. But by such favours, she cemented these ubiquitous servants of the court to her side, and spied on the adolescent emperor in Peking.

The ladies in her retinue were mostly her relations: Lung-yü's two sisters, her nieces, and the intended wife of a nephew who had decided, when he died before the marriage, to live celibate as his widow for the rest of her life – a pious action which would earn her a handsome arch of chastity. But Tz'u-hsi's chief companion was Princess Jung-shou, Prince Kung's daughter, whom she had adopted as her own early in 1862, and who had returned to Tz'u-hsi's side in 1871, when she had lost her husband at the age of seventeen. Ten years later, Tz'u-hsi made her an imperial princess and granted her the privilege of riding in a sedan chair in the Forbidden City – a mark of favour so exalted that even princes kowtowed to her. She was 'austere in manner, plain in appearance, and dignified in bearing' and Tz'u-hsi probably liked her because she was 'noted for her accomplishment in making the most graceful curtsey of any lady of the Court',[13] and Tz'u-hsi was finding etiquette more and more important.

Tz'u-hsi also conquered the jealousy that had made her son T'ung-chih's wives anathema. One of them, Yu-fei, an 'exceptionally clever' woman, in Te-ling's opinion, wrote poetry, and played many musical instruments. 'She showed me several poems which she had written,' wrote Te-ling, 'but they were of a melancholy character.'[14] Tz'u-hsi and Yu-fei, her son's widow, recited together page after page of Buddhist sutras or, meditating on the landscape of the palace gardens, lingered over the haunting poems of the T'ang dynasty, by Tu Fu brooding on his exile or by Li Po urging epicureanism in his earthy drinking songs. Tz'u-hsi's poetic tastes were utterly conventional, and she never composed anything herself; but she was inordinately proud of her calligraphy and painted the characters for Good Luck, Longevity and Happiness on silk scrolls for presentation to loyal officials.

Her ladies-in-waiting and her eunuchs were the immediate victims of her increasingly crotchety temper. She dominated them by sudden outbursts of rage, but also by taking each of them aside conspiratorially now and then and professing particular affection and concern. Each then felt singled out, while Tz'u-hsi laughed up her sleeve, and the next day treated the new 'favourite' ferociously. 'She is very changeable,' said one, 'she may like one person today, tomorrow she hates the same person worse than poison.[15] She also liked to dazzle them with her knowledge, with recitals of the classics, and to reiterate to them the plots of her favourite plays, scoffing at the ignorance they feigned to please her. Her manners were bossy and direct, and she always held her interlocutor with a piercing look straight in the eye. She loved ordering punishments, both petty and serious. Once she ordered two maids to slap each other's face harder and harder in front of her. When she ordered one eunuch, Chao, to take two special dishes as a mark of her esteem to Li Lien-ying, it was pouring with rain, so Chao told one of his subordinates to do it. When he reported Li's thanks to the empress, she retorted: 'Did you deliver them youself?' Chao said he had. 'It is raining outside,' she said crisply, 'so how is it your clothes are dry?' At Chao's confusion, she sentenced him to ten strokes of the bamboo.[16]

Tz'u-hsi was always swift with the rods carried by one of her entourage and her commands were always executed immediately, on the buttocks. Anywhere else was considered too tender. Tz'u-hsi's predilection for corporal punishment seems another indication, besides her ambition, her fastidiousness and her affection for eunuchs, that the teahouse tales of palace amours were idly founded and that her pleasures were found elsewhere. Once when she ordered a beating, she laughed, saying: 'They have not been punished for several days and they are looking forward to it. I will not disappoint them, but give them all they wish to have.'[17]

In the summer, the imperial procession – Tz'u-hsi, ladies, eunuchs, some swinging censers, some carrying her cosmetics, some playing music, some transporting a travelling kitchen – halted in the gardens when Tz'u-hsi called for lunch. She ordered it at any moment and in any place that took her fancy, and the eunuchs set up their stoves and cooked it, or otherwise produced it from thermos lacquer containers, and reheated it. Tz'u-hsi's lunch and dinner always consisted of the same hundreds of dishes, from which she picked and chose her favourites. As these remained constant, the cooks pocketed a good part of the *table d'hôte* allowance by serving up day after day the same dishes she never sampled until the weevils were crawling in them visibly. As Tz'u-hsi sat at her table alone, the spread of dishes before her, she sometimes favoured a lady-in-waiting with a dainty morsel which manners forced her to eat wreathed in smiles. As Tz'u-hsi never offered one of her special delights, the morsel was quite possibly ten days old, and she probably was well aware of it.

Tz'u-hsi was a gourmet of astonishing voraciousness. In spite of the quantities of tribute rice exacted from the farmers and sent from the south to Peking, Tz'u-hsi preferred bread, baked in moulds shaped like dragons, butterflies and flowers, and fried or steamed with sugar, pepper and salt. She drank the fiery Chinese wine, *samshu*, very rarely, and flavoured her tea with flowers – honeysuckle, rose petals or jasmine. She brewed a new blend from the chrysanthemums cultivated in her garden. She invented hams, and experimented, ordering her chefs to dip magnolia and lotus in batter and fry them. A special mushroom, called a monkey's head, which swelled in water, was sent to her from the provinces; she loved delicacies like sea cucumber (really sea snails), shark's fin, ducks' feet and steamed ducks' tongues, of which she ate thirty at a time; she adored pork, especially the rind chopped into tiny pieces and fried, called 'tinkling bells'. Melons were stuffed for her with fruit and seeds and pine nuts and ham and chicken and steamed for hours; she nibbled at sweetmeats and *friandises* all day long. 'I never ceased to marvel', wrote Te-ling, 'at the appetite of Her Majesty.'[18]

Replete, she retired an hour to rest after lunch, while her ladies thankfully sat down, probably for the first time in the day, to their own meal. But by the early evening they were summoned once more to attend upon the Empress. She might want to inspect porcelain newly arrived from the imperial factories in Kiukiang: in 1891, '80 pieces of the finest quality, and 1,204 round articles of the high class kind . . . 1,414 plates, dishes, cups and vases' arrived to be given away as presents on the birthday of the Emperor Kuang-hsu.[19] She might want to order a new robe, or visit the shoe-makers, weavers, dyers, and dress-makers who lived behind the hill at the summer palace. Her attention to detail was tyrannical: she rebuked one of the dyers when her eagle eye picked out that one shade of green had been omitted from the spectrum. Alternatively, she might want to go boating on the dragon barge, while the eunuchs played to her and fanned her in the sun. She had introduced a small steam launch at the summer palace, and she loved to order it over to the shallow end, and then cackle gleefully at the eunuchs' horror when it ran aground and they had to leap, in all their finery, into the water to heave it free. Or she might play dice or dominoes, or paint, or read, or go for another long walk. In her pearl-laden high-soled shoes Tz'u-hsi was indefatigable: trailing her attendants along, she darted into the muddy reeds at the side of the lake after a plant that caught her eye, or trudged through the watered beds of her chrys-anthemums; she spent hours picking ornamental gourds, com-paring their shape and loveliness, and paring and pulping them deftly with a knife. One of her special joys however was rain. 'Taking away all defects,' she said, 'and washing the landscape in soft mystery.'[20] But while she indulged her pleasure in real life watercolour under a huge umbrella, her eunuchs and ladies stood by miserably soaked to the skin. 'It was a characteristic of Her Majesty's,' commented Te-ling, 'to experience a keen sense of enjoyment at the troubles of other people.'[21]

In retirement, Tz'u-hsi was as punctilious as she had been as ruler in her observance of religious ceremonies. The New Year sacrifices at the Temple of Heaven were followed by fifteen days of riotous carnival, of fireworks and banquets and audiences and presen-tations, during which Tz'u-hsi liked nothing better than an afternoon's gambling. She had invented a game, 'Eight Fairies Travel Across the Sea', played on a map of the Chinese Empire, in which eight counters, starting at different points, raced, signifi-cantly, for occupation of the Forbidden City. If Tz'u-hsi won, she tossed the cash in the air and hooted helplessly as her ladies scrambled to gather it up.

The changing seasons, the solstices and the equinoxes, the anniversaries of the birth and death of every Chinese emperor were commemorated in an endless festal cycle. At Tz'u-hsi's beloved groves at the Sea Palaces the empress and her ladies tied gaily coloured ribbons round the trunks and stems of the trees and shrubs and hung them with lanterns to celebrate the Birthday of the Flowers and Trees and the rising of sap at the beginning of spring. At the Temple of Sericulture, also at the Sea Palaces on the North Sea, the empress sacrificed livestock to the guardian deity of the silkworms, and then, with her retinue dressed in bright pinafores, gathered the first mulberry leaves of the year to feed to them. Tz'u-hsi took a keen interest in the production of silk, China's ancient discovery, and often visited the Halls of Sericulture to listen in fascination to the sound of the silkworms gnawing. Each year, she prepared eagerly for her birthday, painting scrolls in her handsome calligraphy and laying up stores of porcelain and jade and bolts of silk and brocade to present to her favourites. She also awaited greedily the poems and paintings of tribute, the quantities of luxury goods, of precious stones and ivory, of spices and delicacies that poured in from all over the empire in celebration. Yet she had little use for them: in 1900, when foreign soldiers penetrated into the Forbidden City, they found an enormous hall piled high with crates. Many had never been opened.

Each year on her birthday, as a Buddhist gesture to the preciousness of all living creatures, Tz'u-hsi redeemed ten thousand caged birds that were the favourite pets of the Chinese, and released them in the gardens of the summer palace. Some always remained, perching on her shoulder and refusing to fly away, which gave her overweening pleasure. She fancied her charisma with animals, and could whistle to birds and lure them to eat out of her hand. But the eunuchs had specially trained the birds for her birthday to gratify her, and her gesture was null and void, for as soon as she retired, the eunuchs scrambled up the trees to recapture them and sell them in the market place.

Tz'u-hsi was extravagantly generous, after the fashion of all Chinese. But she expected others to equal her, and told Te-ling sternly, 'I can see those who gave me things in order to please me, and those who gave because they were obliged.'[22] Also, she delighted in ruining her enemies by sending them prodigal gifts: if they did not respond in kind, they lost face, yet an equivalent present to the throne might break them. Tz'u-hsi herself grew more and more cavalier with money. As her interest in her own death grew keener, she raised extra funds for her mausoleum at the Eastern Tombs where the great Ch'ien-lung and her husband Hsien-feng lay buried. In 1897 she whimsically decided, probably on the advice of geomancers who later took a cut on the profits, that the teak pillars on which the building rested would be more auspiciously placed a few yards further away. At immense cost, the mausoleum was moved.

But her tomb, her birthdays, her feast days and ceremonies, wanderings and meals were insignificant beside the single enduring passion of Tz'u-hsi's life. On the first and fifteenth of every month the theatre came to her. At the Forbidden City, it took place at the Hall of Joyous Sounds, a theatre with three superimposed levels and complex stage machinery and props; at the summer palace, another theatre had been newly bult on the shore of the K'un Ming Lake. A troupe of actors, effeminate, pampered creatures who nevertheless often had families, and who still, in spite of the adulation lavished on them from the highest nobleman to the meanest peddler, were forbidden to sit the state examination, travelled to the court to play all day long for the Empress Dowager. Her most gifted eunuchs, like An Te-hai before his death, and Li Lien-ying in his youth, joined with them, and several plays were performed in succession. Tz'u-hsi made the selection beforehand, and directed them through eunuch intermediaries. She preferred the classics, particularly the Buddhist legends she knew verbatim because she could then chuckle appreciatively when the actors ad-libbed, but she also read new plays submitted to her and thus sponsored a revival of interest in Peking opera.

Princes and officials also attended, sitting in the pit while the empress and the ladies in their boxes were screened from their quizzing by gauze of imperial yellow. Crunching nuts, sipping tea in winter, bamboo-leaf juice in summer, gossiping and swopping anecdotes, the audience attended lazily to the rambling plays. Beneath the stage and facing them stood the musicians, sighing on their morose pipes and flageolets, beating drums, playing two-stringed fiddles and the Chinese guitar, and wailing into the *erh-kuang* (double flute) which gave Tz'u-hsi's favourite genre of drama its particular flavour. The plays' stories were always based on well-known legends or histories, some epic, some comic, some poignant, some bawdy. The latter had probably been banned from court by the 1880s at the latest – Tz'u-hsi's image as Old Buddha might have become tarnished. Three hundred and sixty-five standard plays and hundreds of episodes drew the picture of so many villainous mothers who ruin their sons' lives and murder their daughters-in-law, so many tyrants who usurp the throne, so many favourite concubines and lovelorn emperors, so many intrigues about the succession, that it is a wonder Tz'u-hsi did not bellow for the house-lights. These popular plays may well have provided the genesis of the street scandals about her: in the case of Alute's suicide, she was possibly cast as the wicked mother-in-law who drove her to it, because the latter was a stock character of Chinese theatre; or she figured as a scheming and ruthless termagant because the type had, like the Empress Wu of the T'ang, erupted occasionally into Chinese history and legend. Or it might also be a case of life imitating art: Tz'u-hsi remained highly impressionable to the end of her days.

The Chinese theatre was stylized: a piece of white paper curling around an actor's face and chest transformed him into a ghost; actors carrying black flags represented evil spirits abroad; fireworks heralded the appearance of a demon. Men played all the parts, swaying prettily on built-up boots with tiny shoes attached to imitate 'lily-feet', while other characters were delineated by a rich and vivid vocabulary of face-painting and masks and costumes. Beards and moustaches were twirled and cut and brushed into every shape, eyes and lips diabolically exaggerated in fierce colours, robes magnificently worked and braided and painted to resemble fishes, dragons, beasts of field and fable. The props which Tz'u-hsi often helped to design were often made of coloured rice-paper stretched over articulated split bamboo frames, making them very light, and mischievously alive. In private, she performed in masques and dressed up with her eunuchs. Her favourite rôle, naturally, was Kuan-yin, Goddess of Mercy, with Li Lien-ying as the Goddess's attendant divinity.

After a day at the theatre Tz'u-hsi retired happy. She was always early to bed, for she rose at dawn. Dancing lanterns accompanied her back to her apartments and bobbed in the waters of the lake. Not until 1903 was electric light introduced, when it ruined with its harshness the gold and vermilion chambers made for candlelight or the filtered sun and also altered the routine of the palace household. But at this date, Tz'u-hsi took her evening meal early, smoked her last pipe and was bathed by attendants who sat her in a chair and soaped and rinsed her all over, working downwards. Proper as she was, she exhibited no self-consciousness at all, but 'talked briskly and entertainingly'[23] during her bath to her ladies. Te-ling who attended her in 1903 when Tz'u-hsi was sixty-eight was dumbfounded by the youthfulness of her skin and body and particularly of her breasts. Afterwards, patted all over with extract of honeysuckle, she was put to bed.

Chapter Ten

THE DWARF MEN PREVAIL

In Kwangtung, a forward-looking young Chinese scholar, K'ang Yu-wei, grew up watching the decline of China and, during Tz'u-hsi's days of idleness at the I Ho Yuan, tussled with messianic yearnings to found a new Utopia in the Middle Kingdom. His ideals of reform ran the gamut from practical proposals to visionary iconoclasm: they proclaimed a single government for the world, the abolition of all private property, of marriage and the family, and the complete equality of race and nation.

My appearance in this world [he wrote] is solely for the purpose of saving all living beings. It is for this reason that I do not dwell in Heaven but enter into Hell; that I do not go to the Pure Land, but come to the world of corruption, that I do not exist as emperor or king, but as one of the people. . . . Thus . . . every instant I hold the salvation of the world to be my business, which I perform without regard for my person or my life . . .[1]

When K'ang wrote thus in 1884-5 he was already a maverick and had defied his family's ambitions, spurning the traditional examinations which would have obtained him government office. For he had progressed from orthodox Confucianism in his teens to a mystic absorption with the more arcane writings of Mahayana Buddhism, and in his twenties had retreated into the mountains of Kwangtung, grown his hair long and tousled, and meditated till his head grew light: 'At first wild thoughts crowded my mind like demons, but later my nightmares ceased, and I felt spiritually transcendent, carefree and at ease.'[2] Having cast himself in the ancient mould of the sage, he then suddenly discovered the West, in the flourishing streets of Hong Kong and the bustling, clean foreign settlements of Shanghai, and so he began to devour the new Western literature flowing from Meiji Japan, from the missionary presses, and from Western translators. The scientific, technological and professional knowledge of the West inspired in him a passionate admiration for foreign institutions. Also, unlike many scholars of his day, he was able to make an intellectual leap and apply them to the China around him. Therefore, he was also capable of drawing up a more earth-bound blueprint for Chinese reform that attacked the country's customs and structure with rare originality and daring.

K'ang studied hard to find a Chinese tradition for his views. He interpreted the *Spring and Autumn Annals*, eliminated 'forgeries' from other major classics of Confucianism to prove that the Master himself had implied a concept of progress when he spoke of three eras, barbarism (Disorder), civilization (Approaching Peace) and the Millenium of Universal Peace, towards which all men should strive. As conventional Chinese philosophy had always abided by a cyclical view of history, in which the wheel both turns upon itself, and surrenders to an eternal process of decline, K'ang's *Confucius as a Reformer*, as his later written treatise was called, was disturbingly heterodox. Yet he was sincere in his belief that his readings of the classics were accurate and true to Confucian doctrine, for while he adopted certain Western styles, forbidding his daughters for instance to bind their feet, he enacted such complex and archaic Confucian rites on his father's death that his *li*-conscious gentry relations looked askance at his antics.

'The world of corruption' into which K'ang was one day to plunge was the Manchu court of Peking, symbol and repository of all the most entrenched and dogmatic conservatism in Chinese mores. In 1888 at the age of thirty K'ang, in his conviction that the 'salvation of the world' was his duty, made his first approaches. He wrote to Weng T'ung-ho, the Kuang-hsu Emperor's tutor and an ex-Grand Councillor, and to other ministers at Peking to outline a programme of reform. The emperor was not shown the document, so startling were its contents. But even if K'ang's words threatened to sweep away the privileges on which the Ch'ing dynasty rested, only a few more years of foreign depredations were to pass before they became the one gospel the emperor desired to hear.

As the decisive year of 1894 approached, K'ang Yu'wei and his writings and disciples remained unknown to Tz'u-hsi as she boated and painted and built and postured at the summer palace as ever, with an even grander project in mind. In 1894 she was to be sixty years old, and when the mothers of the K'ang-hsi, Ch'ien-lung and Chia-ch'ing Emperors had celebrated their sixtieth birthdays, the great Stone Road between the summer palace and Peking had become a teeming highway of princes, officials and devoted servants of the Throne pouring forth to do the dowagers homage and present their tribute. Musicians had sung and played, actors had performed, the days had been filled with feasting, the emperors had showed 'dear love' for their mothers, and even given them new pleasure-gardens and palaces. Accordingly Tz'u-hsi, ever lively to tradition, was planning a birthday party that would make the I Ho Yuan resound. All officials were expected to contribute twenty-five per cent of their salary to her birthday fund; silks, robes, furs, jewels, luxuries, and delicacies made the slow and awkward journey through a poverty-stricken, hard-pressed China to the sumptuous court. When Tz'u-hsi took stock of her servants' loyalty, it was worth about thirty million taels.

This birthday party was never held. In 1893 in Korea, still turbulent after the precarious arrangement between Japan and China in 1885, the Tong Hak group of patriots rose in rebellion. They were an obscurantist, ultra-Confucianist group who proclaimed Korea for the Koreans, and wanted to oust both the Japanese, a novel influence, and the Chinese, traditional overlords. Although their rising was swiftly crushed by Korean government troops, the emotions behind the unrest were by no means stifled. A few months later, in March 1894, the leading pro-Japanese reformer was decoyed to Shanghai, murdered, and his corpse hacked to pieces and distributed strategically in Korea as a warning to his sympathizers.

The Chinese army, at the Korean government's request, marched to quell the riots; the Japanese were notified according to the 1885 agreement, and also sent in troops. When they produced an ambitious programme of Japanese-style reforms for Korea, the Chinese, standing on the suzerain's pledge that the vassal country administers its internal affairs as it wishes, declined to cooperate. The Japanese, deciding to ignore China's position as overlord and treat Korea as an independent country, tried to force their plans on the Koreans by direct methods. On 23 July 1894, Japanese soldiers therefore kidnapped the Korean queen and her children, and installed the eighty-year-old father of the king as their pawn on the throne of the Hermit Kingdom. Two days later a British ship, the *Kowshing*, chartered to transport Chinese troops to Korea, was obstructed by a Japanese gunboat, which, after some words, discharged a torpedo, opened fire with all guns and sank the *Kowshing* in half an hour. The Japanese then shot at the struggling survivors in the water and killed 1,130 people. Two days later Japan's puppet ruler of Korea implored Japan's assistance in the war he now declared upon China.

In sorrow and in anger Robert Hart, writing to England, described the provocation: 'China had given no offence, has done no wrong, does not wish to fight, and is willing to make sacrifices. She is a big "sick" man, convalescing slowly from the sickening effects of centuries, and is being jumped on when down by this agile, healthy, well-armed Jap – will no one pull him off?'[3]

In full and weary awareness of the weakness of his vaunted northern army and navy, which had fast declined through Tz'u-hsi's embezzlements and his own nepotism, Li Hung-chang went to war with Japan. Throughout September, October, November, December, January and February, the Chinese struggled hopelessly to defend the vulnerable north-east entrance to their capital. But all engagements, on sea and on land, faced the rejuvenated spirit of an always martial Japan, armed to the teeth with Western-style weapons of the latest device and ingenuity. The Japanese swiftly forged their passage across Korea to the western border, then across the Liaotung peninsula (northern arm of the Bay of Pechili) and drove the Chinese relentlessly back. By November they were arrayed before the Chinese citadel of Port Arthur, fortified and built with advisers from the West, pride of the northern theatre of war Li had established since 1884. On 21 November 1894, in spite of the bravery of the Chinese army, Port Arthur fell to the Japanese.

Across the Bay lay the southern arm, the Kiaochow peninsula, where Weihaiwei, also a fortress of Western design, stood as Port Arthur's complementary defence of the sea approaches to Peking. By 12 February, it too had surrendered; with it, all the fortifications of that area were in Japanese hands. The admiral in charge of Li's model navy committed suicide; he was followed by his second-in-command, then by the general in command of the forts, and then by another commanding officer. In Peking Prince Kung was recalled from the cultivation of his garden to 'piece together the cup which the present ministers have smashed to the floor'.[4] There was little the embittered old statesman could do.

Tz'u-hsi, railing piteously against the heaven that should so punish her, had to cancel her birthday celebrations.

The auspicious occasion of my sixtieth birthday [she wrote] was to have been a joyful event, in which the whole nation would unite in paying to me loyal and dutiful homage. It had been intended that His Majesty the Emperor, accompanied by the whole court, should proceed to offer congratulations to me, and make obeisance at the Summer Palace, and my officials and people have subscribed funds wherewith to raise triumphal arches, and to decorate the Imperial Highway throughout its entire length from Peking to the I Ho Yuan; high altars have been erected where Buddhist sutras were to have been recited in my honour...

Bitterly she added, 'Who would have anticipated that the dwarf men [the Japanese] would have dared to force us into hostilities, and that since the beginning of summer they have invaded our tributary states [Korea] and destroyed our fleet?[5]

She awarded three million taels to the navy fund from her birthday presents and her Privy Purse, a stingy sum considering she had by now acquired seven pairs of honorific titles, and that her income stood at 1,400,000 taels per annum. For she was by this time such a fabulously wealthy woman that in the very year of her country's trouncing by the Japanese, she consulted the English manager of the Hong Kong and Shanghai Bank in Peking – probably on the shrewd Li Hung-chang's advice – about depositing a nest egg of £8,250,000 in gold and silver bullion in a London vault.[6]

The defeat by Japan had revealed the worm that had reduced the stout fabric of China to handfuls of dust. The defeat was appalling not only because the military reforms of decades lay in ruins, not only because Korea, China's buffer vassal, was lost, not only because the decrepitude of the sick old man China was exposed, but particularly because the blow had been inflicted by another nation of the East, and by the Japanese, always the despised 'dwarf barbarians' who had copied Chinese civilization slavishly for centuries and had inspired nothing but supercilious scorn from the true fountainhead of Eastern wisdom in China. As recently as 1871, they had paid tribute to China as vassals. 'Who would ever have anticipated ...' was indeed the question ringing in the shamed heads of proud patricians like Tz'u-hsi.

Obloquy was heaped viciously upon Li Hung-chang. Now seventy-two years old, the great viceroy had entrusted his son-in-law with the military supplies of the army; he had boasted of his northern fleet and concentrated the military defence of north China in his own hands; and he had early pleaded for peace, a suspect action in a humiliated country yelling for vengeance, which became all the more so when it was rumoured that Li was heavily invested in Japanese business and so might not wish to lose his dividends through protracted war. 'Li Hung-chang has invariably advanced himself because of his relation with foreigners', snarled one censor.... 'He seems to have been afraid that the large sums of money, saved from numerous peculations, which he had deposited in Japan might be lost; hence his objections to the war.'[7]

Having thus attacked Tz'u-hsi's loyal minister, whose graft she understood only too well, the censor was fortunate that he was only banished to the post-roads.

While the mood of many officials at court was warlike and vengeful, Li Hung-chang and the emperor, knowing that further battle was hopeless, managed to retain Tz'u-hsi. Indeed, even before the fall of Port Arthur and Weihaiwei, the Chinese had made overtures of peace through other foreign powers. But the Japanese, pleased with their military triumph, and intoxicated with the moral victory over the more ancient civilization, wanted to hammer their advantage and make the proud Chinese eat wormwood on their knees. Echoing the bully days of the British and French in 1858–60, the Japanese rejected the first peace envoys as having inadequate credentials, and held out for a truly eminent representative to come and sue for peace. Li Hung-chang, who had been spared his life, but not his titles, was now appointed ambassador to sail for Japan and submit to China's conquerors, the destroyers of his life's work.

The Japanese terms at Shimonoseki were unequivocally harsh: they demanded the Liaotung peninsula on which Port Arthur was situated, the Pescadores Islands, and Formosa, which at the time of the peace negotiations was under attack from the Japanese fleet; they added a demand for the full independence of Korea; a 200-million-tael indemnity, and the occupation of Weihaiwei until the sum had been raised and paid. Yet these were modified terms, for, on arrival in Japan, the seventy-two-year-old Li Hung-chang had been shot in the cheek by a fanatical patriot, the bullet just missing his eye, and his near-assassination had raised such an outcry from the hitherto inert Western nations that the Japanese had hastily withdrawn original demands for more territory in Manchuria and 300 million taels.

On 17 April 1895, China bent her proud old head to the Land of the Rising Sun and the Treaty of Shimonoseki was signed. It immediately sharpened the savage greed of the powers in the Far East, and simultaneously the lust for reform in the progressive, impatient provinces of Kwangtung and Hunan.

Li Hung-chang had always adhered to the time-honoured Chinese diplomatic principle of playing on international jealousies: 'Use one barbarian to control another.' After Shimonoseki, Li trusted the Western nations to maintain the balance of power in China and to 'request' Japan's withdrawal from the key Liaotung peninsula. As expected, Russia, France and Germany politely did so, and Japan, not entirely unaware of a number of Russian men-of-war in the area, graciously concurred. The indemnity to Japan was raised another thirty million taels in compensation, but – for a time – the Liaotung peninsula was inviolate.

Progressives and reactionaries alike still thirsted however for Li Hung-chang's blood, and the only way Tz'u-hsi could save her loyal standby was to spirit him away to Russia as the Chinese representative to Tsar Nicholas's coronation. In St Petersburg, out of overweening confidence in his own diplomatic skills, or out of frank naïveté, Li Hung-chang neglected his own wise axiom that Russia alone, contiguous to China, would seriously consider seizing Chinese territory, and forgetting the colonization of the Amur lands and the port of Vladivostok in 1858–61, listened instead to the advice of many great officials who had recommended an alliance with Russia against Japan. In 1896 in a secret treaty, Russia and China bound themselves to defend each other against Japan; and in order to make things easier for Russia, China granted her the right to extend the Trans-Siberian railway across Manchuria to the sea, and also, unbelievably, to transport troops and military supplies by rail not only in times of war with Japan, but also in times of peace. Li has been accused of taking bribes from the Russians, but Count Witte, the Russian negotiator, denied the rumour in his memoirs.

When Li returned home in the winter of 1896, other storms distracted his enemies. For a time the foreign powers with interests in China had hesitated where to start on the Chinese spoils before them. Their first move was to secure an audience with the Kuang-hsu Emperor, in the Imperial City itself. It was the first time they entered the City, for Kuang-hsu's audience of 1891 had been granted at the Tzu Kuang Ko at the Sea Palaces, where T'ung-chih had also held court. After securing his final capitulation to their equality, Russia, France, England and Germany began to vie for the privilege of a loan to the indigent China to repay the Japanese indemnity and to repair and retrench. China borrowed from all three and pledged her customs revenue, her *likin* (transit) and *gabelle* (salt) taxes as security. But the powers who had magnanimously intervened to save the Liaotung peninsula did not stop there. In November 1896 Germany's Chancellor informed the Kaiser that 'the Minister at Peking should be instructed to keep his eyes open for an event suitable as a cause for advance'.[8]

Kiaochow, on the same spur as Weihaiwei, was selected by German patrol boats as a suitable German port. A year later, some Chinese bandits robbed a village in Shantung, burning the houses and murdering the inhabitants. Amongst the victims were two Roman Catholic missionaries – Germans. The Kaiser rose to soaring eloquence:

Plentiful atonement for this must be secured by energetic action of the fleet. The squadron must instantly proceed to Kiaochow, seize the port there, and threaten with severest repression unless the Chinese government instantly agree to a high compensation in gold as well as a really effective pursuit and punishment of the criminals. I am fully determined to abandon, henceforth, the over-cautious policy which had been regarded by the Chinese as weakness, and to show the Chinese, with full power, and – if necessary – with brutal ruthlessness that the German Emperor cannot be made sport of and that it is bad to have him as an enemy.[9]

Four days later, the Chinese garrison of Kiaochow was routed. After its capture, the port and the land around for a radius of fifty kilometres was 'leased' to Germany for ninety-nine years, with exclusive mining and railway rights in the area.

The scramble began: Russian warships sailed into Port Arthur, as they were allowed by the secret treaty of 1896, and announced that they had come to stay. Port Arthur was ice-free in winter, Vladivostok was not. Count Witte does this time corroborate in his diary that he paid Li Hung-chang and his colleague 500,000 taels each to expedite the matter: by March 1898, fortified Port Arthur and the merchant port of Talienwan nearby were 'leased' to Russia for twenty-five years, with all mining and railway rights for sixty miles around.

Sir Claude MacDonald, the British minister and the first to have no previous experience of China except as gunnery instructor in Hong Kong, was a stringy, bleary-eyed beanpole with exaggerated waxed moustaches. 'Everyone denounced the appointment,' wrote The *Times* correspondent, George Morrison. 'He was attacked as imperfectly educated ... weak, flippant, garrulous ... the type of military officer rolled out a mile at a time and then lopped off in six foot lengths.'[10] MacDonald voiced Britain's fury and indignation that the balance of power in the Gulf of Pechili had now been upset, and demanded that Weihaiwei should be handed over to the British as soon as the Japanese indemnity had been paid and the town had been evacuated. He also threw in an increase to the area of Kowloon, the mainland opposite Hong Kong. France, panting along beside, clutched thankfully at some anti-missionary riots in Kwangtung to demand a similar ninety-nine-year lease on the port of Kwangchowan, south of Hong Kong. China, like a shop assistant at a bargain counter, yielded helplessly to the snatch-and-grab.

Although the fight over the last loan towards the indemnity to Japan continued violently between Great Britain and Russia, the powers were otherwise most courteous to each other and guaranteed the 'spheres of influence' they had seized for themselves. Germany and Russia agreed that the entire Yangstze basin from

Szechuan to the delta at Kiangsu was British; Britain agreed that southern Kwangtung and southern Yunnan were French; a belt from Kansu across through Shensi, Shansi, Hunan and Shantung was German; Manchuria and Chihli were of course Russian. Freedom-loving principles made the United States fight shy of the seizure of territory; but, alarmed that they might be excluded from the benefits, they secured equal rights and opportunities for all nations in the leased areas, and termed their attitude the policy of the 'Open Door'. While foreign powers so remorselessly apportioned China, they failed to notice the flickering warnings of an almost extinguished spirit of revolt.

When Shimonoseki was signed, K'ang Yu'wei and his talented disciple Liang Ch'i-ch'ao, who had a flair for rousing journalism, were up in Peking together, for K'ang had given into tradition and decided to take the metropolitan examinations. The gathering of all these bright and ambitious candidates in the city always formed a flashpoint, and K'ang and Liang harnessed this energy and petitioned the emperor in a famous, outspoken Letter of Ten Thousand Words. It first carried the signatures of 1,300 scholars, but after threatening placards appeared in the streets many withdrew. K'ang's suggestions were sweeping: the Treaty of Shimonoseki was to be rejected, the ancient examination system and the sale of rank abolished; salaries increased to prevent 'squeeze'; the capital moved from Peking to a thrusting, modern city like Shanghai. Although the petition could do nothing to alter the treaty, it found receptive soil: the earnest Kuang-hsu Emperor, only twenty-three years old, and frustrated by nascent ideals and few men with whom he could discuss them, read the Letter – in an edited version – and liked it so much he ordered its circulation throughout officialdom. According to K'ang himself, Tz'u-hsi read it as well: it was her first encounter with the reformers.

The reformer K'ang Yu-wei's output over the last years had been prodigious and eclectic: he had written many books and delved into much of the history, philosophy and science obtainable through Japan; he had produced, with Liang Ch'i-ch'ao, one of his disciples, an independent newspaper – the first in China – called the *Chinese Progress*, consisting mainly of reprints of missionary translations, and such advanced items as the *Laws and Timetables of British Railways* and extracts from *The Adventures of Sherlock Holmes* – the wisdom of the West. For two taels a day only, K'ang found he could include a thousand of such broadsheets in the pages of the *Peking Gazette* itself and so circulate his ideas among mandarins directly.

He also formed, in the very nerve-centre of Peking, a Society of the Study of Self-Strengthening, and through the Society, his bold original views, his confident utopianism and attacks on obsolescent traditions were heard clearly by many influential men.

Tz'u-hsi had engineered Weng T'ung-ho's dismissal in 1896 from his post as tutor to the emperor, but the friendship she feared still held fast, and Weng's interest in reform and westernization continued to influence Kuang-hsu. Weng visited K'ang Yu'wei, a remarkable sign of esteem from such an august official, and stayed five hours, absorbing attentively K'ang's tangible proposals. Other mandarins, like Chang Chih-tung, now viceroy of Hunan and Hupeh, Wang Wen-shao, a Grand Councillor and Liu K'un-yi, the mild-mannered viceroy of Liang-kiang, each gave five thousand taels towards the movement, although Chang, with his business acumen, wanted the Society to lend its library at a profit, and was reproved by K'ang. Yuan Shih-k'ai, now in his thirties, was then in Peking, as his post as Chinese Resident in Korea had vanished in the Sino-Japanese War, and was training a wing of the new metropolitan army along German lines. Dining with K'ang one night, Yuan plighted himself to the cause of reform, and gave him funds. The foreign legations were naturally helpful with books and maps and information; the Baptist missionary Timothy Richard emerged prominently to serve as mentor to the reformers. But debts and trouble brewing over his newsheet drove K'ang back to his native south. There he finished his controversial *Confucius as a Reformer*, celebrated his fortieth birthday and, in a somewhat unprogressive way, took a concubine.

In 1897, when the Western powers first pounced, K'ang wrote again to his 'Prince', the Kuang-hsu Emperor and urged him vehemently to emulate Peter the Great of Russia and the Meiji Emperor of Japan and reform China. Japan or Great Britain were moreover, he assured the emperor, more trusty allies than Russia; also, if all the ports of the China coast were opened to international trade, the question of seizures and encroachments would not arise. Such a reversal of the principles of Chinese politics for the last half century scandalized the conservative officials who processed the emperor's correspondence, so that although Weng T'ung-ho pressed that K'ang should be received in audience, this letter of his was not even shown to the emperor.

But as the attacks on Chinese sovereignty accelerated through the winter of 1897, the statesmen cast about desperately for another solution. On 24 January 1898, K'ang Yu-wei was at last ushered into the office of the Tsungli Yamen, the Bureau of Foreign Affairs, before Li Hung-chang, Weng T'ung-ho, Jung-lu and Prince Kung. The latter, ailing and elderly, proposed caution, and told K'ang to write down his views and the Yamen would then see; Jung-lu declared angrily, 'The laws of our ancestors cannot be changed',[11] and was the first to leave – but this is K'ang's account and Jung-lu was already anathema to him. After hours had passed in which K'ang demonstrated his plans to streamline China like Japan, he was told to assemble material for presentation to the emperor. He immediately drafted a model for a Bureau of Institutions, with himself as president, which would overhaul the entire administration.

March 1898, when Port Arthur, Weihaiwei, Kowloon and Kwangchowan fell one after another into foreign hands, galvanized the young emperor. Why, he demanded furiously, had the alliance with Russia been made if the Russians had then turned and seized Port Arthur? Why were there never any means to fight back? Why were his ministers like Li Hung-chang so conciliatory all the time? Why did Tz'u-hsi never have any new ideas, and why did she always agree with Li? Why was China so feeble?

He was shown K'ang's works. Then he remembered the outspoken Letter of Ten Thousand Words he had read in 1895 and asked to see it again. In growing excitement he read through K'ang's opus. K'ang's *Study of Political Reforms in Japan* particularly inspired him, and while in the provinces frightened officials impeached the Societies for Self-Strengthening that mushroomed under K'ang's influence, the Son of Heaven himself rallied to the reformers' side. While Great Britain and Russia scrapped over the loan for the last instalment of the Japanese indemnity, Kuang-hsu tried to free China from the indemnities, loans, debts and yet more loans and went to the country. On 4 February he decreed the sale of government bonds to raise the money. His decree marked the beginning of another of China's efforts to derive strength from within herself, and in this was the first gesture of the reform movement. It was sad and telling augury therefore when the decree produced only a fraction of the hundred million taels required and stirred savage feelings in the south against the extortions of the alien Manchus.

In the spring of 1898 Tz'u-hsi was wary of her nephew's new enthusiasms and manoeuvres, but not antagonistic. For the epoch which came to be known as the Hundred Days of the Reform Movement would never have progressed as smartly or as optimistically as it did at the beginning unless Tz'u-hsi and her conservative power block had initially permitted it. The slight, delicate emperor with his melancholy eyes and his slim nervous hands, whose childhood had been tyrannized by her, knew better at first than to defy her wishes openly.

On 11 June, Kuang-hsu inaugurated the reform movement, in a somewhat half-hearted decree drafted by his tutor Weng, whose original enthusiasms had weakened before the dangers he now foresaw: 'We now issue this special Decree so that all our subjects, from the Imperial family downwards may hereafter exert themselves in the cause of reform.... There must be a careful investigation of every branch of European learning appropriate to existing needs, so that there may be an end to existing fallacies and that by zeal, efficiency may be attained....'[12] The next day, Kuang-hsu hurriedly reminded everyone that the Empress Dowager, in her great wisdom and goodness, was responsible for all the new measures, and that officials who received new appointments were to show her the profoundest gratitude.

But Tz'u-hsi was not satisfied that Kuang-hsu and his party were not surreptitiously progressing beyond her reach. On 14 June therefore she banished Weng T'ung-ho altogether from Peking. Her ostensible reason was vapid: 'displaying temper in the presence of the Throne'; a more immediate reason was Weng's recommendation of the notoriously heterodox K'ang Yu-wei to the emperor; but the fundamental one was Tz'u-hsi's keen instinct for survival and for the balance of power in the capital. Her scalpel's accuracy showed itself once again, for in losing Weng, Kuang-hsu lost his only confidant, who in many ways had replaced his own father during his lonely adolescence and the one man who had always calmed his fears and nightmares. But he did not fight for his friend: Weng's sudden half-heartedness and caution had alienated him. Still Tz'u-hsi did not feel secure, but continued to marshal her supporters. Prince Kung, long a trusted defender of the Manchu throne, had on 29 May at last given in to his long illness and died, in quiet and disillusion. Tz'u-hsi commemorated his thirty years of wise counsel and loyal service by her side in a markedly laconic obituary decree and immediately looked about for other support. She lit upon Jung-lu. The same day as Weng was banished, Jung-lu was appointed viceroy of the metropolitan province of Chihli with full charge of the army in the area. After the Sino-Japanese War Jung-lu had returned from exile in the provinces. Now he found himself, after seven years out in the cold, the keeper of the keys of power in the capital.

Kuang-hsu observed Tz'u-hsi's manoeuvres with some pain, but he persevered. On 16 June, seated cross-legged on a large imperial yellow cushion, the twenty-six-year-old emperor of China informally received the scholar K'ang Yu-wei who had so profoundly inspired him. He waved his eunuchs away, dispensed with the formality of the Manchu language and for many hours they held each other in a deep conversation that was to crystallize many, many hopes.

'The four barbarians are all invading us, and their attempted partition is gradually being carried out: China will soon perish', lamented Kuang-hsu, adding in anger: 'All that is being caused by the conservatives.' K'ang agreed enthusiastically, and immediately asked the emperor to set up the Bureau of Institutions he had drafted to handle reforms. Kuang-hsu assented, but when K'ang continued to press him, he 'glanced outside the screen, and then said, with a sigh. "What can I do with so much hindrance?"' K'ang was moved by the sight of the emperor's powerlessness, but he was horrified that he should be surrounded and frightened of spies. But he continued, pointing to the roots of the problem: the Confucian reliance on men of ability, rather than on efficient institutions, the insistence on tradition and precedent, the rigidity of the exams, and the stagnation of the promotion system. 'Today most of the high ministers are very old and conservative. . . . If Your Majesty wishes to rely on them for reform, it will be like climbing a tree to seek for fish.' K'ang suggested that young, lower-ranking officials (like himself) should be used on the reform bureau, by-passing the older men. When he spoke of the examination system, he attacked in particular the 'eight-legged essay' (the formal composition in eight parts). Kuang-hsu agreed sadly and wearily throughout: 'Westerners all pursue useful studies, while we Chinese pursue useless studies. Thus the present situation is brought about.' He then agreed to abolish the old examinations, and urged the reformer to continue. Again and again K'ang thought he should conclude, but the emperor ordered him on. At its close 'there had never been so long an audience' and Kuang-hsu granted the reformer the privilege, reserved for higher officials, of memorializing him direct.[13]

This vital audience was followed by an immediate spate of decrees. Many of the reforms promulgated were concerned with education, for Kuang-hsu, true to his upbringing, believed deeply in its value. A University of Peking was established, with the missionary W. A. P. Martin at its head; Manchus were urged to travel abroad and broaden their minds; schools were established in the provinces to teach applied skills like the preparation of tea and silk – manual labour unknown to the Confucian classroom; inventors and writers were encouraged by the introduction of patents and copyrights; 'unofficial' temples and shrines were ordered to become village schools. Above all, a week after K'ang was received by the emperor, the staple of the old examination system, the eight-legged essay, was abolished as he had promised.

The emperor also stamped his imprimatur on despised careers in trade and commerce by ordering officials to encourage and assist merchants, by setting up a Bureau of Control of Mines and Railways, and by allowing Manchus to take up professions. He turned his attention to another condemned area of activity, the military, and ordered the Manchu Bannermen to adopt Western drill, and soldiers to pass examinations in feats more contemporary than stone-throwing and archery. Journalists were told to write on political matters – a completely novel freedom of speech in China; the reform of the law courts was promised; and on 24 August, the staid old literati of the empire were scandalized to hear that the emperor, accompanied by Tz'u-hsi, would issue forth in full view from the Forbidden City on 19 October and travel *by train* to Tientsin where they would review the army personally. Tz'u-hsi, it was rumoured, was tremendously excited about the journey, her first excursion ever since her youth and the flight to Jehol in 1860.

Scholars who had studied for years to acquire the art of the eight-legged essay in order to obtain office were therefore immediately plunged into a vacuum and found their livelihood and future had disappeared overnight, and that nothing at present had been announced to take its place. The transformation of temples into schools was deeply disturbing to the enormous vested interests of Buddhist, Taoist and all manner of esoteric priests and nuns whose livings and homes had been so summarily destroyed, and who had the superstitious empress's favour. Many potential sympathizers of reform were alienated when the measures struck at their personal interests, and gravitated *en masse* to Tz'u-hsi, their automatic figurehead. But Kuang-hsu must have dutifully submitted to her the drafts of his decrees and she must have agreed to them, so at this stage, it seems she refused to be moved by the conservatives' alarmism.

K'ang bombarded the emperor with his works, and with memorials – sixty-three in three months alone, including his *Record of the Partition of Poland*, so vivid the emperor sat on his throne and wept. Each of K'ang's lengthy memorials was answered by fresh reform decrees, and when at K'ang's suggestion the emperor permitted all officials, whatever their rank, to memorialize the throne secretly, hundreds, making seven a day during the Reform period, poured in from all over the empire. The emperor, keen but inexperienced, had however few people he could trust and no one, since Weng's banishment, in whom he could confide. Yet he desperately needed advice, and the steps he was taking desperately needed consideration. But K'ang himself, whom Kuang-hsu may have seen regularly throughout the first weeks of September, though the meetings were not recorded, had a streak of volatile fantasy, and was anyway a man of letters, not a man of action. Moreover he was not the only reformer to whom Kuang-hsu listened. Others, who did not share K'ang's veneration for the concept of the throne or for Confucian tradition, were a hundredfold more dangerous.

In early September a brilliant, excitable and erratic Chinese scholar called T'an Ssu-t'ung arrived in Peking at K'ang's recommendation from the province of Hunan, where Chang Chih-tung, the viceroy, had successfully sponsored reforms and industries. T'an was thirty-three years old, had suffered during his childhood at the hands of a cruel stepmother, and of a well-meaning but traditional father, the governor of Hupeh, who had misunderstood his son's imaginativeness and brains. In his early loneliness, T'an had steeped himself for solace in the classics, and had, like K'ang, absorbed much of Buddhism's more abstruse side. He too had discovered his vocation was to stir China towards a greater future, 'to break the net of fame, self-interest and traditionalism, lay aside all thought of emperor-worship and blind respect for antiquity; transcend all particular philosophies and religion in favour of the boundless, the unrestricted, the revolutionary'.[14] T'an developed a mystic's belief in the Confucian quality of *jen* (benevolence) which he conceived of as an almost physical force, an electric current that penetrated and transformed. 'When one's knowledge is "real",' he proclaimed, 'there is nothing one cannot do.'[15] Quite unlike K'ang, who was devoted to the Ch'ing dynasty and to Chinese traditions, T'an was profoundly and fundamentally revolutionary. He had written to a friend:

What you mean by foreign matters are things you have seen, such as steamships, telegraph lines, trains, guns, cannon, torpedoes, and machines for weaving and metallurgy; that's all. You have never dreamed of or seen the beauty and perfection of Western legal systems and political institutions.... All you speak of are the branches and foliage of foreign matters, not the root.... Now there is not a single one of the Chinese people's

sentiments, customs, political and legal institutions which can be favourably compared with those of the barbarians.[16]

Liang Ch'i-ch'ao wrote T'an 'shed infinite light and had no equal as a
sweeping and cleansing force . . . for this reason I compare him to a
meteor.'[17]

Although in the terms of 1898 the slogan of K'ang and sympathizers like the viceroy Chang Chih-tung – 'Chinese learning for the
fundamental principles. Western learning for practical application'[18] –
seemed radical, it was tame compared to T'an's revolutionary
vision. After meeting T'an on 5 September Kuang-hsu ceased to be
concerned with schools and steamships and the 'branches and
foliage' but struck out for the root: he had already abolished six
minor government bureaus, and many sinecures and offices,
including the governorships of Kwangtung, Yunnan and Hupeh –
T'an's own father's seat – because all three provinces already shared a
viceroy with their neighbours. Six officials of the Board of Rites,
two presidents and four vice-presidents, had been suspended as well
for waylaying a memorial from a junior reformer as indecent and
thus infuriating the suddenly accessible emperor. The memorialist
had suggested, amongst other things, that Kuang-hsu and Tz'u-hsi
should embark upon a tour of the world together. But on 7
September Kuang-hsu became over-excited: he dismissed Li Hung-
chang from the Tsungli Yamen.

Kuang-hsu had taken K'ang and T'an's strictures against
government sinecures too much to heart, for the dismissal of so
many influential men could only jeopardize the reform movement
itself. Tz'u-hsi would not take the removal of her veteran cam-
paigner and old favourite Li with equanimity. Movement therefore
quickened between the capital and the I Ho Yuan, where she was
enjoying the changing colours of early autumn. The sacked ministers, with other officials equally alarmed at the extent of the
changes and at the threats to their traditions, begged the Empress
Dowager to control the emperor and exercise the power and authority she had over him as the most senior member of the imperial
family and his adoptive mother. Tz'u-hsi listened this time,
although, remembering her pleasure in others' discomfiture, one
suspects she was slyly amused by their fears and lamentations. For
she did not rescind Kuang-hsu's decree and reinstate the ministers,
as she had retained the power to do. Instead she summoned the
emperor to appear before her. She warned him that she knew his
limitations and his weaknesses, she reminded him that she had

placed him on the throne, for which he should be eternally grateful, and told him that she would brook no further reforms that endangered venerable officials. She pointed out that Jung-lu held the province of Chihli and declared that if K'ang Yu'wei, whom she had heard wrote filthy slanders about her, ever came once more near the emperor, she would see that he never could again.

Kuang-hsu rushed a telegram summoning from Tientsin the only soldier he knew to be sympathetic to the reformers' cause: Yuan Shih-k'ai. Then he dashed off a rash, secret note to his only friends, the reformers:

In view of the present difficult situation, I have found that only reforms can save China, and that reforms can only be achieved through the discharge of the conservative and ignorant ministers and the appointment of the intelligent and brave scholars. Her Graceful Majesty, the Empress Dowager, however, did not agree. I have tried again and again to persuade her, only to find Her Majesty more angry. You, K'ang Yu-wei . . . and T'an Ssu-t'ung should deliberate immediately to find some ways to save me. With extreme worries and earnest hopes.[19]

A second note was even hastier, ordered K'ang to leave Peking immediately and go abroad and 'devise every means to save me without a moment's delay'.[20]

K'ang Yu-wei and T'an Ssu-t'ung first received these notes four days later, so frightened had Yang-jui the messenger been to deliver them. They knelt to accept them and wept together. By that date, 18 September, Kuang-hsu had also issued a *public* decree ordering K'ang to Shanghai, an unprecedented step for such a low-ranking official as K'ang, and it combined with Kuang-hsu's notes to panic the reformers. It is a measure of Kuang-hsu's pathos, that, as emperor of all China, his only knights errant were a handful of minor officials, and that his messages of distress to them provoked them to such hot deeds that Tz'u-hsi came storming out of the summer palace at the head of her followers, who were as ever legion.

Chapter Eleven

NEVER THE WORD 'PEACE'

At a private house in Peking, the night before the emperor's messages of distress reached him, K'ang Yu-wei the reformer was dining with friends and sympathizers. Reclining on cushions after supper, they smoked a pipe or two together and listened to plaintive music sung by girls from the Chinese city, songs which filled them with melancholy and foreboding. When the emperor's secret notes reached them, K'ang and his colleague T'an Ssu-t'ung were already in the mood for disaster. In their despair they thrashed about wildly for a solution to the emperor's plight.

The most likely opportunity, it seemed to them, for their enemies to strike at Kuang-hsu was the review of the new army under Jung-lu, due to take place at Tientsin under the eye of Tz'u-hsi and Kuang-hsu together on 19 October, only a month away. Thousands of well-drilled soldiers gathered together, the supreme command held by one of Tz'u-hsi's consistently loyal henchmen, the emperor surrounded and vulnerable, removed from his palace: it was the perfect scenario for a *coup d'état*.

Yuan Shih-k'ai's secretary was present; taking his tears as representative of his master's opinions, remembering that Yuan had himself contributed funds to the reform movement's early days, they excitedly adopted the thirty-nine-year-old military commander, the hero of Korea, as the emperor's champion. Their plan of action was extremist: the firebrand T'an Ssu-t'ung was sent to Yuan Shih-k'ai, 'to persuade Yuan to go to the aid of the Emperor'. As K'ang wrote: 'We asked him to lead several hundred determined men to escort the emperor ... to kill Jung-lu, and to destroy the conservative faction.'[1]

While the reformers plotted, Yuan Shih-k'ai, in ignorance of their schemes for him, knelt before the Kuang-hsu Emperor on his throne at the summer palace and pledged his loyalty. He was a short, thickset man, with a 'powerful neck and bullet head', which 'gave him the appearance of great energy', 'with a keen glance, expressive features, and quick gestures'.[2] 'My family', he told the emperor, 'have received imperial kindness for generations, of course I must place myself entirely at His Majesty's command.'[3] In Korea in the 1880s, Yuan had witnessed Japanese-style reforms at first hand, and

Kuang-hsu thirsted for this direct knowledge. Yuan was also the only powerful soldier who had expressed sympathy with the reform movement; he had raised a superb army, which an English observer, Lord Beresford, had complimented: 'On parade the whole force appeared an exceptionally smart body of men of extremely fine physique.'[4] The emperor admired Yuan and trusted him, but as this first interview took place under Tz'u-hsi's Argus-eyes at the I Ho Yuan, he could not whisper any signals of his imagined peril to Yuan. He created the ambitious official an honorary vice-president of the Board of War – a post far more elevated than either K'ang's position as secretary to the Tsungli Yamen, or T'an's similar post on the Grand Council.

Jung-lu meanwhile, alerted by Kuang-hsu's summons of Yuan Shih-k'ai to the capital from the army headquarters at Tientsin, had received messages and even deputations of grieving and scared old officials begging his help. To ensure his grip on the situation, Jung-lu redeployed his troops: one general, the ex-robber chieftain Tung Fu-hsiang, who with his unruly Moslem troops had caused so much trouble during the Mohammedan rising in the west but who had since won his pardon by fighting on the imperial side, was dispatched with his forces to the Northern Gate of Peking; other troops held the Tientsin-Peking road and the newly-built railway. But Jung-lu also wanted the young general Yuan back under surveillance, and therefore, when Yuan returned to the capital from the summer palace after his audience with the emperor, he found a telegram from Jung-lu awaiting him. It described hostile movements of British and Russian warships in the Bay of Pechili where tension over the recent leases of Port Arthur and Weihaiwei was still running high, and ordered Yuan's immediate return to the command of his army in the area. The political contents of the telegram were completely but plausibly fabricated, but everyone, the reformers included, believed the ruse, and it only exacerbated their agitation and frenzy.

In the temple where Yuan was staying in Peking it was midnight when he sat down and took up his brush and ink to draft a reply to his commanding officer Jung-lu. Suddenly T'an Ssu-t'ung, in 'informal clothes', uninvited and unheralded, burst in and asked to see Yuan in confidence. He congratulated him on his new vice-presidency, and then, when Yuan led him into a quiet chamber at the back of his apartments, declared abruptly: 'Jung-lu lately proposed to dethrone and murder the emperor. Did you know that?' The passionate young scholar then played on Yuan's ambitions by saying that the reformers had continually recommended Yuan's promotion but Jung-lu had always opposed it. 'He is outwardly very nice to you,' pursued T'an. 'But in fact he is both suspicious and jealous of you. . . .' Thus stinging Yuan's avidity, he then produced a document the reformers had drafted, on which these hectic orders were written:

Jung-lu plans to dethrone and murder His Majesty. Traitor! Must be done away with as soon as possible. . . . Give him [Yuan] a mandate in the Vermilion Pencil, ordering him to call on Jung-lu with his troops, arresting and executing Jung-lu. T'an takes over the Viceroyalty and Commissionership. . . . Yuan and his troops come to Peking to guard the Forbidden City and besiege the Summer Palace. . . .[5]

Even Yuan Shih-k'ai's daring and ambition baulked at such a murder – of his superior officer, the viceroy of the most important province in the north – and at such a coup – the seizure of the capital and capture of eminent statesmen for whom all his education had instilled the greatest reverence. Above all, laying siege to both imperial palaces was an act of the greatest treachery, unless the emperor had decreed it, and of this Yuan had no proof. In Yuan's account, T'an then sped breathlessly on: 'The old rotten . . . [Tz'u-hsi] must be got rid of, or our country will perish. That will be my job. You need not bother.' At this stage Yuan could bear no more: 'Her Majesty's regency of over thirty years has delivered China safely out of many disasters', he remonstrated. 'She is widely loved. My soldiers are taught to be loyal. I cannot turn them into rebels.'[6]

In K'ang's version however no mention is made of getting rid of Tz'u-hsi, and Yuan only plays for time, putting forward pragmatic objections. 'To kill Jung-lu would be as simple as killing a dog', K'ang claims Yuan said. 'But all the officers in my camp are his men, and the guns, bullets, and powder are all under his control.'[7] Also, Yuan only had seven thousand men to Jung-lu's one hundred thousand, and he could hardly count on the loyalty of his entire force in such a hazardous and deadly enterprise. So he temporized: if the Son of Heaven had decreed the coup, then he could and should, in all duty, obey; but if he had not, Yuan would, as a practical man of ambition, weigh out the winner and side with him.

At Yuan's hesitation, T'an produced Kuang-hsu's messages of distress. But as the notes only asked for help against Tz'u-hsi's obstructionism, and did not specify how much help should be given, and furthermore were written in black ink, and not in the vermilion pencil of a decree, Yuan exclaimed: 'Heaven above me, I, Yuan Shih-k'ai have never been ungrateful to His Majesty. I will not put my liege in jeopardy. The whole subject must be thought over with care, and a foolproof plan is required. I must confess I have no courage to become a public enemy.'[8] T'an taunted him for cowardice, and drove on sarcastically: 'If you decide against it, please go to the summer palace and report to Her Majesty. You will get power and wealth there.' Yuan reacted furiously to the insult, and, even at his own later admission, renewed his pledge of unswerving loyalty to Kuang-hsu: 'What sort of man do you think I am? My family has received imperial benevolence for three generations now. Do you think I am crazy enough to turn traitor? I will risk my life for what is good for my emperor and this country.'[9] T'an Ssu-t'ung stood up, exultant, and 'visibly moved': the soldier, it seemed, had been wooed and won.

Tz'u-hsi returned to the Forbidden City. But even her presence was unable to prevent Kuang-hsu from receiving Yuan Shih-k'ai again on 20 September. Ostensibly it was a formal audience of no consequence, in which Yuan prostrated himself to thank the emperor for his new vice-presidency. In practice it was crucial, for when Yuan tactfully, without betraying the reformers' plans to the empress's spies, sounded out the emperor himself, he found himself the bearer of a secret vermilion decree, which authorized him to seize Jung-lu, march a force to Peking, surround the summer palace and hold Tz'u-hsi prisoner until the reforms were in full swing.

But the emperor's secret decree is now lost; if indeed, it ever existed. For neither Yuan Shih-k'ai, nor K'ang Yu'wei, nor Jung-lu, nor any of the protagonists ever quote it directly. Neither do any of the reformers mention how they informed the emperor of the measures they had taken to 'save' him, or if they informed him at all. In all probability the enthusiastic and childish emperor received Yuan Shih-k'ai on the morning of the twentieth in all ignorance of his friends' dark plans of the night of the eighteenth, and no decree changed hands. Instead, when Yuan sounded his emperor, Kuang-hsu only expressed in nebulous terms his great trust in Yuan's support of the visionary reform movement, and so confirmed Yuan's suspicions that the reformers had acted on their own initiative. Kuang-hsu, well-intentioned, desperate but ill-advised, locked in helpless innocence in the Forbidden City while his allies and his enemies conspired far away from him, presents a spectacle of far more poignancy and conviction than Kuang-hsu the reforming hell-raiser party to a *coup* in his own capital.

After Yuan rose from the foot of the throne on the morning of 20 September, he took the train back to Tientsin, where ceremony and music greeted him on the platform to congratulate him on his new appointment to the Board of War. Then Yuan headed straight for Jung-lu's quarters, and kowtowing to the proud Manchu general, he told him, immediately, and at his own admission, of the night's clandestine plans: 'His Majesty is filial to the empress, but there are rogues forming cliques in the capital, who are putting the Throne in a dangerous position.'[10] For Yuan had made the perilous decision between the emperor's desires and leanings as an individual and his role as an institution, and had decided that Kuang-hsu the person had transgressed against his sacred function and that it was his, Yuan Shih-k'ai's, duty to restore him to the paths of right-eousness. He therefore foreswore his pledge and for 'the good of my emperor and his country' made a clean breast of all he had heard and seen in Peking to his superior Jung-lu.[11]

When he revealed Kuang-hsu's secret message accusing Tz'u-hsi of standing in the way of his reforms, Jung-lu was astounded, not only by the emperor's shockingly unfilial words, but above all because Tz'u-hsi's intelligence system had failed to pick up such treason. He immediately ordered Yuan to accompany him on the next train from Tientsin to Peking. On arrival they raced through the bustling crowds already agog with rumours – the decree ordering the reformer K'ang Yu-wei to leave Peking had set the scandal-mongers buzzing – and made straight for the Forbidden City. Exacting access from the bewildered doorkeepers, charging through the baffled and uneasy eunuchs who dared not stop the viceroy of Chihli even though he had no appointment with the empress, Jung-lu found Tz'u-hsi near the North Lake of the Sea Palaces. She was sanguinely making the annual sacrifices to the deity of the silkworms in the Hall of Sericulture.

Jung-lu kowtowed and begged forgiveness for intruding on her without permission. The sixty-three-year-old empress demanded angrily to know his reasons. He told her of the urgency of his news and begged a hearing. Then he described the reformers' plot to encircle her palaces and hold her prisoner, to kill him and seize power in the capital and Chihli. 'When I sought Your Majesty', wrote Jung-lu later, 'in secret audience and laid before you the details of the plot, once more did Your Majesty, without a moment's hesitation, respond to our prayers and resume control of affairs, swiftly visiting upon evildoers of that treacherous crew the might of your august displeasure.'[12]

Once more indeed and swiftly too: Tz'u-hsi ordered the troops of Jung-lu and Yuan Shih-k'ai to the capital, and once all the city gates were in her soldiers' hands by the following morning, she swept into Kuang-hsu's apartments: 'Do you know', she thundered, 'the law of the Imperial Household for one who raises his hand against his mother?'[13] She struck the emperor across the face, some say – and if she did, it was the only blow of the *coup* – and then ordered the palace guards to seize him and take him to the Ying T'ai, the island on the south lake of the Sea Palaces. 'There was nothing I could say,' remembered Kuang-hsu forlornly in later years, 'but I had never even suggested that Yuan Shih-k'ai, or anyone else, raise a hand against Her Majesty.'[14]

The dawn had just broken that morning of 22 September 1898 over the lotus-covered lakes of the Sea Palaces when the young emperor of China was hustled into the prison where he would stare out the following years. The Ying T'ai, or Ocean Terrace, was, ironically, the island paradise which Tz'u-hsi herself had much improved and adorned, but it was linked to the mainland by a narrow pathway and a drawbridge only, and Tz'u-hsi's soldiers stood guard over this single escape route. All Kuang-hsu's personal eunuchs had been changed; fourteen had been executed at Tz'u-hsi's orders. When the Pearl Concubine pleaded to share his prison with him, she was arrested and confined to her rooms. Only Lung-yü, his thin-lipped empress, Tz'u-hsi's niece, was allowed to live with him. From that day they ceased to speak at all.

Tz'u-hsi, advised by Jung-lu's faction, issued what announced to an abdication in Kuang-hsu's name:

From this day forth her Majesty will transact the business of the government in the Side Hall of the Palace, and on the day after tomorrow we ourselves at the head of our Princes and Ministers shall perform obeisance before her in the Hall of Diligent Government. . . .
The words of the Emperor.[15]

She had resumed the throne once more; this time there was to be no 'yellow curtain' and even the decrees would, at her convenience, be issued in her name. She pressed mercilessly on: Kuang-hsu was made to recant publicly, for in a long decree in his name, Tz'u-hsi enumerated each of his reforms and abolished them. The six sinecures were restored; the *Chinese Progress*, the paper that was to have been the government and the movement's mouthpiece, was suspended; the right to memorialize the throne was withdrawn from minor officials; temples and shrines were reinstated; the old examinations were re-established. 'For over two centuries this system has worked most satisfactorily. . . .' explained Tz'u-hsi.[16]

Brutal as Tz'u-hsi's restoration was, the reforms had been largely illusory. An avalanche of decrees had poured from the Forbidden City in under three months, ordering radical alterations to administration, education, army organization and the recruitment of officials. There had of course been little time to set them in motion, but also Kuang-hsu had not outlined how they should be carried out, or what should take the place of abolished institutions. This was left, in the fashion of China, to the provincial officials to organize, and they, bemused, degenerate and often opium-ridden, had helplessly done little or nothing. Only the governor of Hunan, Ch'en Pao-chen, was enterprising and efficient enough to obey the decrees of the Hundred Days.

Tz'u-hsi therefore cashiered Ch'en; and not satisfied with Weng T'ung-ho's banishment, she now cashiered him too, 'never again to be re-employed, and kept under supervision by the local authorities'.[17] She had known him intimately for thirty years, for he had been her son T'ung-chih's tutor and her Grand Councillor in the early days, yet she had no gentleness or friendship for him. But the quarry whose scent Tz'u-hsi had really got in her nostrils was not Weng, but K'ang himself and his confederates, and she forced Kuang-hsu's reluctant hand to pen the death-warrants of his few friends. But K'ang Yu-wei, the seer who had brought about his emperor's ruin, had embarked in gloomy ignorance for Tientsin and Shanghai on the very day of the *coup*. Urged by his friends to disguise himself and shave off his long moustaches, he had refused, since 'I felt that death and life were predestined'.[18] In a half-hearted way he had tried to summon foreign aid for the emperor, but Sir Claude MacDonald, the British minister, was away; and the missionary Timothy Richard had no influence. Then K'ang had passed miraculously unmolested through Tientsin, and through the next port, Chefoo, where the senior official was absent when K'ang's arrest warrant arrived by cable, in a cipher to which the clerks did not have the key. So K'ang languidly picked pebbles on the shore and ate some pears as he waited for the steamer for Shanghai. Once embarked, he was approached by a British consul, told of the *coup*, and of the emperor's rumoured death. 'My heart was so heavy that I had no desire to live',[19] he wrote later, and scholar to the last, extemporized a four-line poem. But, however stricken, he was well enough to escape safely to Hong Kong, under the escort of two British warships, and thence to Japan, where he joined his disciple Liang Ch'i-ch'ao, who had also eluded the authorities. At his home in Canton, K'ang's family were searched, his relatives scattered, his belongings confiscated, and his house stripped and sealed.

T'ang Ssu-t'ung, thirty-three years old, who had thrust the reform movement so confidently on Yuan Shih-k'ai's shoulders, the prophet who had proclaimed so buoyantly, 'When one's knowledge is "real", there is nothing one cannot do',[20] stayed behind defiantly in Peking. He was arrested, arraigned before a tribunal consisting of Jung-lu and other fiercely reactionary Manchu grandees, and sentenced with five others to instant decapitation. K'ang's younger brother, guilty only by kinship, was amongst them.

'The Six Gentlemen of the Reform Movement', as they came to be known, were China's first political martyrs to progress, and to a movement of whose exact nature and potential T'an Ssu-t'ung was unaware when he irrepressibly shouted before baring his neck to the executioner's sword: 'I am willing to shed my blood, if thereby my country may be saved. But for everyone that perishes today, a thousand will rise up to carry on the work of Reform, and uphold loyalty against usurpation.'[21]

On the Ocean Terrace, Kuang-hsu sickened. His appetite was gone, his health, always delicate, deteriorated. He performed the religious ceremonies required of the Son of Heaven for the Feast of the Tutelary Deities two days after the *coup*; but two days later, an edict informed the people that he had been ill since May, and that 'all medical treatment had proved ineffective'.[22] A famous doctor, Chen Liang-fang, was summoned from far Soochow to minister to him. Although he was not permitted to examine the Son of Heaven personally, but only to kneel before his throne and listen to Tz'u-hsi's expatiations on Kuang-hsu's symptoms, the doctor managed to diagnose severe ulceration of the throat and tongue, and high fever – both caused by grave nervous tension. He also discovered Kuang-hsu's lung condition. But this disease was only incidental to the emperor's true sufferings: he had had a nervous breakdown. In later years, though for the sake of appearances he sat at Tz'u-hsi's side during audience, he would slip out, bored, for no one consulted him, or dared to attend to what he said if he spoke. One official recalled that he even drew huge pictures of a mighty dragon, his own emblem, and tore them up in despair, or painted a tortoise, a reptile odious to the Chinese for its supposed homosexuality, pinned it to the wall, shot it with arrows, then cut it up with scissors, and 'threw the pieces in the air like a swarm of butterflies', muttering under his breath the name of his Judas, 'Yuan Shih-k'ai. Yuan Shih-k'ai.'[23]

Kuang-hsu had threatened Tz'u-hsi's survival, and, as had happened time and again before, all her cruelty and tenacity set hard when she felt herself to be, in the Chinese image, as precarious as piled eggs. This time her personal animus found justification in Chinese orthodox thought: Kuang-hsu had, she thought, virtually plotted matricide, and there was no crime in the Confucian canon more heinous than a dereliction of filial piety, especially in an emperor, the moral example to his people, who 'must show a dear love to his mother'. Her *coup*, and her subsequent tormenting of the wretched Kuang-hsu were therefore distastefully sanctimonious: she brandished before him not her hurt affections, not her fears for herself, but moral righteousness. For she only saw herself, China, and its problems, and was helped to see them by the men beside her, through the prism of that narrow traditional morality of which she was, as Empress Dowager, the principal guardian and interpreter.

In 1899 a decree announced that P'un-chun, adolescent son of Prince Tuan, member of the Imperial Clan, Tz'u-hsi's own great-nephew, was to officiate at the imperial ceremonies, for Kuang-hsu was too ill. To the legations, it seemed that Tz'u-hsi would see to it that the emperor would never recover. They warned China they would be most displeased if anything happened to him, and demanded that one of their own physicians should examine him. The French legation's doctor duly arrived at the Forbidden City, was received at a suitable distance, pronounced himself satisfied that the emperor was alive and convalescent, and returned to the legations to titillate the gentlemen after dinner with Gallic scandal about the emperor's personal inadequacies – which he certainly would not have been allowed to glimpse.

This last foreign affront was merely the most recent barb in a whole quiverful Tz'u-hsi had recently received from the legations, and it landed in the heart of the xenophobia that had seethed unseen and unheard, since 1860, and the sack of the summer palaces. In her own country, K'ang Yu-wei, arch-traitor in her eyes, had been spirited away under British protection; in 1896 the revolutionary San Yat-sen, ensnared into the Chinese legation in London to be brought home to justice, had had to be released under extreme pressure from the British government. In 1898 and 1899, the powers annexed Kiaochow and Weihaiwei and Port Arthur, and China had been casually split into spheres of foreign influence.

The reformers' adulation of Japan's progress, in the context of such foreign encroachments, as well as coming so soon after the defeat of China by Japan, made their movement particularly disagreeable to Tz'u-hsi and the traditionalists who supported her. For one of the revealing features of the reform movement is that during the heady and ill-fated Hundred Days the greed of the powers continued unabated and even increased. Throughout, demands for railways and mining concessions, for territory, spheres of influence, and privileges rained down on the Tsungli Yamen. Italy had her eye on Chekiang; Japan, sore at the sight of its prize Port Arthur disappearing into the jaws of Russia, wanted Fukien opposite newly-acquired Formosa. The Yamen parried helplessly, but the powers had given up even a pretence of diplomatic cajolery: 'Unless the very moderate terms already demanded are immediately complied with,' Great Britain informed China in August, at the very height of the Reform, 'we shall, in addition, require the concession of another line on the same conditions [they had already demanded three railway lines] . . . and additional demands will be preferred as the result of further delay.'[24] The Yamen, floundering, had conceded everything to everyone, and had therefore made it quite apparent to the conservatives that the reformers' predilection for foreigners in no way quenched foreign thirst, and was not therefore a new version of the ancient Chinese craft of disarming the barbarians by a show of friendship.

On the other hand, after Tz'u-hsi's *coup d'état*, the picture changed. On 15 December, she tartly informed the powers that 'no more railroads could be built, and that it would therefore be unnecessary for the foreign representatives to submit any new proposals to build them'.[25] Then, in her own hard-liner fashion, she retained one reform from the whole litany Kuang-hsu had promulgated: military self-strengthening. As she herself put it in a homely image: 'When we have been choked, it does not follow that we are to cease eating, merely for fear it may happen again.'[26] A policy of re-arming was familiar to her, for she had attempted it with Prince Kung in the sixties and Li Hung-chang in the eighties. So throughout the winter of 1898 and 1899 she reinforced Kuang-hsu's decree that generals should adopt the latest Western techniques and buy Western armaments. An army of steel, springing spirited and valiant from the very dragon's field of discontent with China's ceaseless appeasement of the foreigner – the field the reformers had unsuccessfully begun to reap – would now challenge foreign demands.

Jung-lu, the ever-loyal paladin, became head of the Grand Army of the North, with four armies grouped under him; Yuan Shih-k'ai found 'power and wealth' and was appointed in 1899 acting governor of Shantung to defend that coast with his army; Tung Fu-hsiang's reckless Mohammedan soldiery remained quartered barely twenty miles from Peking in the emperors' ruined Hunting Park; Yü-hsien, mere prefect in the spring of 1898, noted only for his rabid chauvinism, had been raised to governor by 1899; Kang-i, a notorious, superstitious and arrogant Manchu of the old school, became Tz'u-hsi's chief fund-raiser, nicknamed Lord High Extortioner as he scoured the provinces for revenue for the new defence policy.

Tz'u-hsi continued to circulate China with fighting words. Volunteer militia were to be raised alongside the regular army, and drilled and trained for the defence of families and villages. But her indications as to who should be enrolled were vague and ambiguous: sometimes the footloose and the poor, bandits and vagrants were exhorted to join up patriotically, at other times decrees enjoined the same militia to suppress banditry and protect their homes from ruffians. While she ordered China's military reconstruction, she also disentangled diplomacy in the provinces. The Tsungli Yamen in the capital was increasingly under pressure: one missionary stoned, and the Yamen might spend days wrangling with the foreign diplomats over the just retribution. In January 1899 Tz'u-hsi freed the Yamen from all but questions of state that affected the whole of China: she decreed that all viceroys, governors, and Tartar-generals had ex-officio powers as Tsungli Yamen members, and that therefore foreign matters were to be dealt with by them locally. She was following her long-held leanings towards provincial autonomy, and her Confucian belief in men of ability. 'The successful accomplishment of my object does not depend upon these innovations commanded by me, but really upon the calibre and conscientiousness of the official.'[27] In the same decree, she made a controversial move, and gave Christian missionaries equivalent ranks with Chinese officials: bishops were to rank with viceroys, and so forth. Indignation flared immediately among anti-Christian elements at such honours, and Protestants, fearing Chinese opinion, refused to accept them unlike the Catholics; but although Tz'u-hsi's prejudice was no less keen, she hoped to absorb Christians into the Confucian social framework, just as Buddhists and Mohammedans had been before, for once inside the system, they could be disciplined and controlled.

From the remote heart of the Forbidden City, Tz'u-hsi radiated that emotional solipsism that had made China seem to her as a little girl and to her contemporaries the grandest, nonpareil nation of the world, and her decrees, unlike Kuang-hsu's that had acknowledged the West's advances, struck ringing chords in the provincial gentry, and in the idle and arrogant literati.

In March 1899 her strong-arm policy met triumphant confirmation. Italy, lagging somewhat behind in the race for concessions in China, demanded lease of San-men Bay in Chekiang. Great Britain supported her claim, and gunboats lazed menacingly off the coast. Tz'u-hsi reacted fiercely: the Tsungli Yamen sent the Italian minister a curt note that his demand could not even be considered, telegrams summoned troops from provinces as far flung as Kansu to Peking in the event of a struggle, secret decrees ordered that if the foreigners attacked, China should fight. The Italian minister, cursing his luck that he and only he should be so frustrated, was disavowed by his government. Resistance had achieved what had eluded decades of diplomacy: a victory of face, a victory of consequence over a foreign power.

On 11 November 1899, Tz'u-hsi, gave vent to her new feelings:

Our empire is now labouring under great difficulties which are becoming daily more and more serious. The various powers cast upon us looks of tiger-like voracity, hustling each other in their endeavours to be the first to seize upon our innermost territories. They think that China, having neither money nor troops, would never venture to go to war with them. They fail to understand, however, that there are certain things that this empire can never consent to.... There is an evil habit which has become almost a custom among our viceroys and governors which, however, must be eradicated at all costs. For instance, whenever these high officials have had on their hands cases of international dispute, all their actions seem to be guided by the belief in their breasts that such cases would eventually be 'amicably arranged'. These words seem never out of their thoughts: hence, when matters do come to a crisis, they, of course, find themselves utterly unprepared to resist any hostile aggression on the part of the foreigners. We, indeed, consider this the most serious failure in the duty which the highest provincial authorities owe to the throne, and we now find it incumbent upon ourselves to censure such conduct in the most severe terms.... Never should the word 'Peace' fall from the mouths of our highest officials.... With such a country as ours, with her vast areas, stretching out several tens of thousands of *li*, her immense natural resources, and her hundreds of millions of inhabitants, if all would prove their loyalty to their Emperor and love of their country, what indeed is there to fear from any strong invader? Let us not think of making peace, nor rely solely upon diplomatic manoeuvres.[28]

Such a policy was subtle as the serpent. Foreign aggression was to be resisted; but what constituted foreign aggression? Some provincial authorities, seconded by the majority of Chinese, found the Christian missionaries themselves colonists. And if the missionaries were colonists, the foreign concessionaries were so a hundredfold. Yet Tz'u-hsi had also, repeatedly, since the 1860s, decreed that missionaries and foreigners were to be granted the protection and rights guaranteed in the treaties.

When Tz'u-hsi dealt the death blow to Kuang-hsu's period of reform, many of her subjects rejoiced because they interpreted it as a gesture against foreign influence and foreigners. Only one week after the *coup*, some foreigners riding in Peking were attacked by a mob. In October the legations fanned the fears of further foreign aggressions by bringing up over a hundred soldiers from Tientsin for their protection. The riots and incidents multiplied: at the end of October a band of imperial troops, under the ex-brigand Tung Fu-hsiang, spontaneously attacked a member of the British diplomatic staff. Sir Claude MacDonald, the minister, demanded the immediate withdrawal of Tung's braves living in the Hunting Park on the flank of the capital – another instance of foreign interference – and, sulkily, Tz'u-hsi and the Tsungli Yamen gave in and ordered Tung to remove his troops to 'guard the coast' east of Peking.

Anti-foreign riots continued to pepper the course of the winter of 1898 to the spring of 1900. An English missionary was murdered, possibly with official connivance, in Kweichow; a French priest was tortured and killed in Hupeh. In the provinces which had experienced foreigners at close quarters, grievances fomented, particularly in Kiaochow, the birthplace of Confucius, where the Chinese therefore bitterly resented Christianity. The Germans there, the British in Weihaiwei, the Russians in Liaotung made the populations restive, and when the foreigners decided that they, as leaseholders, were entitled to the Chinese taxes gathered in those areas, sporadic and ugly bouts of violence and even murder broke out.

Tz'u-hsi's *coup* had effectively set a torch to the bonfire of xenophobia, for Kuang-hsu had, to China's great pity, lacked the moral stamina and coolness to carry out the reform movement that might have extinguished it. K'ang Yu-wei was a scholar, unfit for action, and Kuang-hsu's nursery and schoolroom terrors of Tz'u-hsi had been combined with K'ang's bookish view of her as some historical monster like the Empress Wu. Tz'u-hsi had been unduly excited by the reformers while they, on their side, had vituperated quite unnecessarily against her. From the south she still received a stream of filth and abuse from K'ang Yu-wei, who accused her in the newspapers of murdering Niuhuru, her co-empress, of poisoning Alute, of causing Hsien-feng to die of 'spleen and indignation', of mischief with a spurious eunuch, and even of branding Kuang-hsu's feet with irons[29] – allegations quite unworthy of an inspired philosopher. But men like K'ang Yu-wei, who believed fervently in the Confucian state, had to blame China's disintegration on personalities and not on the system itself, and Tz'u-hsi, the conservative symbol of all that was loathsome to them, was the reformers' scapegoat. They had sincerely believed that her removal, together with Jung-lu, her military arm, would send the spirit of reform coursing through China. It was only the revolutionaries, like Sun Yat-sen, who knew that her fall should be but a first step towards the overthrow of the antiquated despotism and the dynasty.

K'ang later disclaimed responsibility for the vital trigger of the *coup*: Kuang-hsu's dismissal of senior officials. K'ang had, it was true, always advocated the creation of a completely new Bureau, staffed with younger men of advanced views, who could have set the reforms in motion without upsetting the sinecures of ageing civil servants. But a time would have inevitably come when the reforms struck at the petrification of China and the idle reactionaries would have had to lose their jobs. Nevertheless K'ang, as an ardent and loyal supporter of tradition, should have glimpsed the slender chance that if Tz'u-hsi had been contained within the movement, given the credit, kept informed, if she had been 'soothed and bridled' she might have endorsed the movement and brought with her the block of public opinion that aligned itself solidly behind her. She loved personal power; but with the proviso that its objectives must seem to be the support of the Ch'ing and the strengthening of China, she does not seem to have minded in what specific political form her power manifested itself.

When Kuang-hsu appealed for help the reformers overreacted, under-estimating hopelessly the vested interests behind Tz'u-hsi, who was, as she had been since 1861, the genie of the *status quo*. They feared that Tz'u-hsi would deal a *coup de main* to the movement, and, in consequence, the Hundred Days were blighted by a chimera, which, conjured by fear, brought the very object it feared into being. From then on, like clouds in a windy sky, Kuang-hsu's vision of reform metamorphosed into a new and wilder monster. 'Never

... the word "Peace",' Tz'u-hsi had proclaimed, and in doing so, she became the lamplighter for a cause that was to convulse the Chinese empire and the Ch'ing dynasty in the first throes of its certain and approaching death. For she had, inadvertently, placed herself at the head of the Boxer partisans.

Chapter Twelve

BURN BURN BURN
KILL KILL KILL

From the spring of 1898 gangs of youths, few of them much older than nineteen, gathered in the northern provinces and particularly on the borders of Shantung and Chihli. In the farming villages, in the dust-filled streets, in the market squares, they made public demonstrations of their cause. One boy in a circle of others closed his eyes, folded his hands and began chanting; dropping to his knees, he then drew figures and cabalistic signs in the dust, and invoked the spirit. As he worked himself up into a frenzy, as his gestures became wilder and wilder, his expression more and more exalted, his recitation more excited, his companions would ask him who he was and what he wanted. He was a great man of history, he would reply, swaying, eyes shut, and all he wanted was a big sword. What would he do with his sword? they clamoured, and sometimes handed him one. Rising, still chanting, he began to thrust and parry, to weave and plunge in a series of callisthenic exercises – shadow boxing. He would, he shouted, 'Uphold the great Pure Dynasty and Exterminate the Barbarian'.

At other times, a member of one of these gangs, dancing in wild contortions, would call to his companions to strike him. Like Baldur the Beautiful he would stand, flushed, before them as they hit him with the blades of their swords and shot at him with arrows or even cartridges, and in his trance, feel not a thing. At other times the youths would rehearse a rigmarole of theatrical gestures: as in Chinese plays, they mounted imaginary horses, fought with imaginary weapons, and waved handkerchiefs over buildings to set them on fire. While they practised their strange rites, young men and women with them clutched at members of the crowd which had gathered to watch the possessed boy. They told them in excitement that their movement made them invulnerable; they thrust handbills into their hands or pasted posters up on the mud walls of the village. Heaven was angry with the foreigner and all his works, they proclaimed, and particularly with his religion, Christianity, and they had come to purge China of this venom.

The scandalous conduct of Christians and barbarians is irritating our Gods

179

and Geniuses, hence the many scourges we are now suffering. . . . The iron roads and iron carriages [railways] are disturbing the terrestrial dragon and are destroying the earth's beneficial influences. The red liquid which keeps dripping from the iron snake [rusty water from the oxidated telegraph wires] is nothing but the blood of the outraged spirits of the air. . . . The missionaries extract the eyes, marrow and heart of the dead in order to make medicaments. Whoever drinks a glass of tea at the parsonage is stricken by death: the brains burst out of the skull. . . . As for the children received in orphanages, they are killed and their intestines are used to change lead into silver and to make precious remedies. . . .[1]

At first, the tracts provided crazy recipes to ward off the poison foreigners poured down wells, or charms or prayers against their evil. But by the spring of 1900 the gangs declared themselves more dangerous: they wore red scarves round their heads, stamped with the character of Happiness, red coats, red bands round their wrists and ankles, banners embroidered with their slogan, and their placards had become explicit:

After this notice is issued to instruct you villagers, no matter which village you are living in, if there are Christian converts, you ought to get rid of them quickly. The churches which belong to them should be unreservedly burned down. Everyone who intends to spare someone, or to disobey our order by concealing Christian converts, will be punished according to the regulation when we come to his place, and he will be burned to death to prevent his impeding our programme. . . .[2]

By that spring the name of the roaming youths was on everyone's lips: I Ho Ch'uan, Righteous Harmony Boxing. In short, the Boxers.

The Boxers might just have been another illicit secret society such as had always proliferated throughout China. Magic callisthenics had certainly been practised as early as 1815, if not earlier, as a feature of an esoteric sect; and their charms, spells and incantations were selected to occult Buddhism or Taoism in character. The Boxers might have constituted another peasants' revolt, to be crushed as mercilessly as the Taipings, the Nien-fei and the Moslems had been throughout the sixties and seventies. But they differed in an aspect of paramount importance: they were sworn to defend and uphold the ruling Ch'ing dynasty, not to tear it down. In 1900, with that boundless Chinese capacity for syncretism, Buddhists, Taoists and Moslems (Tung Fu-hsiang's troops were still near Peking) found common cause with establishment Confucianists in a swelling tide of nationalism against the enemy – the foreigner and his doctrine. Footloose, wild and ruffianly, the Boxer volunteer looked every inch a rebel, but he was the self-appointed guardian of the dynasty, and at a time of seething discontent throughout the empire, Tz'u-hsi was naturally affected by this loyalty.

The crowds who gathered wide-eyed round the possessed Boxers as they punched and chanted, and who picked up their inflammatory literature, would have remained indifferent to their threats, their message and their antics if the Boxers had not touched live wire. The peasantry was, through the stultification of Chinese society, ignorant and superstitious. In the provinces, around Peking – Shantung, Chihli, Shansi and Manchuria – foreigners had exacted leases; trains now hurtled and crashed through the fields; telegraph wires dripped 'blood' and moaned like uneasy spirits in the wind. The harsh indemnity of the Sino-Japanese war led, in a despotic system like China's, to unremitting tax on the poor; the foreigners' steamships that now travelled inland waterways, further south on the Yangtze, had stolen work from the porters and junk-pullers and sailors; the coastal trade had suffered throughout China because foreign steamers were superior to Chinese junks.

Of the three main categories of foreigners living in China – diplomats, merchants and missionaries – it was the missionaries who were most feared and most avoided. For they extended privileges and protection to their converts and, as no alteration had been made to the treaties, the abuses that had exploded thirty years before into the Tientsin massacre were still rife. Christian preachers in China also continued to make the tragic blunder of using the scientific and medical knowledge of the West to proselytize: if we can cable messages through the air, if we can cure your children, then our religion must be the true one, our god the true god. Such a gospel did not convert the people to Christianity, but made men who hated and despised Christianity (as did some of the most erudite men in China) hate and despise the Western advances with which the religion had been identified. The treatise by 'the most heart-broken man in the world' that had first appeared in 1861, continued in various forms to spread a contagion of prejudice. Missionaries were vehemently vilified in popular cartoons. Superstitious suspicions were so deep-rooted that one missionary even saw 'common people ... drawing water out of the wells in a time of great drought, and pouring it upon the roads in the hope of draining off the poision which they believed to have been thrown in by the Christians'.[3]

All three categories alike alienated peasants, gentry and officials by their continued exploitation of the extraterritorial clause, which placed them, to all intents and purposes, above Chinese law. Resentment had been present for decades, ever since China was first galled by the first treaty; but since then, the Sino-Japanese war, the excision of China's tributary nations and of her ports had fomented the rancour, and when, in Shantung and Chihli, the winter of 1898–9 turned out to be one long and bitter haul of flood and famine, when the harvest of 1898 failed in Shantung, when the Yellow River engulfed hundreds of villages over two thousand six hundred miles in a savage overspill in August 1898, rendering thousands homeless and making it impossible to sow the next year's crops, when locusts descended to devour the meagre remains, then the squatters, the out-of-work, the homeless, the discontented and the dispossessed longed for a reason, a cause and a scapegoat. The Boxers both sprang from this misery and pain and fed it.

Tz'u-hsi's decrees of November and December 1899 ordering the recruitment of voluntary militia to defend China against foreign aggression reached provincial officials at precisely the time when the Boxers' increasing numbers and popularity were becoming a headache. There had been a few incidents of Chinese Christian convert deaths; but when some officials, treating the Boxers as rebels, had attempted to disperse them, the governor of Shantung, Yü-hsien, flew into a rage: here were the 'patriotic militia', and government troops were murdering them in his province.

The crucial question therefore became whether to absorb the Boxers into the military defence framework of the Chinese state, or to suppress them as dissident, unruly elements, Tz'u-hsi, twisting about as usual for a consistent policy, could not make up her mind. But one thing filled her with overwhelming rejoicing: this cry from the very throats of the people, that the Mandate of Heaven had not run out for the Ch'ing.

Here was a people's army, sprung spontaneously to the defence of their country and herself. Her xenophobia had been increased by the reformers who had made it clear that westernization in China would entail her disappearance; and by the leases of Kiaochow, Port Arthur, Weihaiwei and Kwangchowan. Whenever there was an anti-foreign outbreak in a province, foreigners demanded the dismissal of the responsible official: in the last year she had shifted or lost several governors, eminent and needed men. She grudged foreign interference altogether and reflected, with her inimitable ability to voice the orthodoxy of the moment, the prevalent chauvinism: 'Let them live as they please,' she said of the missionaries, 'make such medicines as they desire; which may be good enough for all I know – and teach their own religion – but to people who are receptive. It is just because we are not receptive that they strive to compel their own ideas upon us. The foreigners are the curse of China today. . .'[4]

In spite of her antipathy, Tz'u-hsi invited the ladies of the legations to tea in the Forbidden City on 13 December 1898, to celebrate her sixty-fourth birthday and to cement good relations between East and West after the *coup d'état*. Mrs Conger, wife of the American minister, led the party of seven ministers' wives and was extremely impressed by Tz'u-hsi's gentle cordiality. For Tz'u-hsi presented each lady with a huge pearl ring set in gold, offered each of them a jade cup of tea with both hands, and, drinking from it first and then passing it to them, had murmured, 'One family, all one family'.[5] Nevertheless, in her hall of audience each morning, the dispirited Kuang-hsu silent at her side, Tz'u-hsi deliberated the worth and nature of the Boxers with her ministers. At the beginning of 1900 the councillors and members of the Tsungli Yamen were a mediocre crew – so many men of talent were dead, like Prince Kung, or disgraced, like Weng T'ung-ho, or lying low, like Li Hung-chang, now out of his enemies' reach as viceroy of Kwangtung and Kwangsi. Prince Ch'ing, weak, useless and dishonest, was head of the Tsungli Yamen; another Manchu, Shih-to, was so colourless he had managed to survive on the Grand Council, without any distinguishing act, since 1884; Jung-lu, also of course Manchu, was the Council's presiding adviser. The Grand Secretariat, which had for several reigns paled in importance as a decision-making organ next to the Grand Council now rose in the ascendant; it too was at this time almost entirely composed of Manchu diehards, including Kang-i, a man of impressive slowness and stupidity.

For the first time Tz'u-hsi found that the balance of progressives and reactionaries which she had maintained throughout her years of power had collapsed. The hegemony of hereditary Manchu princes and dukes, who normally lived obscurely but richly in their palaces in Peking, enjoying their privileges and stipends, now left their feather-beds and began to take a fatal interest in politics.

From the brothels and the concert halls, the theatres and the pleasure gardens, the Manchu aristocracy came eagerly to the Forbidden City to participate in the renewal of the dynasty's mandate. Since the 1860s, when the first reforms had diminished Manchu pre-eminence in China's affairs, their education had been overlooked, and since then their fall had been precipitous: they were coarse, crude, violent and unfathomably ignorant. Their lives were spent in futile idleness and hedonism, and *nostalgie de la boue* had overcome them. One story of Manchu decadence was recorded by an official:

It was a very hot day [he recalled] and so friends had invited me to join them. . . . At the table next to us sat a young man of about eighteen: his face was as black as soot and he looked thin and ill-nourished. His queue was plaited round his head and he had inserted a bone hairpin in his hair, after the manner of the Peking hooligan class in summertime. He wore no socks and was stripped to the waist.

He sat, with legs crossed, on the ground, drinking wine. His conversation was full of vulgar oaths and the lowest Pekingese slang. . . .

All of a sudden I observed . . . two officials . . . both wearing the button of the third rank and peacock's feather. . . . They approached the young beggar, and reverently addressed him: 'Your Highness's carriage is ready. . . .'[6]

It was young men like this princeling, Tsai-lien, grandson of the Tao-kuang Emperor, who joined Tz'u-hsi's councils of state, changing their rags for resplendent Manchu military uniforms of lacquered leather, with eighteen sable tassels dangling from their jewel-encrusted helmets, to prostrate themselves before her and recommend that the Boxers be enrolled as government troops.

Prince Tuan, the younger brother of the make-believe beggar, was the ringleader of the Manchu princes who now announced, as if indulging another fad, that they were Boxers. Prince Tuan was 'an evil-visaged man, his face marked with smallpox scars, his eyes small and ferret-like',[7] with an expression of brutish ferocity. He was born under a cloud that would never leave him: he had been blasphemously conceived during the mourning period for his grandfather the Emperor Tao-kuang, and when he became heir to his uncle Prince Jui, in 1894, the scribe mistakenly wrote the similar character Tuan instead, but the court had been thrown in such confusion by the Sino-Japanese war that the error was never rectified. So mistaken Prince Tuan he remained. Significantly, he had married the daughter of Kuei-hsiang, Tz'u-hsi's brother, and had thus become her nephew by marriage.

As this period threw all Tz'u-hsi's failings into magnified relief, it would be a matter for surprise if her nepotism had not displayed itself. Prince Tuan, determined, thrusting and confident, caught that elderly eye that had always liked a contrast to the staid seclusion and effeminacy of the palace. The listless Kuang-hsu grated more and more on her nerves. As her own sister's son, he had also failed to consolidate her family's position by producing an heir to the throne through her niece, his wife Lung-yü. But Prince Tuan had an adolescent son, P'u–chun, also of her flesh and blood, and of royal lineage, built like a prize-fighter, and every bit as rowdy and overbearing as his father. In January 1900, calling a special audience of the princes and ministers, Tz'u-hsi wrung a cruel confession of impotence from Kuang-hsu: 'Our protracted sickness renders it impossible for us to hope for a son, so that His late Majesty remains without heir. . . . We have accordingly prostrated ourselves in supplication before our Sacred Mother, begging that she may be pleased to select some worthy person from among the princes of the blood as heir to His Majesty T'ung-chih. . . .' Accordingly Tz'u-hsi chose P'u-chun, her own great-nephew. Kuang-hsu was forced to decree: 'Our gratitude at this is unbounded, and obediently we obey her behests, hereby appointing P'u-chun to be Heir Apparent and successor to the Throne.'[8] When the legations refused to comment on the appointment, and withheld the congratulations due to the new heir apparent's father, Prince Tuan sulked and his Boxer sympathies hardened.

Tz'u-hsi indulged the Boxers tentatively at this stage, only partly because they were loyal to the Manchu dynasty. Her real attraction to them was superstitious, for she had become, at the age of sixty-five, a remarkably credulous woman. Her childhood in the rougher world of the fervent south, her early experiences of the heady lamaism of the huge Buddhist monasteries at Jehol in 1860–1, her reliance on portents, stars, omens and, in short, the supernatural, fostered by the loneliness of a despot's position and her old age, all combined to erase the superficial veneer of educated classicism and Confucianism. She was really deeply disturbed by the Boxers' claims to invulnerability. Their displays were, it was true, very affecting, for all the chicanery of blank cartridges, blunt arrows, together with the genuine fits that convulsed the youths, did render them, like fakirs, temporarily impervious to pain. When Yuan Shih-k'ai lined some Boxers up against a wall before a firing squad and had them all shot dead, the Chinese, as superstitious as their empress, retorted: if they were dead, then they had not been real Boxers; alternatively, they only seemed dead, and would return. In Newchwang in Manchuria, just north of Port Arthur, one English customs official recalled a towering Boxer who was arrested during the riots there, executed and thrown into the sea. The crowd believed he would return, and days later, sure enough, his corpse was washed up: even in death, he still wielded his sword, and seemed, with the movement of the water, to strike at the cable of a Russian ship moored by the quay.[9]

Such eerie tales hummed through the Forbidden City and the summer palace, sped to Tz'u-hsi's ears by scared eunuchs and women. Li Lien-ying, who reputedly believed in the Boxers' super-human powers and encouraged his empress, must have influenced her, for no doubt Li had seen the Boxers in action which Tz'u-hsi could not, trapped as she was in the inaccessible enclaves of the palace. When the foreign ministers demanded that the Throne should repudiate the Boxers, Tz'u-hsi simply could not bring herself to thrust aside a heaven-sent force of champions, for if she did, it might turn against her own creaking rule and bring it down:

When peaceful and law-abiding people practise themselves in the mech-anical arts for the preservation of themselves and their families, or when they combine in *village fraternities for mutual protection*, this is in accordance with the public spirited principle enjoined by Mencius of keeping 'mutual watch and giving mutual aid'. Some local authorities, when a case arises, disregard this distinction, and listening to false and idle rumours against all alike as being seditious associations, mete out indiscriminate slaughter. The result of *this failure to distinguish between good and evil* is that men's minds are filled with fear and doubt. This proves not that the people are lawless, but that the administration is bad.[10]

Her instructions were therefore twofold, and in her mind independent: to strengthen China against foreigners by raising patriotic train-bands, and also, as she had repeatedly decreed since 1861, and once again in 1898, to tolerate Christianity and foreigners according to the rights granted them in the treaties, because otherwise, China knew the character of their vengeance. She refused to admit to herself that the double policy was, from the point of view of the Boxers and the foreign ministers, wholly untenable.

With such ambivalent leadership each important official responded differently: Yü-hsien, who after a missionary death in his area, had been removed at the demand of the foreign powers from his governorship of Shantung, became governor of Shansi. There the Boxers prospered and multiplied, aided and abetted by the provincial administration, and, presumably, by its purse. The fact that Tz'u-hsi appointed him governor elsewhere immediately after his removal from Shantung shows the high favour in which she held his pro-Boxer views. Yü-lu, viceroy of Chihli, tried to tread the imperial tightrope, to cajole the Boxers into remaining a *defensive* and not aggressive force. But by the end of May, when gleeful bands of red-turbaned hooligans were setting fire to railways, occupying buildings and burning Christian houses to the ground, Yü-lu telegraphed 'persuasion can no longer disperse them. The commanders, if hesitant and tolerant, will certainly lead to calamities.'[11] In Shantung, the resourceful Yuan Shih-k'ai, the acting governor, ignored repeated admonishments that the 'people' must be persuaded to disperse, not crushed by brute force, and hounded the Boxers out of his province. 'These Boxers,' he replied to the Throne in May, 'gathering people to roam on the streets and plundering over distances of several hundred miles, cannot be said to be defending themselves and their families; setting fire to houses, kidnapping people, and offering resistance to government troops, they cannot be said to have no criminal activities; plundering and killing the common people, and stirring up disturbances, they cannot be said to be merely anti-Christian.'[12]

Although Yuan's policy effectively rid Shantung of the Boxers, it was disastrous, for it drove them north into Chihli, and then on to the capital itself. But the keyholder of power in Peking the powerful Jung-lu, what line had he adopted? Jung-lu was as helplessly undecided and hesitant as Tz'u-hsi herself: as late as July 1900, when the Boxer conflagration was blazing, Jung-lu was still racking his brains over it. He wrote to a friend, the viceroy of Fukien: 'By themselves they cannot be fully trusted, but it seems to me . . . that one might profitably use them to inspire, by their fanaticism, the martial ardour of our regular troops.' Though he disagreed with the Manchu princes over their efficiency in combat, his assessment remained pretty naïve:

As a fighting force they are absolutely useless, but their claims to supernatural arts and magic might possibly be valuable for the purpose of disheartening the enemy. But it would be quite wrong, not to say fatal, for us to attach any real belief to their ridiculous claims, or to regard them as of any real use in action. . . . These Boxers are not trained troops, but they are ready to fight, and to face death. It is indeed a gratifying surprise to see any of our people display courage, and to witness their enthusiasm for paying off old scores against the foreigner; but. . . .

At the end of this troubled rigmarole, Jung-lu decided that, in southern China, and Fukien at least, the Boxers should not be encouraged: 'the main thing is to prevent the throne's decree becoming an excuse for the banding together of disorderly characters.'[13]

But in April 1900 the Boxers had still not yet reached the capital proper, and Tz'u-hsi, surrounded by conflicting counsel, sat on the fence. In response to reiterated demands from the foreign ministers that the throne should suppress the movement, she again at the end of May pleaded for a distinction to be made between 'good and bad elements' among the 'militia'. Meanwhile, the placards and posters and pamphlets multiplied; rowdy incidents increased; mission buildings and property were burned and looted. General Nieh took the field to clear some Boxers in early June, and was coldly rebuked, although Tz'u-hsi herself then issued a decree that if the bad elements 'refused to reform', imperial troops could disperse them.

At the legations, the ministers, as out of touch with the real state of affairs in their European seclusion as Tz'u-hsi was in the court, turned a deaf ear to the warnings of the missionaries and to the Bishop of Peking, Favier, who, alert to the urgency as early as 19 May, had declared that the anti-Christian propaganda was only a cloak for a projected wholesale slaughter of foreigners, and had requested military protection for his Northern Cathedral. Sir Claude MacDonald, though personally pooh-poohing the fears of his colleagues, agreed to call up guards from Tientsin. On 24 May the British Legation celebrated Queen Victoria's eighty-first and last birthday; on 30 May there was more champagne, dancing and music from Sir Robert Hart's Chinese band, the 'I-G's Own'. On 31 May, three hundred and sixty-eight international guards arrived at the legations; eighty-three Germans and Austrians followed three days later. The Tsungli Yamen had given permission for thirty guards for each legation. Twice that number had arrived.

If anything was needed to inflame Boxer rage further, or to lend credence to Prince Tuan's warnings to Tz'u-hsi that the foreign powers were bent on parcelling China between them, it was the arrival of the troops. On 28 May the railway station, symbol of foreign oppression, was burnt down at Fengtai near Peking; on 4 June the telegraph between Peking and Tientsin was cut at Paoting, near the capital; on 7 June two English missionaries were murdered; on 7 June also, Belgian railway engineers and their families were mobbed; on 9 June the sanguine members of the legations became truly alarmed for the first time: their splendid grandstand at the Peking racecourse, symbol of all their kind held dear, was burnt down. So Sir Claude, transgressing the sovereign rights of a country theoretically at peace, cabled for more reinforcements from Tientsin to protect the legations in Peking. Yet the guards had already stirred up enough unrest, and had already exceeded the quota allowed by the Yamen.

On 10 June, a mixed international force of two thousand-odd soldiers under the British admiral Seymour set out from Tientsin. The news of the advance triggered off the Boxers massing themselves in the fields outside the capital. On 11 June the chancellor of the Japanese Legation, Sugiyama, was murdered by Tung Fuhsiang's quarrelsome Moslems, at the southernmost gate of the capital. In Peking, as news of the armed advance spread, Prince Tuan had his point made: the foreign devils were aggressively bent on conquering and devouring China. As Seymour's force followed the smashed railway line to Peking – this time no Chinese porters came to the foreigners' aid – Tz'u-hsi yielded to the war party and gave Prince Tuan his way. He was made head of the Tsungli Yamen, replacing the prevaricating, alarmed Prince Ch'ing. On 13 June, under the auspices of Prince Tuan, the tatterdemalion, violent, bloodthirsty, starveling, red-robed boys, armed with rusty gingals and old rifles they hardly knew how to handle, with bamboo spears, huge old double-edged broadswords, and all manner of makeshift weapons, burst into the capital. They were quartered in the palace of Prince Tuan's cousin Prince Chuang, and their shout, 'Burn burn burn, kill kill kill' began to reverberate through the streets.

The legations occupied an area sandwiched between the wall of the Imperial City and the wall of the Tartar City, and formed a complex of houses, streets, canals and gardens, a happy hunting ground for an urban guerrilla or sniper. The few members of the legations who were young or courageous enough to fight immediately saw the vulnerability of their position, and set to work with the guards to build barricades and to sandbag the exposed outer perimeter and openings in the defences at crossroads and bridges. After the Boxers' entry into Peking, the legation residents were increasingly nervous and their rash and repeated acts of aggression against the tumultuous hordes outside must have helped to provoke the conflict. During the second week in June, legation soldiers shot at their pickets, and at any Chinese wearing 'any bit of red in his uniform.'[14] The Americans 'had seen a few Chinese in the distance and accordingly arranged to fire volleys every quarter of an hour down the road on the off chance of hitting anyone who might be coming along'.[15] On 15 June, the American minister reflected happily that nearly a hundred Boxers had been killed already. The rescue parties that hunted out Chinese converts and brought them back to safety in the legation compound were gallant and distinguished operations, for, without doubt, the converts were the most conspicuous targets of the Boxers' hatred. Yet even Morrison, The *Times* correspondent, one of the most attractive foreigners in China, failed to see how provoking such knight errantry might be. On 16 June he wrote in his diary: 'Christian captives with hands tied being immolated ... 5 already dead. Rescued 3. One accidentally killed. All Boxers killed; one only dared face us. I killed myself at least 6.'[16] But if only one dared face the rescue party, then the others must have been shot in the back as they fled – and war had not been declared by China on any other country or vice versa.

On 11 June an elegant party of foreign staff went to the station to meet Admiral Seymour and his reinforcements. There was no train, hardly any station and certainly no admiral. Puzzled and unhappy, the foreign party returned to the legations. Inside the compound there were diplomats, bankers, traders, merchants, tradesmen, missionaries, the rescued Chinese Christians, customs officials, and Chinese servants – a heterogeneous community speaking a score of different languages and numbering nearly five thousand people. Outside, thousands of Boxers, of imperial troops and Chinese lay between Peking and the shore, where Admiral Seymour's two thousand-odd men were beating their way through increasingly unkind territory.

Although they had passed unmolested through the lines of the imperial troops under General Nieh, whom they had found even friendly, Seymour's forces were attacked by Boxers on 13 June and driven back on to Tientsin. In Peking Tz'u-hsi now saw the Boxers' exploits with her own eyes: from the Forbidden City she watched the Eastern Cathedral, and then the Southern Cathedral go up in flames; all over the city she heard the explosions of rifles and the crackling of fire. On 16 June at noon she called an urgent meeting of her ministers. The discussion was heated and stormy: several young secretaries of the government boards warned against a full-scale attack on the foreigners; Kuang-hsu roused himself from his apathetic and invalid gloom to plead, weeping, that the Boxers' claims to unvulnerability were so much poppycock and that they should be suppressed. But Tz'u-hsi remonstrated: 'If we cannot rely upon the supernatural formulas, can we not rely upon the heart of the people? China is weak; the only thing we can depend upon is the heart of the people.'[17] After a prolonged and troubled debate, Tz'u-hsi forced her desires upon the Council and once again it decided that the 'good elements' among the Boxers would be conscripted, the rest pacified, and the foreign advance on Peking stopped.

But such a policy was so much waste vermilion pencil; it was unenforceable. That night the legations and Tz'u-hsi watched from their windows the burning of the huge Ch'ien Men, vast triple-tiered gateway to the Tartar City itself, which danced and blazed splendidly in the darkness, engulfing in its flames the richest quarter of Peking of furriers and *antiquaires* and jewellers and silk merchants. The Boxers had set alight shops that sold foreign medicines, but in that dusty-dry season, everything around had caught fire.

The destruction of the gate was an evil omen for the Ch'ing dynasty, and Tz'u-hsi had all mentions of it expunged from the annals of the reign. No amount of censorship on paper could however disguise the fact that the Boxers could no longer be sifted and controlled. Prince Tuan, fearing that such arson and terrorism might tilt Tz'u-hsi against the Boxers, concocted a letter by which the Powers demanded that all military affairs and all China's revenue should be placed in their hands. Such was Prince Tuan's fantasy, and in the light of the recent threatened partition of China, it was within the bounds of probability. Prince Tuan's document then stated – uncultured and uncouth as he was, he knew exactly where to sting Tz'u-hsi – that the Powers demanded the restoration of the Kuang-hsu Emperor's authority, and a special residence for him on his own. Tz'u-hsi, jaw set, eyes burning, produced his preposterous forgery at her council meeting on 17 June. So humiliated was she by its effrontery that she could not bring herself to read the whole of it, and left out the demand for the emperor's independence. 'Now,' she cried, 'now they have started the aggression and the extinction of our nation is imminent. If we must fold our arms and yield to them, I would have no face to see our ancestors after death.'[18] Quoting the *Book of Odes*, she added typically, 'Let us exterminate them, before we eat our morning meal.'[19]

Jung-lu was not present, but when he heard, he believed the document spurious. Other members of the Tsungli Yamen, who had not taken delivery of it from any representative of the foreign diplomatic body, must also have suspected it. But it was impossible to accuse a prince of the royal house of fraud, and so they remained silent. Tz'u-hsi and Prince Tuan must have felt cheated when her ministers did not immediately roar for war to the death, but continued to press caution on her. But she need not have worried: the international force under Admiral Seymour would force the issue to crisis-point.

For on 16 June Admiral Seymour, beaten back towards the sea by the Boxers, struggling with many wounded, decided that his only line of retreat lay towards the Taku forts, scene of earlier British summer campaigns. He served an ultimatum on the Chinese: 'To occupy provisionally, by consent or by force, the Taku forts' by 2 am on the 17 June. The Chinese opened fire an hour beforehand. But with the help of two destroyers that glided up silently under cover of dark, the forts fell bloodlessly into Allied hands. Yü-lu, viceroy of Chihli, notified the court of the Allies' ultimatum, but failed to report the fact that the forts had been captured.

Yü-lu's report confirmed the contents of Prince Tuan's document: the foreigners were provoking China in order to destroy her. Tz'u-hsi coldly informed the legations of the ultimatum and equally coldly gave them twenty-four hours' notice in which to leave Peking under the protection of government troops. At the legations, huddled behind sandbags, the residents were beginning to enjoy a putting green that had recently been laid in case of a siege. When they heard the ultimatum, a fierce and heated quarrel broke out between the different nations' ministers and other respected members of the foreign community. Sir Claude MacDonald twirled his waxed moustaches and decided that they would obey the Yamen and leave at once. But such a departure would abandon all the Chinese with foreign connections, whether converts or not, to the mercy of the Boxers, and George Morrison of *The Times* became enraged: 'If you leave Peking tomorrow,' he declared, 'the deaths of every man, woman and child in this huge unprotected convoy will be on your heads, and your names will go down in history, and be known for ever as the wickedest, weakest and most pusillanimous cowards who have ever lived.'[20]

Sir Claude nevertheless prevailed. The only minister who sided with Morrison, who agreed that to surrender the converts in their charge would be unpardonable and that Chinese protection was a dead letter, was the German Baron von Ketteler, a florid, excitable man with a flaming temper who had only a few days before caught a teenage Boxer wearing scarlet insignia outside the legations and beaten him with his walking stick to within an inch of his life. It was Ketteler who, the next day, unable to endure the tension as the assembled ministers waited for the Yamen's reply to their acceptance of the ultimatum, set off in his official chair, with his interpreter by his side, to accost the Chinese spokesman personally. As he jolted towards the Tsungli Yamen, a Manchu Bannerman, in full uniform, rode up to him, and taking aim, shot him dead at point blank range. Ketteler's interpreter, wounded in both legs, dragged himself back to safety and gasped the news to the legations. Even Sir Claude had to admit regretfully that now they could no longer leave with any hope of safety.

That afternoon at 4 pm, the exact hour when Tz'u-hsi's ultimatum expired, the Chinese army fired the first volleys of the siege of the legations. As he returned from settling some Chinese converts in their quarters, Professor Hubert James, a kindly distrait old man, was captured, and later tortured for three days, murdered and his head spiked and displayed. At the barricades, an Austrian sailor and a French volunteer each caught a Chinese sharpshooter's bullet. In the Forbidden City, Tz'u-hsi heard the sound of rifle fire as she drafted a declaration of war. For on 21 June 1900, the Empress Dowager Tz'u-hsi decreed, in the name of the Emperor Kuang-hsu, that China was at war with Great Britain, the United States, France, Germany, Italy, Austria, Belgium, Holland and Japan. Her presentation of the facts as the Chinese saw them, was, ingenuous in its candour:

Ever since the foundation of the dynasty, foreigners coming to China have been kindly treated. In the reigns of Tao-kuang and Hsien-feng they were allowed to trade, and to propagate their religion. At first they were amenable to Chinese control, but for the past thirty years they have taken advantage of our forbearance to encroach on our territory, to trample on the Chinese people, and to absorb the wealth of the Empire. Every concession made only serves to increase their insolence. They oppress our peaceful subjects, and insult the gods and sages, exciting burning indignation among the people. . . . Hence the burning of chapels and the slaughter of converts by the patriotic braves.

The Throne was anxious to avoid war, and issued edicts enjoining protection of legations and pity towards converts, declaring Boxers and converts to be equally the children of the state. . . .

A dispatch was yesterday sent by them calling upon us to deliver up the Taku forts into their keeping. Otherwise they would be taken by force. These threats are a sample of their aggressive disposition in all matters relating to international intercourse . . .

With tears have we announced in our ancestral shrines the outbreak of war. Better is it to do our utmost and enter on the struggle than to seek self-preservation involving eternal disgrace. All our officials, high and low, are of one mind. There have also assembled, without official summons, several hundred thousands of patriotic soldiers [Boxers]. . . . Even children carry spears in the defence of their country.[21]

The same day Tz'u-hsi dispatched a more graphic missive to her Boxer Prince Tuan: 'The foreigners are like fish in the stewpan. For forty years have I lain on brushwood and eaten bitterness because of them.'[22]

Chapter Thirteen

MEN OF THE PEOPLE

It was high, burning summer; a warm, dry wind blew sand down onto Peking from the deserts of Mongolia, and in the Forbidden City the wide courtyards became dustbowls. But Tz'u-hsi, who had always cared so much for her comforts, did not escape to the cool breezes and ponds of the I Ho Yuan, but withstood the heat of Peking. She had undertaken the enterprise of great moment that she had always nurtured, ever since, as a young woman of twenty-five, she had fled from Peking before the advance of the French and British, ever since she had returned to find foreigners obstreperously in residence and the summer palace a heap of charred rubble and ash. As she had said to Tseng Chi-tse twenty-two years before: 'How can we forget our grievances for a single day? But we must gradually make ourselves strong. . . .'[1]

Now China was strong, and she and her chosen advisers felt that all its pent up rancour and revenge could now be successfully loosed upon the foreigner to drive him from China. Nevertheless, as a man who suddenly finds the love-object he has cherished for years within his grasp almost recoils from reaching out to touch it, and hesitates where to begin, Tz'u-hsi, gnawing sleeplessly at the problem, cast about and hesitated and changed her mind every few days, according to whoever had her ear.

Outside, in the crucible of the city, the Boxers swaggered in their red sashes and ribbons and brandished their ramshackle weapons. Prince Tuan reorganized the traditional 'Tiger' troops, Manchu Bannermen with tiger skins thrown over their shoulders and tigers' heads mounted on their shields; on the other hand, Tung Fu-hiang's Kansu Moslems, white-turbaned, weatherbeaten and hardened by years of campaigning in the open, were equipped with Western weapons – rifles and carbines. Jung-lu's Grand Army of the North, or Headquarters army, were also up-to-the-minute in Western armaments. Banners, gold, scarlet and blue, triangular and square, with fretted borders, embroidered with emblems and characters fluttered over these tens of thousands of motley, ill-assorted soldiery arrayed outside the terrified legations.

They had combined to raze shops owned by foreigners or selling foreign goods; to reduce the Christian churches, except the Northern Cathedral, to smoking ruins; to plunder and burn the missions scattered throughout the city. The Northern Cathedral, monument to much ill-feeling, where the Bishop of Peking, Favier, was immured with twenty-two nuns, three thousand four hundred converts, eight hundred children and a mere clutch of sailors – forty-three men only for their defence – was now being besieged; the legations were being stormed.

From Tz'u-hsi's point of view the first task was to rid Peking of the foreign representatives; then the way would be open to expel all foreigners, and to return to splendid isolation. Afterwards the foreign army – which even now was cutting its way through the same forts, the same territory between Taku and Tientsin that Elgin and Gros had trampled in 1860 – could be routed. In Tz'u-hsi's eyes, this road between the coast and the capital was the crucial theatre of the war, not the battle taking place just over the side of her high and purple walls. Her orders were discreetly worded, but clear: 'The work undertaken by Tung Fu-hsiang should be completed as soon as possible so that troops can be spared and sent to Tientsin for defence.'[2]

The assault on the legations was therefore, for the first few days, fierce and sustained. On 21 June a band of roaring Boxers streamed over the north bridge, pennants flying; the next day, Tung Fu-hsiang's men rushed the north-east corner. Together these attacks drove the handful of defenders out of the Austro-Hungarian legation, out of the customs buildings, out of the Italian legation, out of the French legation, cutting foreign-held territory by a third (although the French were able later to regain half their building). Two days later the German and American guards on the actual wall of the Tartar City to the south – a vital position because it commanded four directions from above, and unlike many sniping posts had the medieval crenellations for shelter – were swiftly and effectively attacked. The pickets fell back before the onslaught and to the horror of the other defenders abandoned the wall. The Chinese had now penned back the legations into a series of highly combustible wooden buildings, low-lying in the main, with picturesque pleasure gardens growing between them, where ironically the love-arbours and temples gave excellent cover. Nevertheless, the Chinese occupying the wall could pick out, as casually as in clay-pigeon practice, any movement in between the buildings. The only remaining enclave of any strength that the foreigners occupied was the British legation compound itself.

On 23 June Tung Fu-hsiang's troops set out to do something none of the old China hands had thought possible: they tossed lighted firebrands into the Hanlin Yuan, Forest of the Ten Thousand Pencils, the seat of Chinese academe, the oldest library in the world, where unique copies of ancient Chinese wisdom were deposited, bastion of learning in a country founded on scholarship. But the Hanlin Yuan stood contiguous to the north wall of the British legation, and a north westerly was blowing the sand-storms of the Gobi desert into the capital. The Chinese intended to smoke the foreigners out, like so many moles from a troublesome lawn.

But the conflagration did not spread as the Chinese had hoped. From the eight wells in the British legation compound, teams of drawers passed buckets, bowls, ewers and vases of every description to the front line to quench the flames, while providentially the wind, which had been blowing north for weeks, quietened and died. When a few foreigners made a foray to rescue what treasures they could, the found 'ruins, the ornamental pool. . . . choked with debris; wooden printing blocks, manuscripts, and books were lying scattered about, trampled into the mire.'[3]

Although this particular stratagem had failed, it remained inconceivable to Tz'u-hsi, as she heard the singing of bullets and saw the flames over Peking, that the handful of besieged foreigners could hold out much longer. She now swayed towards forcing Seymour's capitulation first, for if his force were crushed, the legation members could be easily dealt with, either by marching them out of the country under escort, as had been proposed before the attack on the Taku forts and the declaration of war, or by wholesale butchery. Therefore she wavered. The news from the coast was blissfully encouraging: dispatch after dispatch from the viceroy of Chihli announced victory against the foreign expedition.

But the victory was a question of interpretation. It was true that the Chinese army had beaten Seymour back to the Taku forts, and that once there, he had had difficulty extricating himself, and had left troops behind to garrison them, thus further depleting his numbers, already thinned by the wounded. It was true that the Chinese had captured two foreign gunboats. It was true that as Seymour tried to hack his way back from Taku to Tientsin through country alive with Boxers, he had lost his orientation and become trapped in a village, Hsiku, north of Tientsin, which he did not even know existed. It was true that in the first skirmishes outside Tientsin, the foreigners had the worst of it. But Yü-lu the viceroy failed to report to his empress that the Taku forts were in foreign hands, and that, therefore, the international force had a base of operations, that it could land troops and enter China when it wanted, that the Peiho river to Peking was open – that, in short, victory was hardly the apt description.

Jubilant at Yü-lu's slant on the situation, Tz'u-hsi issued her only completely unambiguous decree of support for the Boxers – the very next day after the burning of the Hanlin Yuan, 24 June, which shows how truly superficial her vaunted respect for learning was. Without equivocation, she appointed as generals of the Boxer volunteers Kang-i, the notorious reactionary Grand Secretary, and Prince Chuang, Prince Tuan's cousin, who had given his palace over to the Boxers as their headquarters on their arrival in Peking. She thus formally acknowledged the thirty thousand members of the movement in the capital as imperial soldiers, and they were then organized into one thousand four hundred bands. Tz'u-hsi triumphantly described Yü-lu's 'victories' and declared:

The Boxers who helped the troops so much in these actions are men of the people; with them, the State need not use a soldier nor spend a dollar. Even the little children wielded arms in defence of their altars and fields. In all their dangers, the spirits of their ancestors, of the gods, and the sages, protect them. The myriads of the people are actuated by one ideal.

We hasten to publish this edict in praise of the patriotic Boxers, and to assure them that those of their number who are in distress will be cared for. When these troubles are over we intend to bestow on them special marks of our favour. Let these people's soldiers still continue, with united hearts and utmost efforts, to repel aggression and prove their loyalty, without failing, to the end.[4]

In this radiant mood Tz'u-hsi ordered thousands of bags of rice to be freely distributed among her ragged, adolescent, country-bred deliverers.

But whether Tz'u-hsi wished the movement to spread throughout China or not, more wary minds were bent on preventing it. When she had first declared war, she summoned her governors and viceroys to her aid: they were to advise her how it should be conducted; furthermore, they were to send troops immediately to defend the capital from the aggression of the foreigner. To the west her missive successfully inspired an epidemic of cruel tortures and atrocities perpetrated against Christian missionaries and their protégés by the bloodthirsty Yü-hsien, who presided with relish over the gory execution of the foreign devils. In Manchuria, several priests and foreigners were murdered or executed – one was even burned alive. In Chekiang twenty-seven members of a Protestant mission were massacred by a marauding band. The movement was powerful but it did meet with resistance: in Shantung Yuan Shih-k'ai continued to defy the throne's directives, and dispersed the Boxers by force. In the south, the viceroys, powerful independent men like Chang Chih-tung, the reformer, of Hupeh and Hunan and Liu K'un-yi, the virtuous but opium-smoking viceroy of Liang-kiang, swiftly sent the throne a solemn warning that to wage war on the world would bring nothing but calamity on China . They begged Tz'u-hsi to give orders for the Boxers' suppression and for the protection of foreigners. In early June Chang had telegraphed that the Boxers were 'staging a rebellion on the pretext of anti-Christianity'.[5]

Meanwhile, together with the crafty Li Hung-chang at Canton, they conferred by telegraph, and decided that the Boxers were a rebellion against the legitimate power of the ruler and that all orders to encourage them were issued by Prince Tuan who had gained illegal influence over the throne. They decided therefore to construe Tz'u-hsi's order 'to unite together and to protect their territories'[6] as an order to suppress trouble – not the foreigner, but the Boxers. They accordingly refused to send troops to Peking as requested. Chang Chih-tung, however, who always liked to play it both ways, progressive and traditionalist, sent five thousand troops but cannily suggested they dawdle *en route*. In his own province Chang drove the Boxers to ground, as did the other viceroys in the south. Furthermore, these self-willed men joined forces to make the foreign powers in the treaty ports of the area agree not to sail up the Yangstze in gunboats or stage any of their favourite displays of force at such a turbulent and sensitive time, and they continued, in the face of the Throne's explicit orders, to pay back the war indemnities and the foreign loans. By their courageous unilateral action, the great southern viceroys not only contained the Boxers, but saved China from full-scale war.

In Peking, where the struggle was now concentrated in spite of Tz'u-hsi's wishes, Prince Tuan, grown swollen-headed with Tz'u-hsi's support, overreached himself and forcing his way into the Forbidden City with some Boxers at his heels, claimed that some of her personal attendants were clandestine Christians, and that if a Boxer struck them on the forehead a cross would appear. Immediately he and his followers began striking the squealing eunuchs and maids. Te-ling, Tz'u-hsi's lady-in-waiting, claimed that Tz'u-hsi later said she allowed the prince's presumption in her precincts in such an uncharacteristically meek and mild fashion because she feared reprisals from the Boxers otherwise. Another famous diary (supposedly kept during the siege by an eminent Manchu, Ching-shou, but proved later to be forged in order to exonerate certain leading protagonists of the Boxer uprising like Jung-lu) described an incident on the night of the twenty-fourth: Tz'u-hsi, painting a design of bamboo on a silk scroll, was violently interrupted by the ex-bandit Tung Fu-hsiang, who began to reproach Jung-lu roundly for withholding heavy artillery from his troops. In both accounts, Tz'u-hsi, infuriated at such a lack of decorum, re-evaluated the Boxers in whom she had placed such trust. But whether the cause was intrigue, or moodiness, or simply panic again at her dilemma, Tz'u-hsi certainly veered the other way, and on 25 June, the long bronze trumpets of the Chinese troops wailed out a message, and the incendiarism, the stoning, the war-whooping stopped and quiet was restored to the legations.

A Chinese messenger appeared on the north bridge, near the British legation and announced that a dispatch from the Tsungli Yamen was on its way. The strained, besieged legations waited; three days they waited in the unaccustomed silence, but no further messenger appeared, and on the night of the twenty-eighth the siege began again, this time in earnest. Prince Tuan and primitive longing had again prevailed over Tz'u-hsi's hesitation.

This second phase was to last until 17 July – three weeks, day and night, but especially night-time harassment, ambushes, sniping, fires, explosions and noise. Yet with remarkable nerve, at the very height of the siege, Tz'u-hsi sent trenchant telegrams: to Queen Victoria, pleading that as two old women they should understand each other's difficulties, to Tsar Nicholas and to the emperor of Japan. To all three she outlined the necessity for their countries to remain on good terms with China – not, it must be pointed out, China's need to remain on good terms with them. To Britain the reason was trade, to Japan the Eastern alliance against the West, to Russia, the ancient border dependency and friendship of the two countries.

By the middle of July the legations were well and truly suffering the results of their greed and intolerance. The guards and one hundred and twenty-five volunteers defended them valiantly, and on the night of 2 July they ambushed their old position of the Tartar City wall and recaptured it. Sir Claude MacDonald, as Commander-in-Chief, issued orders on diplomatic visiting cards. The missionaries and priests prayed. With that genius for adminis-tration of colonial powers, an efficient bureaucracy had already been established – committees for supplies, sanitation, fortification, watches, health, transport, posts and communications. The women devoted themselves to sewing – monogrammed pillowcases, silk pyjamas, damask curtains and bales of the best China brocade became sandbags, making the barricades look like a New Year's carnival; the Chinese converts did the heavy work and the dirty work, often with extreme courage under fire. They were pitifully undernourished on a diet of grain, though occasionally one of the defenders, breaking the rule against wasting ammunition, would shoot a passing crow for them to eat. The few ponies they had were allotted to the legations' staff and the active soldiers – and how they regretted eating their best racehorses and hunters. A Norwegian missionary, Nestergard (nicknamed Nearest-to-God) went stark mad; one of the babies born was christened Siege; a German, believing his last hour was at hand, played the March of the Valkyrie in a 'soul agony' on the piano; the libraries that had not burned down were ransacked for tales of previous massacres: Lucknow and Cawnpore were lengthily discussed.

The beleaguered were tormented not so much by the direct attacks as by the strain of siege conditions: they could not see their assailants, shells and bullets sang past their heads from unidentifiable vantage points; the temperature during July was often one hundred and ten degrees in the shade; every few days the summer rains swamped the corpses lying unburied on the defence perimeter, breeding disease and asphyxiating the legations with the stench. Flies proliferated in the pestilential air. The unceasing noise, not only of gunfire and cannon, but also of fire crackers, set off all night to harass them, preyed dreadfully on their nerves. Yet the curious thing was that, when the noise did cease, from time to time, the stress of not knowing what the Chinese were up to was, some felt, almost worse. While daily the spirits of the besieged flagged at the disappointment that Seymour's force had still not arrived, it was the knowledge that it must be on its way, that he could not fail them, that sustained them throughout their trial.

At the Northern Cathedral, the tragedy was acute. There, hundreds of Chinese were defended by the unforgettable gallantry of a twenty-three-year-old Breton sailor Paul Henry, who drilled some of the converts with makeshift pikes, managed to steal a cannon from the imperial troops besieging them, and with that to hold the Boxers at bay for as long as the far better equipped legations. And there, where so many Christian converts, the Boxers' greatest *bêtes noires* were housed, there was no reprieve, not even for one night.

Valiant as the defenders of the legations and the Cathedral were, it did strike many of them as odd that they were able to hold out quite so effectively. The more religious wondered that the hand of Providence restrained the assault, for so many shells flew wild, so many rifles were discharged skywards, only one gun was fixed on the lethal position on the Imperial City wall when the Chinese possessed hundreds they could have manoeuvred there, and because, principally, a handful of soldiers, lamentably short of fire power, with one mongrel cannon – of British make, with an Italian gun-carriage, and Russian ammunition – could stave off thousands of fresh, well-armed Chinese.

'I have tried', wrote Jung-lu to the southern viceroys, 'to give protection and to bring about a reconciliation.'[7] 'If one weak country fights more than ten powerful countries, danger and ruin will follow at once. Moreover, when two countries are at war, it has been customary from far antiquity not to injure the envoys. The founding of the dynasty by our forefathers was an arduous task; how can it now be lightly thrown away by believing in the heretical brigands?'[8] Jung-lu's ascendancy in the province of Chihli had been weakened by the rise of the Manchu princes and their Boxer armies, and so though he was commander-in-chief of the imperial troops in the area, he had been dithering – not the best thing for a commander-in-chief to do. It was this irresolution on the part of one of her most reliable military men that continued to throw Tz'u-hsi into equivalent confusion and indecisiveness. 'The various legations', Jung-lu also explained to the southern viceroys, 'were united and daily fired their rifles and guns, killing innumerable officials and people. Four times they attacked the Tung-hua Gate, but were repulsed by the troops of Tung Fu-hsiang. They occupied the wall ... it was therefore impossible for the Headquarters Army [his own] and Tung Fu-hsiang's troops not to defend their positions and make counter attacks.'[9] Nevertheless, he tried desperately to remain a defensive force and throughout those central weeks of the siege, until 17 July, Jung-lu reined in the imperial troops, and let the Boxers, ill-equipped, rash, hot-headed, young and enthusiastic, hurl themselves fruitlessly against the legation barricades.

There is also some evidence that Jung-lu was ill at the time. He was on sick leave when the decisive meeting of 17 June was held and Prince Tuan produced his forged letter, and was therefore only able to doubt it later. He was again absent when Tz'u-hsi decided to declare war on the Powers. In his telegram to the southern viceroys, Jung-lu excuses himself: 'Later I was ill and could not move; still during my leave I submitted seven Memorials. . . .'[10] He may have feigned sickness to avoid responsibility, but at sixty-five, he was an old man with only three more years to live.

In the palace Tz'u-hsi was torn helplessly between Prince Tuan, Jung-lu, her desires and her judgement. On 1 July she denounced the Boxers – whom only a week before she had so lovingly acclaimed – as 'untrained bandits', 'disorderly characters', 'rebels' and announced that 'the population passed completely out of control' and that 'the Throne was by no means averse to give orders for their suppression, but had it reacted with undue haste, the result might have been a general conflagration, and our efforts to protect the Legations might have ended in a dire calamity'.[11] Though this may have been a ruse to cover her actions for posterity, it might equally well reflect her genuine puzzlement. At the beginning of the war, she had wanted to use the Boxers as auxiliary, official troops to rid China of the foreigner; now she wanted to use them to that end, but claim afterwards that they had risen spontaneously and accomplished it without high government authority; by mid-July, she was to change her mind again altogether. Her problem was, as it had always been, that she met circumstances as they happened, often according to whoever was advising her, and was never able to foresee and forestall them.

Her volte-face was complete for a simple reason: because, from the main theatre of the war, Yü-lu reported no more victories. Japanese, Russians, French, British and American, plus a token representation of Austrians and Italians, making fourteen thousand troops in all, had been able to land at the British-garrisoned Taku forts, prise the remnant of Seymour's expedition out of his bewildered encampment at Hsiku and march, ten thousand strong, on to Tientsin. There they relieved the foreign settlements which were besieged by Boxers and stormed the ancient battlements of the Chinese city. The Chinese troops defending Tientsin did however inflict great losses on the international force as it tried to take the town by frontal assault. Finally on 14 July, after the walls had been encircled and attacked on all sides, the Japanese troops blew up one of the massive gates, scaled the wall, and effected the capture of Tientsin. The town was immediately savagely plundered, each nation outdoing the other in committing greater horrors. Also, to compound the distress of the Chinese, General Nieh, one of Jung-lu's chosen leaders, who had fought to scatter the Boxers throughout the summer with immense independent courage, was killed in battle with them on 9 July.

The double calamity – the loss of one of her finest generals at the hands of the Boxers, and the capture of one of the most strategic cities on the route to Peking at the hands of the foreigners, made Tz'u-hsi turn again in despair to the sober warnings of her southern viceroys. She was also exasperated with the continued resistance of the legations: 'There has been enough firing for the past few weeks to kill off every foreigner in China several times,' she remarked crossly. 'And so far there is hardly anything to show for it.'[12]

Between 14 and 18 July the legations, in the darkest depths of ignorance as to what was actually happening in the world outside their barricades, suddenly received many ambiguous, impossible and fragmentary notes from Chinese messengers bearing flags of truce. They were not written on official paper, were signed 'Prince Ch'ing and others' – hardly usual in Chinese ceremony – and begged the ministers, yet again, either to leave for Tientsin or to find refuge, taking ten people each, in the Tsungli Yamen. Whether Tz'u-hsi authorized these communications, or whether they came from Prince Ch'ing, who had been ousted from the Tsungli Yamen by the belligerent Prince Tuan, is not known; but they certainly reflected her desperation. On 18 July she ordered a cease-fire in the siege of the legations.

To her earlier telegrams abroad, she now added one to the Kaiser, apologizing for Ketteler's death, and others to the presidents of France and of the United States. She then proclaimed, with magnificent two-faced effrontery:

The reason for the fighting sprang from a disagreement between the people and the Christian converts. We could not but enter upon war when the forts at Taku were taken. Nevertheless, the Government is not willing lightly to break off the friendly relations which have existed. We have repeatedly issued edicts to protect the Ministers of the different countries. We have also ordered the missionaries in the various provinces to be protected. The fighting has not yet become extensive. There are many merchants of the various countries within our dominions. All alike should be protected. . . .

She ordered lists of foreign casualties and damaged property to be drawn up, and she once again condemned the Boxers. 'The vagabonds who have been burning houses, robbing, and killing the people these many days, have produced a state of chaos. . . .'[13]

In the legations the nerves of the beleaguered jangled at the awesome silence that now reigned. Soldiers, who only the day before had been murdering them, now became 'most friendly and came close up to our barricades to talk'.[14] One young Chinese even turned up to see the legation doctor to have a slashed ear dressed – he was a trumpeter in Sir Robert Hart's brass band. The Japanese were able to buy rifles from their attackers. Sir Robert Hart received official letters from the Tsungli Yamen. One asked where he was; the other what should be done about the customs dues in Nanking. Later he received another letter from the Yamen, suggesting he should write to the Powers and tell them all was well with the legations. He responded by ordering winter suits from his tailor, which duly arrived in Peking in October just as the cold season started. To the utter amazement of the besieged, gifts also poured in from the Yamen, with Tz'u-hsi's compliments and greetings. Though there is some doubt as to who actually sent them – it may have been Jung-lu – it would be typical of Tz'u-hsi's artlessness to send fine white flour and fifteen cartloads of melons and vegetables to the men, women and children whose slaughter she had advocated and encouraged only days before. But undeniably the most bitter news for the men under siege was a note received during the lull, on 28 July, from the British consul at Tientsin. Incoherent and muddled as it was, it seemed to inform the legations that the relief expedition had not yet started out. If an ingenious Chinese spy in the pay of the Japanese had not invented the most superb victorious Allied march on Peking, the foreigners there might have surrendered altogether, so total was their despair at the consul's news.

The peaceable decree of 18 July which had inaugurated the truce was wrung from a reluctant Tz'u-hsi; in it she had rejected both her heart's desire and her fears that had formed when the Boxer movement grew. Susceptible as she was to outside advice, it only needed one wilful persuader, and she would adopt the Boxers again. Prince Tuan and his degenerate cousins were discredited: their promises to sack the legations and hold the Taku-Tientsin-Peking road had proved empty. Jung-lu and Prince Ch'ing and other moderates in the Tsungli Yamen urged the policy she found humiliating, and after so many warlike utterances, quite simply embarrassing. So when Li Ping-heng, viceroy of Szechuan, a conservative patriot, arrived in Peking, in answer to her summons to the governors and viceroys, eager to carry out her commands to exterminate the foreigner, she needed no persuasion. On the night of 29 July, the cease-fire came to an end, and the legations were once more under siege.

Li Ping-heng had distinguished himself in the war against France over Annam in 1884 and was a model Chinese of the old school, haughty, scrupulously honest and utterly devoted to the Dragon

Throne. As one of China's abler officials he had been shamed in a way no Chinese of the old style could endure when at the request of the foreign powers he had been removed from the governorship of Shantung after the death of the two German missionaries there in 1898. His already developed xenophobia had therefore been confirmed, and he was now bent on avenging himself, and his country upon the foreigner.

On 26 July he told Tz'u-hsi, 'Only when one can fight can one negotiate for peace.'[15] In her magnanimity she immediately bestowed on him the highest honour of riding in the Forbidden City precincts and travelling in a sedan chair with two bearers. She also, more vitally, made him Deputy Commander of all the Northern Armies, thus yet again undermining Jung-lu's authority over his troops.

In the renewed spirit of war, two members of the Tsungli Yamen who had protested continually with great wisdom and courage against the use of the Boxers, were immediately arrested and decapitated. The last effort to raze the legations and murder their inhabitants began.

The rescuers' force, overwhelmed by the heat, at sixes and sevens with each other over the complexities of the plural alliances, were meanwhile still loitering in Tientsin. Nearly two months after the start of Seymour's original relief force, the now powerful international army had failed to press home a hundred miles to save the foreign community they knew were in the gravest danger. If Peking were taken, sharing China between so many countries would be so very problematic, they felt; above all they feared that they were too late already. But on 22 July the amassed soldiers heard from Sir Claude MacDonald that the victims were still alive. Still the lumbering machine of international co-operation could not rouse itself to action.

Tz'u-hsi's novel and underlying hope during the new assault at the end of July was that if all foreigners in the legations in Peking were massacred, there would be no witnesses to her misrule and she could then play, as she was so adept at doing, the helpless old woman at the mercy of unkind and unmanageable circumstance. Her hope might even have been realized, so dilatory was the relief force at Tientsin, if the British General Gaselee had not arrived there at the same time as the stern Li Ping-heng took over in Peking. Both were catalysts, and both precipitated the fatal clash.

Gaselee was a solid dignified and gallant Victorian, and he was utterly horrified to find that the besieged were still imperilled in

Peking and no one was making a dash to save them. Astutely, he transformed the problem of international co-operation into international rivalry. Soon, each country was competing in eagerness to be first into Peking, and by 4 August, twenty thousand troops were streaming out of Tientsin.

Either the sun beat down mercilessly on the expedition or summer rain swamped it as it made its painful way along the uprooted railway line, through country devastated already by the months of battle – between imperial troops and Boxers, between Boxers and foreign troops, between foreign troops and the Chinese. Twenty-five miles away it met the regular Chinese army and routed them. At news of the defeat on 6 August, Yu-lu, the moderate viceroy of Chihli, shot himself. On 9 August the fiery Li Ping-heng led out his men from Peking and engaged the Allies twice. Twice the Chinese were scattered. On 11 August, old fashioned patriot that he was, Li took poison in his disgrace and died. The next day the force pressed on, entering T'ung-chow, scene of the capture of Parkes and Loch forty years before. Ferociously they looted it, murdered the inhabitants and burned it down. One eye witness, the French novelist Pierre Loti, who accompanied the expedition as correspondent for *Le Figaro*, described the inferno of rotting corpses, of wells choked with suicides, of women who killed themselves rather than fall into the hands of the soldiers, of streams and fields fetid with gore.

The Forbidden City was in tumult. Tz'u-hsi frantically summoned her ministers: Jung-lu eight times and Prince Tuan five times in two days. Her grief found expression in savage, crazed acts of ridiculous futility. She ordered the executions of three more ministers who had advised caution in the council meetings, and had shown sympathy with foreign ideas and people – probably to silence their testimony both to the world and to her own miserable conscience. At the same time, she appointed Li Hung-chang plenipotentiary in charge of the peace negotiations. Ever since 18 June she had repeatedly begged him to come to Peking to advise her throughout, and he had continually, out of some sly instinct for survival, delayed. Though she informed the legations the peace terms would be negotiated by Li, she could not bring herself to release her quarry, and on 13 August a Krupp gun was fitted on to the wall of her Imperial City to bombard the legations in one last eternal night of siege. The alarm bell sounded twice in the legations that night, calling every single man or boy who could handle a weapon to the defence. The crude reinforcements, the amateur breastworks, the scanty ammunition unbelievably held once more, for the defenders' spirits were riding high: they had heard three days before from Gaselee that he was definitely on the way, and in the distance they could now hear the unmistakeable fire of Maxim guns – guns only the oncoming foreign expedition could be carrying.

The turmoil in the city, the month of disorganized and changing commands, the stream of conflicting edicts from the Throne, had demoralized both the Boxers and the Chinese soldiers defending Peking. The Boxers were volunteers and were not paid; the regulars' pay was weeks in arrears. On the night of the thirteenth, no resistance to the onslaught of the fourteen thousand Allied troops was offered, except at one gate where the Japanese fought their way through. As the conquerors of the capital of the Chinese empire marched through the streets, the inhabitants fled for their lives. Ponies, camels, carts and sedan chairs heaped with the few household belongings the fleeing Chinese could gather together fell pell-mell into the streets and made for the hills. Shutters went up, boards were nailed to the gates, shops closed as the force pressed forward to the legation quarter. Hundreds of women, in the ancient fashion of the Chinese, threw themselves down the wells of their houses; men committed suicide by hanging to avoid the dishonour of such a defeat.

On 14 August at 3 pm, British Rajputs and Sikhs crawled through the Water Gate under the Tartar City wall in the southern defence perimeter of the legations, and the central gates of the quarter were flung open to receive the rescuing British troops. General Gaselee, seeing two American ladies who had survived the ordeal, joined in the general emotional tears and delirium, and was so overcome he kissed one of them 'reverently on the forehead'.[16] But to the rescuers, the many non-combatants of the siege presented an extraordinary and disappointing aspect: 'To us they looked as if they had just come out of a bandbox. . . .'[17] The siege of the legations was over: in fifty-five days, sixty-six people had been killed, and a hundred and fifty wounded. In the death toll, the Chinese Christians who had toiled alongside the Europeans were not counted.

Amid the excitements, the services held to thank the Lord for their deliverance, the exchange of news and anecdotes, no one spared a thought for the beleaguered Northern Cathedral. Hundreds of men and women were still trapped inside, still shelled by the remains of Chinese Boxers and soldiers. Their stand had been heroic on a scale unknown in the legations: fourteen cannon had bombarded them, and there had been no lull at any point. Paul Henry, the young Breton who had organized the defence with such gallantry and inspiration, had been shot in the throat two weeks earlier. One hundred and sixty-six babies had died of famine or wounds. But the intrepid foreigners of the international force forgot about them. They were already engaged in organizing skirmishing parties to harry the bedraggled exodus of Chinese civilians, and had already trained their guns on the Imperial City itself. 'The sight of these guns,' cooed the American minister's wife, Mrs Conger, in a letter home, 'bombarding the Forbidden City gates, was wonderful to us. We were in a battle!'[18] It was therefore left to the Japanese – the only non-Christians in the party – who had been delayed by their battle at the gate of Peking, to rescue the nuns and children and Chinese left in the battered church. On 16 August they relieved the Northern Cathedral.

In the palace, when the foreign troops first entered the city, Tz'u-hsi was combing her hair. A shot rang through the window of her room and clattered on to the stone floor. 'We heard bullets flying, making noises like the cries of cats. . . . Another miaow was heard and a bullet flew in through the window. It dropped to the floor and bounced and rolled. We examined it closely.'[19] One of the Boxer princes rushed in and gasped the news: Peking had fallen. Tz'u-hsi, in tears, called a meeting of her ministers. Three came. At daybreak on 15 August she ordered the emperor, the young empress his wife, and the heir apparent to come with her. She stripped them of their jewels and finery, and disrobing herself of her rich embroideries, dressed herself in the rough blue cotton of a peasant. Pulling out her hair ornaments, and loosing her long black hair, she bound it up again in a cotton scarf; taking off her rings and her jade nail-protectors, she cut off her six-inch-long nails, badge of her caste, and, remembering to tell Li Lien-ying to bury her treasure in the remotest corner of the palace, she set forth.

The sickly emperor, even more stricken than her at the events he had in his unauthoritative way tried to prevent, followed her, and after him the boisterous and coarse teenage heir apparent whom she had appointed to humiliate him, and the pinched empress Lung-yü, her niece, whom she had forced upon him as his wife. She settled herself in the cart of one of the Imperial Clan, put the emperor in the cart of a general, and the empress in the cart of a commoner. The heir apparent rode on the shaft. As they began to draw away in these tumbrils, symbol of her shattered ambitions, the Pearl Concubine, the Kuang-hsu Emperor's spirited and pretty favourite, threw herself to her knees before Tz'u-hsi. She begged her to remain in the capital, not to flee the foreigner and bring everlasting dishonour to the dynasty and endanger the empire. Tz'u-hsi, seeing in the strong-willed concubine the shadow of her former self at the time when she too had been in her twenties, hearing in the Pearl Concubine's words that pride and dignity she had now so conclusively forfeited, flung a furious order to the eunuchs standing by. And they, in their terror at the horrors of the moment, obeyed. Before the very eyes of the emperor who it seems had loved her, the Pearl Concubine was thrown down the well and drowned in the north-east courtyard of the Forbidden City, and Tz'u-hsi's penitential procession rumbled on.[20]

Chapter Fourteen

A TYPHOON
IN THE APPLE TREE

'Before, I was just like a piece of pure jade,' wept Tz'u-hsi, 'every-one admired me for what I have done for my country. But [now] the jade has a flaw in it . . . and it will remain there for the rest of my life.'[1]

Through a country already swarming with refugees, mutinous soldiers and renegade Boxers, Tz'u-hsi's ignominious procession scrambled on. Even fears for her life could not however prevent her stopping at the summer palace and leaving her niece Lung-yü there with orders to pack up all the valuables and send them to Jehol. Then she hurried blindly on, making – with some Manchu instinct – for the safety of the dynasty's homeland beyond the Great Wall. Only a handful of eunuchs went with her, and they were too scared to think of equipping the Sacred Chariot with food or water or clothes. When she reached the Wall, after two days' ride, she had shared one plate of millet porridge with Kuang-hsu, that was all. A detachment of hungry, unpaid and angry Manchu guards had joined her; various Boxer leaders, including the ferrety Prince Tuan, had slunk shamefacedly into the line of carts; Li Lien-ying, Chief Eunuch, having made up his mind that neither the bandits nor the Allies nor the Boxers could murder her now, joined her on the third day. Once they had penetrated the Wall, and travelled north a little way beyond it, they found that further journey through the wild mountains of Manchuria would, at that time, be extremely dangerous. The Boxers had erupted in the three Manchurian provinces; the Russians, seeing in the havoc a chance to 'help' the Chinese to keep order, as they had done in Ili during the Moslem rising in 1871, had seized Manchuria and were in the process of establishing a Russian protectorate over it. So the Sacred Chariot wheeled south, to pass through the mountains of Shansi to the inland province of Shensi, where the great ancient capital of the T'ang dynasty, Hsian, would make a princely refuge.

At Huailai, north of the Wall, Tz'u-hsi ate her first meal for three days: two eggs and some 'stretched noodles' that were very much to her fancy. There, too, the magistrate gave her his dead wife's robes to wear, and she and Kuang-hsu had been able to exchange their carts for the more comfortable wicker sedans. Her Chinese hair-style, her flat shoes, her simple dress changed her markedly, and with her few missing teeth, stripped of all the paraphernalia that gave her rank, she must indeed have seemed an ordinary, small, plump old woman. Beside her, the emperor became more and more dishevelled: the hair on his shaved forehead sprouted, his face was dirty, his queue undone, his cotton clothes clung to his body in the humidity and heat. But once they entered the province of Shansi, their flight became more dignified: a cook was hired, officials were sent to gather tribute to finance the throne; the number of fugitives with them was swelling fast. A strong-minded, short-tongued, imperious forty-year-old Chinese, Ts'en Ch'un-husan, who impressed Tz'u-hsi with his masterliness, was put in charge of provisions. At one stage, a rogue soldier dashed in front of Tz'u-hsi's sedan and shot at her. Ts'en Ch'un-husan leapt to shield her. The bullet missed them both, and Ts'en then, in front of the empress who had ordered so many executions but had probably never seen one, lopped the soldier's head from his body with one stroke. Ts'en also immediately stopped the looting that had already broken out among the Bannermen and attempted to arrest the eunuchs' graft – they were already squabbling over the size of their share of the tribute money coming in – but over them Ts'en had to face a formidable opponent, the Chief Eunuch, Li Lien-ying. For although Tz'u-hsi accused Li Lien-ying of encouraging her to adopt the Boxers, the eunuch enjoyed her great favour.

Tz'u-hsi still clung to some tatters of her Boxer dreams. For just as her husband Hsien-feng's utterances in 1860 had become more and more warlike as he drew further from the capital, the belligerents, who preponderated in her entourage (for she had either left the moderates in Peking, or executed them in the last spasm of the siege) influenced her still. On 31 August she appointed Prince Tuan a Grand Councillor, urged the disseminated troops of the empire to rally and stand against further advance by the Allies, and defend the rear of the imperial procession. On 10 September, as that critical summer was mellowing, Tz'u-hsi and the Kuang-hsu Emperor arrived in Taiyuan, capital of the province of Shansi, where the harsh governor, Yü-hsien, received the court with much pomp, laying out the gold and silver plate ordered for the Ch'ien-lung Emperor's passage in 1775, which had never been used. Then the old patriot described to her how on 9 July 1900, in obedience to her declaration of war, he had rounded up forty-five Christian mission-aries and some of their converts, and executed them in the courtyard of his *yamen*. Such a massacre, authorized by an official in cold blood, was unusual, even at the acme of Boxer atrocities, and accounts for one fifth of the total missionary death toll during the troubles. The heir apparent, when he heard Yü-hsien's tale, seized one of the broadswords that did the deed and paraded up and down flourishing it and shouting curses on Christians, while Tz'u-hsi praised Yü-hsien happily. 'You did splendidly ...', she said, 'in ridding Shansi of the whole brood of foreign devils.'[2]

But even her old and rigid mind was unsettled by her novel circumstances. The dangers, the hunger, the hardships, and the humiliation had been eye-openers; the fall of Peking – twice in one lifetime – was trauma enough. But, as she puffed consolingly on her water-pipe at each halt in her flight and meditated on her condition, there was one revelation that far exceeded all the others: for the first time in fifty years she saw the state in which the Chinese people lived. The squalor, poverty and sheer misery of her subjects had been closed territory during all her years of power. She now reproached her councillors for not painting it to her in its true light, and realized, probably for the first time, that improvements and reforms were not intellectual word games but vital and urgent necessities.

'Meanwhile the once crowded Peking is a desert,' wrote Sir Robert Hart, who had survived the siege to find that all the customs' archives and records, his life's work, his own diaries and belongings had been burned, 'and the first few days of foreign occupation have seen much that need not have occurred and will certainly be regretted.'[3] For in the abandoned city of Peking, the Allies' rickety collaboration had expired in a frenzy of revenge and plunder. The city had been split into areas, each administered by a different power, and soon ugly squabbles broke out about the lion's share of the loot. When the soldiers discovered that their prize had slipped through their fingers, that the court who had brought this upon them had escaped, they exploded in fury. Skirmishing parties tore down the streets stealing furs and silks and jewellery, jade and food; foreign soldiers penetrated the Forbidden City for the first time, looting, and burning what they could not loot. All Tz'u-hsi's theatre scenery and costumes went up in flames. Even the missionaries and the diplomats joined in: the wife of the British minister, Lady MacDonald, was seen scavenging her way with the worst.

Until the Russians had prevailed on the other Allies to desist, the Forbidden City had been shelled. In return for its kind offices, Russia hoped to wrest Manchuria from China, as in 1860 Vladivostok had been the prize of trifling diplomatic assistance. The Russians also suggested that the other powers should follow their example and retreat to Tientsin. When no one obliged, they returned to Peking themselves. Although they had protected the Forbidden City for their own ends, they plundered along with the rest elsewhere. The young empress Lung-yü's packing had not been very effective, for Morrison of *The Times* reported on 24 September: 'The systematic denudation of the summer palace by the Russians had been completed. Every article of value is packed and labelled.'[4]

Tz'u-hsi grieved bitterly when she heard of her loss, but what truly horrified her was that the foreigners had intruded on her intimate apartments, had lain down on her bed and scrawled graffiti on her walls; that the Americans had quartered their troops at the Temple of Agriculture, over which the Stars and Stripes now flew bravely; that the British had occupied the Temple of Heaven, desecrating both those hallowed shrines; and that when the British decided to bring the railway up to the main gate of the Tartar City itself, they laid the tracks straight through an old and sacred cemetery.

For the besieged the aftermath was disappointingly flat and many of the young who had shown nerves of steel at the time were prostrated afterwards. There was a celebration banquet, but it was postponed many times, and when it was finally held, 'there was nothing in the way of speeches, etc. to distinguish it. . . .'[5] There was a triumphal march through the Forbidden City a fortnight after the relief, but there was hardly anyone in Peking to witness it except the occupying forces themselves. And there were a few exemplary executions of Boxers in public.

But later, after the German relief force arrived (at the end of September), the punitive parties became more frequent. The Kaiser had exhorted his men 'just as the Huns one thousand years ago, under the leadership of Attila, gained a reputation by virtue of which they still live in historical tradition, so may the name of Germany become known in such a manner in China'.[6] The latterday Attila, Field-Marshal von Waldersee, admitted that 'our policy, apart from the punishment of the Chinese, followed no definite purpose. The Kaiser had, it is true, vague ideas in regard to the partition of China. The chief factor was, however, the desire to play a part in world politics. . . .'[7] This desire led Attila to ransack and burn, with the French and the British, the town of Paoting, scene of the massacre of railway officials, and to pursue throughout the spring of 1901 (that is, during and after the peace negotiations), the Chinese troops who

213

garrisoned Chihli and Shansi and prevented access to the court in Hsian. All these were, many felt, pretty tame reprisals: for the real quarry, Tz'u-hsi herself, had escaped.

If deserted Peking was frustrating for the soldiers, it was doubly so for the diplomats. The court had fled, there was no government; and until the now aged Li Hung-chang made up his mind to obey Tz'u-hsi's *twelfth* decree ordering him to Peking, there was only Prince Ch'ing as negotiator, and he was at best a muddler. Jung-lu had been appointed plenipotentiary by Tz'u-hsi, but as the nominal commander of the Chinese army, he was *persona non grata* to the Allies and was prudently lying low in the country. Ch'ung-ch'i, Tz'u-hsi's fourth nominee as negotiator, the cold-hearted old Mongol who had weathered the death of his daughter the empress Alute so well, and who, at the age of seventy-one, had fought alongside the Boxers in the assault on the Northern Cathedral, had committed suicide by hanging himself twelve days after Peking fell. His son and many of his family had followed suit.

The Chinese were dilatory about the negotiations, but the foreign powers were anxious and fretful. 'There would seem to be no choice between three courses – partition, change of dynasty, or patching up the present Manchu rule', summed up the scrupulous Sir Robert Hart, and added 'the present dynasty is far from effete, its mandate runs through all China.'8 Though the Inspector-General in his loyalty exaggerated the strength of the Ch'ing mandate, the Powers did find, after all their cries of vengeance on Tz'u-hsi, and much menacing and bland talk about partition, that it was rather more complicated. The republicans in the south in 1900 were not yet organized enough to rule the country and the reformers had no figurehead. The Kuang-hsu Emperor had had all the fight kicked out of him by the *coup* of 1898, and again by the recent catastrophe and the death of his favourite. Some of K'ang Yu-wei's followers had seized on the disorder caused by the Boxers to form a Protect the Emperor Society on the Yangstze in Hankow and plot the emperor's restoration, but Chang Chih-tung, the viceroy, reneged on his original sympathies with the reform movement and flushed out the conspirators. Their attempt had fizzled out without drawing even so much as a cough from the emaciated emperor. In 1900, the Powers therefore fell back on Tz'u-hsi as the only leader of character who commanded enough obedience and respect to be restored to the Dragon Throne.

Li Hung-chang, when he finally and reluctantly arrived at Taku on 18 September under the protection of his long fast friends the

Russians, discovered that the Powers had decided, as the southern viceroys themselves had done, to consider the recent troubles a rebellion against the legitimate authority of the Throne. It was a diplomatic manoeuvre, transforming the Boxer uprising into the misnamed Boxer Rebellion. On this basis, if Tz'u-hsi co-operated in her former colleagues' punishments, her rôle in the 'rebellion' could be overlooked. Grudgingly, Tz'u-hsi acquiesced, and from the safety of Taiyuan degraded some of the Boxer leaders to commoners, and handed others, including Prince Tuan, over to the Imperial Clan Court for punishment.

Although the Powers were by no means satisfied by this small gesture, they laboriously continued to negotiate the peace proposals in Peking. At the beginning of October the French produced a draft plan, and by 22 December all eleven of the impatient Powers had signed the Collective Note based on the French proposals. The Note contained no mention of the threatened partition of China, or of personal punishment for Tz'u-hsi, or of the restoration of the emperor. Instead, it declared that the Taku forts were to be destroyed, the road to Peking from the sea occupied at strategic points by foreign troops, the legation quarter fortified and garrisoned, the import of arms forbidden; any high official in whose jurisdiction an anti-foreign disturbance occurred was to be 'immediately recalled, without the possibility of being given new posts or of receiving fresh honours'; that the commercial treaties were to be altered according to the Powers' wishes. The old abuses remained, particularly extraterritoriality, and the difficulties of China were not reduced, but exacerbated. Militarily, commercially and domestically, the Powers could therefore command China's affairs. As the republican Sun Yat-sen later commented: 'China's position was worse than a colony. She was at the mercy of the powers, yet there was no one paternalistic colonial power to whom she could turn for mercy.'[9]

Above all China was to pay 'an equitable indemnity'. In May 1901 this blood price was fixed at 450 million taels, or £67 million. The sum was to be paid back by 1940 and was secured on the revenue of the customs, thus transforming the Chinese bureau into 'a debt collecting agency for the powers'. Thus would proper reparation be made for the 'crimes unprecedented in human history, crimes against the law of nations, against the laws of humanity, and against civilisation'[10] which China had committed: two hundred and forty-seven missionary dead, sixty-six dead at the legations and thirty thousand Chinese converts.

But Tz'u-hsi had feared for her life and for the dynasty, and both were safe; she had fled to Hsian, she had ordered several barriers of troops to hold the provinces behind her and prevent the punitive expeditions that at least one power – the Germans – had certainly planned. Although Li Hung-chang had begged her to return to the capital and speed up the discussions, she had refused, for she had been too frightened that once there, the Allies would seize her as a war criminal. But now, hearing of their surprising magnanimity towards her personally, and prompted eagerly by Li Hung-chang, she ignored the stupidity and shortcomings of the Note, and accepted it in all her egotism by imperial decree from Hsian on 27 October.

Li Hung-chang, having sealed with his name the last of the series of crippling agreements with foreign powers of over thirty years' diplomacy, collapsed in Peking. He was seventy-seven, white-haired and white-bearded, and his huge frame had shrunk with age, for he was partly paralysed in both legs and could only walk to the negotiating table supported by his servants. By 7 November he was dead, and Tz'u-hsi ordered that a shrine should be built in Peking in his honour.

Tz'u-hsi baulked however at the Powers' demands for punishment of the Boxer leaders, her friends. But on 11 November Jung-lu, old and ill, joined her in Hsian and silenced her remonstrations. For the sake of a few Manchu princes, she could not risk the peace of the empire again. At the beginning of February, Prince Chuang was sent the 'silken cord' and permitted by the Throne to hang himself; Prince Tuan himself and his younger brother were exiled, and delighted to be spared they trotted off happily to banishment in Ili. The fantasy of Tsai-lien, his elder brother, who had played at beggars in Peking, came true: he was to remain a commoner for life. Yü-hsien, governor of Shansi and ogre of Christians, was humiliatingly executed on 22 February 1901. But Tung Fu-hsiang's quarrelsome Moslems might rise in revolt if they lost their independent and beloved freebooting general: all the court could do was deprive Tung of his ranks and offices.

Once Tz'u-hsi's hawks had been removed, she became truly contrite. She also probably began to believe the story she had invented to clear herself: that 'the Boxers, after bringing about a state of war, took possession of our capital and dominated the very throne itself. The decrees issued at that time were the work of wicked princes and ministers of state, who, taking advantage of the chaotic conditions of affairs, did not hesitate to issue documents under the imperial seal, which were quite contrary to our wishes.'[11] She ordered history to be rewritten: all her edicts and decrees favouring the Boxers were expunged from the annals of the dynasty.

Tz'u-hsi also became somewhat more affable with the emperor. One official noted that she began to include him in discussions, and to ask after his health. However, Reginald Johnston, the English tutor of P'u-i, Kuang-hsu's successor, observed that Kuang-hsu's apartments at the summer palace had bricked-in windows and doors, so that he could neither see over the lake, nor leave freely except through one exit left open.

Nevertheless, on 8 January 1901, Tz'u-hsi issued in the emperor's name a demand for reform closely modelled on his 1898 policies:

We have today received Her Majesty's orders and learn she is now throroughly bent on radical reform. Nevertheless . . . there is to be no talk of reaction or revolution. . . . The teachings handed down to us by our sacred ancestors are really the same as those upon which the wealth and power of European countries have been based, but China has hitherto failed to realise this and has been content to acquire the rudiments of European languages or technicalities, while changing nothing of the ancient habits of inefficiency and deep rooted corruption.[12]

She then ordered vigorous officials like Chang Chih-tung, Yuan Shih-k'ai, Liu K'un-yi and Ts'en Ch'un-hsuan, now governor of Shansi, as well as her henchmen Prince Ch'ing and Jung-lu, to report their proposals for reform to an entirely new Board of State Affairs.

If, instead of maiming China with the exorbitant indemnity, the Powers had been able to co-operate with Tz'u-hsi over the reforms, both financial and other, her new drive to alter China's structure might have been more successful. For she did give evidence, at the late age of sixty-six, of an astonishing change of political heart. On 2 October 1901, she ordered that the viceroys' proposals should be implemented at once.

On 20 October, convinced of the forgiveness of the Powers, Tz'u-hsi left Hsian in a blaze of pageantry – with silk banners, painted lanterns, and flowers and branches held high. In Peking all the clauses of the Collective Note had been met, and consequently Peking and Chihli had been evacuated, except for the posts which it had been agreed would be held by foreign soldiers. Tz'u-hsi nevertheless travelled slowly north-east, for she had developed a taste for tourism and showed her usual insatiable curiosity about the landscapes and the temples and the monuments they passed. At Kaifeng, on the Yellow River, she spent a few weeks: it was 'as pleasant as the hunting trips of the Han dynasty, when the soldiers carried feathered insignia, and danced for the Court, or when they feasted in Ch'ang Yang Palace'.[13]

When she anxiously consulted her astrologers for an exact hour and day propitious for her momentous re-entry to her capital, they informed her that 7 January 1902, at 2 pm precisely, was of good omen. On 30 November, shriving herself of the last clinging taint of Boxerism, she banished from the palace and degraded to commoner status the heir apparent, who had somehow survived to plague the court by his brawls and his scrapes all this time. From Kaifeng the imperial procession began toiling north. Miles of pack animals, horses, mules, carts, litters loaded with the spoil of over a year in Hsian that Tz'u-hsi, even in the most rigorous of self-mortifying moods could somehow not refuse, laboured through the frosty winter towards Peking. 'Banners flew in the air,' wrote one official. 'Everyone was silent. The only sounds were the steps of the horses and grinding of the wheels of the carts in the sand. A city of silk stretched for miles along the river bank and the accoutrements of one thousand soldiers flashed like fire. It was like ten thousand peach trees in full bloom in the spring time.'[14] Two hundred and fifty miles further north, at Chengting, in Chihli, the Belgians offered her the hospitality of their newly built railway. Four freight trains preceded her with luggage, and she followed in a carriage fitted with a throne and upholstered in imperial yellow. At Fengtai she exchanged the Belgian train for the newly constructed British rail. It was her first train journey, and the first time Chinese crowds had been able to stare at the Son of Heaven, his 'mother' and his empress and concubines and eunuchs. In her curiously composed and naïve way, Tz'u-hsi did not flinch at this sudden exposure. Instead, she chatted and smoked in her compartment with the Chief Eunuch, and let her ladies run about giddily on the platform before the marvelling spectators. Once only she flashed an order with her famous determination. Yuan Shih-k'ai had found the carriage reserved for officials a trifle cramped, so had ordered another one to be hitched to the train. Tz'u-hsi, noticing the manoeuvre and asking why, forbade it, and Yuan Shih-k'ai was confined to quarters. At the South Gate of the Chinese City, the auspicious and traditional entrance for the Son of Heaven, Tz'u-hsi and the imperial retinue exchanged the train for a peacock-feather-trimmed chair, and travelled north to the gate of the Tartar City, where Kuang-hsu, who had preceded her, knelt on the pathways strewn with imperial yellow sand and greeted her.

'Wearing very voyant embroideries,'[15] Tz'u-hsi stood stock still, ignoring her attendants who fussed to escort her to her chair. For on the charred wall of the Tartar City, where only a year and a half ago her soldiers had battled with the legations, the foreign community stood to watch her re-entry into Peking. She looked up at them, and her old and wrinkled face broke into a small smile, revealing her blackened and missing teeth, as she raised her hands together under her chin, and bowed gently several times to them, in the Chinese fashion, until from the men and women, crowded above to catch a glimpse of the monstrous dowager, there came a spontaneous burst of applause.

Promptly eight days later, Tz'u-hsi received the diplomatic body in the Forbidden City. She sat on a large throne, with fans of peacock feathers behind her and piles of propitious fruit. Kuang-hsu sat on a smaller throne at her left side, the place of honour in China. A few days later, she received the ladies of the foreign community. During these audiences, she murmured her replies to Prince Ch'ing, who knelt before her, and he conveyed them to her visitors. But she also inaugurated more informal banquets, at which she appeared and talked to the ladies. The feast was at first laid out on brilliant scarlet oilcloth, with mounds of auspicious apples and pomegranates as decoration. When she learned later foreign opinon of such a table, she was deeply mortified: on all subsequent occasions, white linen cloths, champagne, silver and cut glass vases of flowers were produced. In the summer the ladies were rowed by eunuchs across the lake of the summer palace to a picnic on the island. Tz'u-hsi was considerate and well-informed: she congratulated one on the birth of a grandchild, or offered confolences on the death of a parent.

She lavished gifts on her guests: *jui* (may-your-wish-come-true) sceptres of jade, rings of gold and pearl, ornaments of jade, bales of silk were presented at all audiences, and afterwards she sent the ministers' wives and their friends her own Pekingese – doctored, so they could not breed from them. She dispatched feasts in towering baskets to their private houses. She was overwhelmed therefore when the legations requested that such generous gifts should cease. Often, she wept, taking one of the foreign lady's hands in hers: 'I deeply regret all that occurred during those troublous times. The Boxers for a time overpowered the government, and even brought their guns in and placed them on the walls of the palace. Such a thing shall never occur again.'[16]

Tz'u-hsi was too rigid, too narrowly indoctrinated for this apparent transformation to be sincere or profound. Once, for instance, she offered to show her guests her private apartments in the Forbidden City. They filed through with alacrity, commenting excitedly on her furniture and ornaments. Everything, however, had been changed: Tz'u-hsi's attendants had spent a day, and a great deal of money, changing the furniture and silk hangings, so that no foreigner should know her real taste, or her intimate surroundings.

Nevertheless, just as Tz'u-hsi loved seeding and paring the ornamental gourds in her gardens, so she did now begin to whittle at her heritage in earnest. She decreed that Manchus and Chinese could now marry; that footbinding was illegal, that the several time-honoured sinecures abolished in 1898 were abolished once more, that the eight-legged essay was to be shelved, and that history, geography and sciences would be examined as well as the Confucian classics; that Chinese and Manchus of the Imperial Clan were to study in the West and in Japan; that state schools were to be opened for students of all ages, and even for girls, and that the pupils were to be taught military skills. In 1903 she contravened all Confucian prejudice and established a Ministry of Commerce to encourage and organize business and industry; in 1905, to give impetus to the modern schools, she abolished the traditional exams altogether. They had been held since AD 622 every two or three years in exactly the same way on exactly the same subjects. She streamlined the bureaucracy, eliminating more sinecures, and promoting the boards of government into fully-fledged ministries on Western lines. She abolished the Tsungli Yamen, replacing it with the Wai-wu-pu, or Ministry of Foreign Affairs. Catching a whiff of the strong nationalist China-of-the-Chinese feeling blowing up in the south, she recovered the customs, so long a foreign-administered concern and ordered that it be run by Chinese. The Inspector-General, Sir Robert Hart, took the news calmly, but admitted, as he helped with the transition, that it was 'not a pleasant winding-up of fifty years' service'.[17] He tried to resign and take his leave to return to his home in England, and to his native Ireland, the country he had visited only once since he had arrived in China in 1854. 'I should prefer to go to Heaven . . . via London rather than direct' he had written.[18] But business compelled him to stay, and he died in China on 20 September 1911.

In 1906, when Tz'u-hsi converted the customs to Chinese hands, she also began to reorganize the legal system, abolishing confession by torture and death by the slicing process and other penalties to bring Chinese law in line with other countries, so that the oppression of extraterritoriality could be lifted. That same year, she outlined a ten-year plan for the suppression of opium, by raising the taxes enormously, and by giving farmers who grew the drug compensation and advice on the planting of new crops. She banned its import, and won, for the first time, Britain's co-operation. But she added a human touch of her own, which shows perhaps her own intermittent use of the drug: that people over the age of sixty were allowed a pipe or two for consolation. Above all, she sent a commission of enquiry to Europe, the United States and Japan, of eminent officials including a Manchu member of the Imperial Clan, to investigate the workings of *constitutional* government. As the commission was about to step on the train at Peking, a young revolutionary hurled a homemade bomb at them. It exploded in his hand, blew him to pieces and injured two of the party. But the commission persevered, and set out a few months later. When they returned and reported, Tz'u-hsi announced, in 1906, unlikely as it may seem, that China would have a constitutional monarchy.

The desperate gesture of the young revolutionary was prophetic: for although Tz'u-hsi's reform decrees make a formidable and impressive list, many were blighted, many mere ornamental gourds. For China was almost bankrupt. The swingeing Boxer indemnity had been piled on top of the rash of loans of 1898, and they in turn on top of the crippling debt of the Sino-Japanese war, which in turn had merely followed decades of mismanagement and penury since the Tao-kuang Emperor had died in 1851, leaving the treasury drained. In 1911, when the first revolution brought the dynasty crashing down, and payments defaulted, the foreign debt stood at eight hundred to one thousand million taels. During this last spurt of her life, Tz'u-hsi's plans, particularly her educational reforms, needed money, and were therefore dead letters; in other matters, the reforms were emperor's new clothes: the 'constitution' for instance, which was anyway scheduled for 1917, reserved certain absolute rights for the emperor, the right to summon and dismiss a national assembly at will, and supreme command of the legislative, executive and military forces. Only the opium campaign showed signs of success, for it caught the rising tide of popular patriotism in the south. But that same tide was swelling with students returned from abroad, intoxicated with revolutionary, or at least republican dreams, and it was a tide that believed in the revival of a proud, Chinese nation, not in a two-thousand-year-old imperial fossil administered by usurpers from Manchuria.

After Jung-lu, suffering from a recurrence of his asthma, died in April 1903, thanking the empress his mistress for her bounty towards him for nearly fifty years, Tz'u-hsi turned to the lacklustre Prince Ch'ing and made him head of the Grand Council. Ts'en Ch'un-hsuan, now viceroy of the provinces of Kwangtung and Kwangsi, in audience with the emperor and Tz'u-hsi, accused Prince Ch'ing, in his blunt and courageous way, of flagrant corruption, of accepting bribes and selling offices, and questioned the sincerity of Tz'u-hsi's reforms when she retained such notorious men. She refuted him angrily, but he continued to reproach her, teling her brutally that her reforms were null and void. Whereupon she wept, of course. 'Politics', he told her, 'are like planting a tree. Trimming the leaves and the twigs is all very well, but the root is the government in Peking. If the people digging the soil there are corrupt, the root is rotten, and so although I can trim the leaves and the twigs (the provinces) and it looks pretty, when the wind blows the tree will fall, and when the tree falls, what point is there to the pretty twigs and leaves?'[19]

But Tz'u-hsi could not bring herself to dismiss the seventy-year-old prince, and so she confirmed the opinion, bruited fiercely in Japan, and in the southern and Yangstze provinces by men like Sun Yat-sen, that the Ch'ing mandate was running out. For the four headings of Sun's revolutionary manifesto were 'Restore China' (to the Chinese), 'Establish the Republic'. 'Equalize Land Ownership'; and above all, 'Drive out the Tartars', for 'the extreme cruelties and tyrannies of the Manchu government have now reached their limit'.[20] 'It would be easier to change a tiger into a lamb,' wrote one of Sun's followers. '[For] the hundreds of thousands of office-holding parasites of China today have a political power over the Throne which will never again even allow the beginning of such a reform.... Deceptions and false pretences will continue to be advanced by Peking.'[21]

Also Tz'u-hsi's old enemies the foreigners were double-crossing her in the south. For while foreign interests in 1901 had favoured a restoration of the Ch'ing, it had been a measure chosen *faute de mieux*. Now they were investigating the new republicans with some curiosity, hoping – quite wrongly as it transpired – to get more change from them, by offering them the protection of extraterritoriality and political asylum. In 1903, for instance, the editors of the rabidly anti-Manchu newspaper *Supao*, printed in Shanghai, were arrested. By Chinese law, their heads were forfeit, but the diplomatic body intervened and they received sentences of two and three years, which, to the further exasperation of the Chinese, they served in the jail of the foreign settlements in Shanghai.[22]

Truly it seemed the Mandate of Heaven had expired. From 1904 the Russians fought the Japanese on Chinese territory for the possession of Manchuria, and China could do nothing. Tz'u-hsi's reforms had been designed as dams, but in the Chinese saying 'a typhoon can begin at the top of an apple tree and an ant hole is large enough to cause a dyke to fall', and the flood waters were rushing through, for China was riddled with holes. Heaven even frowned on Tz'u-hsi's immaculate appearance and struck her a personal blow. On the right side, her face became slightly paralysed, the mouth drooped, and was occasionally convulsed with an uncontrollable tic. If she noticed an official staring at her collapsed physiognomy, or if a spasm seized her in company, she flew into a violent and humiliated rage.

Yet otherwise she lived, a stiff and decorated doll in a window pane, her former life of ritual and luxury, divorced from the realities she had so frighteningly glimpsed. She boated on the lake amid the lotus at the summer palace; she picknicked in her grottoes and on her marble boat; she gossiped with her eunuchs and her ladies. She was revealed the wonders of photography and enjoyed posing dressed up as the Goddess of Mercy, Kuan-yin. She indulged her new appetite for tourism, and even for trains, and travelled to the Western Tombs, and to the Eastern Tombs, where she inspected her own mausoleum with great interest. She was delighted that she outlived Queen Victoria, and compared herself complacently to the British ruler.

Tz'u-hsi also resumed her former vices. Kuang-hsu was tormented by neglectful and insolent eunuchs; when he complained that his food was stale and unpalatable, nothing was done; when electric light was installed in 1903, his apartments alone were omitted; when he saw Tz'u-hsi being photographed he confided sadly to Te-ling: 'I see Her Majesty having so many photographs taken and even the eunuchs are in the picture.... If it is not risky for us we might try it some day.... But I think we must be very careful.'[23] There are no extant snapshots of Kuang-hsu.

In order to trick the malevolent spirits who had prevented her sixtieth birthday celebrations in 1894, she held her seventieth birthday a year early, in 1903, and received the ostentatious congratulations of her subjects amid an orgy of feasting and theatricals and religious ceremonies. Her seventy-third birthday (seventy-fourth by Chinese reckoning) the last of her life, was no less splendid. Yuan Shih-k'ai, her viceroy in Chihli, presented her with two fox-fur-lined gowns, two pearl and filigree phoenixes, a piece of calambac studded with gems, and a six-foot-long branch of coral. The Dalai Lama flattered her fervent Buddhism and came to pay homage to the Dragon Throne in person, reviving memories of sweeter days. But in 1907, Tz'u-hsi had suffered a slight stroke; the following year her birthday festivities were too much even for her stout frame and she was attacked by dysentery. Simultaneously Kuang-hsu took to his bed. His many complicated maladies, kept at bay over ten years now by herbal treatments, massage and rest, were finally beginning to overwhelm him. And, although the Dalai Lama had rushed a sacred image of the Buddha to Tz'u-hsi's tomb to ward off malignant spirits, Tz'u-hsi knew that she too was dying. On 13 November she rallied from her bed of dysentery to appoint the third child emperor of her life: P'u-i (son of Prince Ch'un II), two years old. He became emperor of China, the last to ascend the Dragon Throne, and after thirty-three years, ritual heir to the T'ung-chih Emperor, Tz'u-hsi's son, whose spirit had remained unattended and unworshipped all this time. The new emperor's mother was Jung-lu's daughter, and thus did Tz'u-hsi, placing Jung-lu's flesh and blood on the throne, pay tribute to her lifelong friend. P'u-i's grandfather, Prince Ch'un, had been married to Tz'u-hsi's sister, but his father Prince Ch'un II was the son of a concubine, so that by blood he was not related to Tz'u-hsi. In spite of this, she appointed him Regent during the minority of P'u-i. She did not altogether leave out her family, but recommended that the child emperor and the Regent Prince Ch'un II should consult the empress Lung-yü, her niece: 'should there arise any question of vital importance . . . the Regent shall apply in person to her for instructions, and act accordingly'.[24]

On 14 November Tz'u-hsi, happy at the dynastic arrangements which had always been her playground, and delighted that she had dashed the ambitions of Yuan Shih-k'ai and Prince Ch'ing who had hoped together to rule for the latter's son, was well enough recovered to visit the feverish Kuang-hsu. In one last gesture of defiance to the woman who had held his life in mortgage over thirty years, the emperor refused to be moved to the Palace of Peaceful Longevity, or to wear the Robes of Longevity prescribed for the Son of Heaven on his deathbed. He lay back on his imperial satin cushions, and with his last strength, scribbled a curse – if gossip can be believed – on Tz'u-hsi, who had put him on the throne, broken his power and murdered his favourite, and on Yuan Shih-k'ai who had betrayed him to serve her. 'We were the second son of Prince Ch'un when the Empress Dowager selected us for the Throne. She has always hated Us, but for Our misery of the past ten years, Yuan

Shih-k'ai is responsible, and one other. When the time comes I desire that Yuan be summarily beheaded.'25 The 'one other' may have been Jung-lu, or even maybe Li Lien-ying. Then, in the presence of Tz'u-hsi, his empress Lung-yü and the Lustrous Concubine, the Kuang-hsu Emperor died, at the Hour of the Cock (5–7 pm) on 14 November 1908.

By the next morning, Tz'u-hsi's robust frame had recovered enough to rise at dawn and hold a Grand Council to discuss the consequences of the Kuang-hsu's Emperor's death. At lunch, frail as her insides were, she could not resist a huge helping of her favourite dish of clotted cream and crab-apples. Seized with dysentery again, she fainted. She was carried to her apartments, dressed in the Robes of Longevity. Weakly she dictated her valediction to the empire over whose disintegration she had presided for nearly fifty years. In it she recalled the death of her lord the Hsien-feng Emperor; the great rebellions like that of the Taipings that had ravaged China for twenty years; her co-regency with Niuhuru and the comparatively settled and successful years of the T'ung-chih Restoration; then the time in 1898 when 'once again it became my inevitable and bounden duty to assume the Regency'; and the proclamation of the constitution. But Tz'u-hsi skated over the fateful impact of the West upon China, the single most important feature of her reign; and she did not mention the Boxer uprising, in which for the first time her personal identity and desires found concrete expression. 'Looking back upon the memories of these last fifty years,' she said, 'I perceive how calamities from within and aggression from without have come upon us in relentless succession, and that my life has never enjoyed a moment's respite from anxiety.'26

Turning her face towards the south and straightening her limbs as was proper, Tz'u-hsi died, on 15 November at the Hour of the Goat (1–3 pm). The coincidence of the deaths of the tragic Kuang-hsu and the tyrannical woman who had adopted him as her son was indeed remarkable. A Dr Chu, who practised Western medicine, was called in to tend Kuang-hsu's last illness when Chinese herbal remedies failed. His examination was still a charade, during which both Kuang-hsu and Tz'u-hsi sat enthroned, while the doctor, forbidden to touch the august body, knelt and listened to Tz'u-hsi's detailed account of the failing emperor's symptoms. But he was nevertheless able to diagnose Bright's disease of the kidneys, for Kuang-hsu had chronic incontinence, brought on by the slightest emotional strain, sudden noise, or an unexpected gesture; he had terrible backache; his lungs had deteriorated – twelve years before, a different doctor,

Chen Liang-fang, had diagnosed a condition already a decade old even then; his pulse was feeble; his mental condition severely depressed. Dr Chu had ordered internal and external medicines to be made up at the foreign hospital; and after several visits during the course of a month, the pain in the spine and the incontinence were both much relieved. But Dr Chu then reported how in September, when Tz'u-hsi had herself fallen ill, he saw Kuang-hsu for the last time, writhing in an agony of stomach cramps, on his bed: 'He could not sleep, he could not urinate, his heart beat grew faster, his face burned purple, his tongue had turned yellow – symptoms which', the doctor cryptically added, 'had no connection with his previous illness.' That was Dr Chu's last visit, three days before the emperor died. Leaving the imperial apartments, the doctor noticed that the dust was standing deep on the furniture: the eunuchs had already stopped caring for their master.[27]

Tz'u-hsi, in some last throe of spite, fearing that if Kuang-hsu survived, the truth would out and her name be blackened for ever, might have had him poisoned by eunuchs, as Dr Chu so unmistakeably implies; alternatively, Yuan Shih-k'ai, fearing for his life if Kuang-hsu, whom he had betrayed, survived the Empress Dowager whom he had served, bribed the eunuchs to murder him – for a rumoured thirty-three thousand dollars. Yet again, the eunuchs themselves, fearing for their fat privileges if the reforming emperor ruled once again, dispatched him themselves. Kuang-hsu had however always been a delicate child, from the moment when as a three-year-old baby he was brought wailing into the palace, and he had been seriously ill for several years with several unpleasant physical disorders, as well as his breakdown in 1898. Yet in 1905, Hart had reported: 'The emperor was looking very bright and healthy: I never before saw him looking so well, but instead of thirty-four, he has the face and figure of sixteen.' Tz'u-hsi was however looking old and tired.[28]

In essence, there is no evidence except gossip and conjecture to point to Tz'u-hsi's last possible crime; and in many ways she seems too commonplace, her spite too mean, to have connived at all the deaths history had lain at her door. So the Kuang-hsu Emperor became yet another unquiet wraith to jostle in the crowd who now haunted her tomb.

The court astrologers whom Tz'u-hsi had always consulted burned offerings and star-gazed in order to find a year, a day and an hour auspicious for her burial in the magnificent mausoleum she had constructed at much expense according to the same astrologers' geomantic oracles. Finally, after her catafalque had waited nearly a year, the resplendent funeral procession swayed out of the Forbidden City. Officials in mourning robes of white, Buddhist priests and lamas in saffron with crested hair-cuts, eunuchs by the thousand, camels, llamas, musicians playing dolefully, the Dalai Lama himself, everyone garlanded with flowers walking under state umbrellas, cavalry with their banners flying, streamed towards the Eastern Tombs. For four days the funeral procession travelled through the countryside while the people burned paper money, paper attendants, paper food and paper clothes to conjure guardian spirits and riches for Tz'u-hsi to take with her into the tomb.

Li Lien-ying, his big frame sagging with age, his face deeply lined, followed the bier in tears. On 9 November at 7 am precisely, Tz'u-hsi was sealed within the vault where her husband Hsien-feng and Niuhuru, her co-regent for twenty years, were also interred. Tz'u-hsi's funeral cost the nation one and a half million taels, the Kuang-hsu Emperor's a third of that sum. Her personal fortune was put at £22 million in gold and silver bullion. She had volunteered none of it towards the Boxer indemnity.[29]

EPILOGUE

The Ch'ing dynasty survived Tz'u-hsi a bare three years. Republicanism in the south flared into revolution: from Wuchang in Hupeh, the first city to fall to the 'rebels', the movement quickened and spread. Yuan Shih-k'ai, banished from Peking and stripped of office by Kuang-hsu's brother the Regent, was now the only efficient leader of the only army loyal to the Ch'ing in the north, and was recalled to defend the dynasty. For the second time in his life he betrayed that trust, and joined the revolt. At Nanking, Sun Yat-sen was declared President of the Chinese Republic, but in the face of Yuan's superior military strength, he resigned and Yuan took his place. The child emperor announced from the Dragon Throne that 'the will of providence is clear and the people's wishes are plain'[1] and abdicated on 12 February 1912. Yuan Shih-k'ai moved into the Imperial City, but permitted the court to live on in the Forbidden City in all its splendour. For the third time, Yuan turned his coat: in 1915, he proclaimed himself emperor, the first of a new – Han Chinese – dynasty. But his reign was a nine day wonder, and a year later, ridiculed throughout China for the vanity of his ambitions, he died. In 1917, a northern warlord marched into Peking and proclaimed the restoration of the Ch'ing. K'ang Yu-wei, Tz'u-hsi's 'arch-fiend', now subdued, returned from exile, and loyal servant as he had always been to his Manchu masters, drafted a new constitution. Twelve days later, republican planes flew over the Forbidden City and dropped three bombs on it. Though they caused little damage, the restoration was over. In 1924, the emperor, eighteen years old, was driven from the palace. He took refuge in the Japanese quarter of Tientsin, and throughout his life he was tossed from one great power to another, until he died, a clerk, in the People's Republic of China in October 1967.

Tz'u-hsi's oblivion might have remained undisturbed. But, in July 1928, twenty years after her death, the sumptuous mausoleum in the countryside east of Peking was dynamited, and bandits crawled into the dark vaults to despoil the coffins of the emperors. They robbed Ch'ien-lung and Tz'u-hsi of the treasures buried with them, and hacked Ch'ien-lung, his wives and concubines to pieces. Tz'u-hsi they stripped to the waist, and flung her to one side, face to the ground, her silk and ribboned pantaloons half pulled down. 'Very gently,' reported the commission of enquiry afterwards, 'we turned the Jade Body on its back. The complexion of the face was wonderfully pale, but the eyes were deeply sunken and seemed like two black caverns. There were signs of injury on the lower lip.'[2]

NOTES

1 Roland Allen, *The Siege of the Peking Legations*, 1901, p. 29.

2 The word 'mandarin' was coined by the Portuguese from *mandar*, to command, with echoes of *mantra*, the Indian religious chant sung by a minister, or person in authority. It is neither a translation, nor a transliteration of a Chinese word, so pedants avoid it. But it is picturesque, so I will not. The button in their caps and the *p'u tzu*, embroidered plaques, worn by mandarins denoted their ranks as follows: First rank: ruby button, crane, (civil); unicorn (military). Second rank: coral button, golden pheasant (c); lion (m). Third rank: sapphire button, peacock (c); leopard (m). Fourth rank: lapis lazuli button, wild goose (c); tiger (m). fifth rank: crystal button, silver pheasant (c); bear (m). Sixth rank: white jade button, heron (c); tiger cat (m). Seventh rank: gold button, mandarin duck (c); mottled bear (m). Eighth rank: worked gold button, quail (c); seal (m). Ninth rank: worked silver button, jay (c); rhinoceros (m).

3 Sir John Barrow *Travels in China*, 1804, p. 77.

4 China was divided into eighteen provinces, each province into circuits and each circuit into prefectures.

5 Edward C. M. Bowra *Papers of the Bowra family*, entry for 1896 in Kiukiang.

6 Te-ling, *Two Years*, p. 251 (Tz'u-hsi only had one sister, so Te-ling's memory is inaccurate.)

7 *Ibid*

8 E. H. Parker, *John Chinaman*, 1901, p. 63

9 I. T. Headland, *Court Life in China*, 1901, p. 222.

10 In J. O. P. Bland and E. Backhouse, *China Under the Empress Dowager*, 1914, Hui-cheng's death is dated 1838, and the authors say that Tz'u-hsi and her family preceded him to Peking where he was to take up a new post. In Yung-ling. *Recollections of the Late Ch'ing Palace*, Hui-cheng dies at his post in Fukien in 1850. But I have followed Arthur Hummel, *Eminent Chinese of the Ch'ing Period*, p. 295, as he is the most reputable source.

11 The Chinese do not refer to themselves as 'Chinese' or to the country, as 'China', but to the 'people of Han' (as we might say 'sons of Adam') and to the 'Middle Kingdom'.

12 The following provinces formed viceroyalties: Chihli, Kiangnan or Liang-kiang (inc. Kiangsi, Kiangsu and Anhwei), Fukien & Chekiang, Shensi & Kansu, Hu-kuang, (inc. Hupeh and Hunan), Szechuan, the Two Kwangs (inc. Kwangtung & Kwangsi), Yunnan & Kweichow. The following provinces also had governors, subordinate to the viceroy: Kiangsi, Kiangsu, Anhwei, Chekiang, Shensi, Hupeh, Hunan, Kwangtung and Kwangsi, Yunnan and Kweichow.

13 Mary C. Wright in *The T'ung-chih Restoration*, 1967, gives the following figures (p. 55, footnote): 1644–1912 Viceroys: 209 Manchus, 18 Mongols, 77 Chinese Bannermen, and 288 Chinese. Governors: 171 Manchus, 18 Mongols, 10 Chinese Bannermen, 573 Chinese. On the government boards, Li-fan Yuan and Censorate; 328 Manchu, 18 Mongol, 77 Chinese Bannermen, 262 Chinese.

14 Arthur Waley, *The Way and its Power*, 1934, p. 181.

15 Rev. Justus Doolittle, *Social Life of the Chinese*, 1866, Vol. I, p. 22.

16 The Chinese date someone a year old from the day of his birth, and therefore Tz'u-hsi, born in 1835, celebrated her decades in 1844, 1854, and so on, and she completed a Chinese 'cycle' (sixty years) in 1894. Also, the Chinese reckon age not

from the birthday itself, but from New Year's Day. Therefore Tz'u-hsi, born in November 1835, was considered two years' old on New Year's Day 1836, or in Chinese style, two *sui*. I have used European reckoning of age, but where it is important to see it from the character's point of view, as on Tz'u-hsi's birthdays, I have used Chinese age. In March 1850, when Hsien-feng succeeded, he was twenty *sui*, but eighteen years old.

17 The official mourning period was three years, but it was customarily shortened to two years and three months, the weaning period of a baby in China, and therefore the time a child should spend grieving for a parent.

CHAPTER 2

1 H. S. Brunnert and V. V. Hagelstrom, *Present Day Political Organisation in China*, 1912, pp. 13–24.

2 Jonathan Spence, *Tsao Yin and the K'ang-hsi Emperor, Master and Bond-servant*, 1969, p. 12.

3 Matignon, J–J., *Superstition, Crime et Misère en Chine*, 1899, p. 186.

4 Mencius, (trans D. C. Lau) 1970, VI A 8 p. 165.

5 Barrow, *Travels*, p. 115.

6 Eric Chou, *The Dragon and the Phoenix*, 1970 p. 133.

7 Te-ling, *Two Years*, p. 251.

CHAPTER 3

1 Hummel, *Eminent Chinese*, p. 295, quoting confidence made to Ch'u Hung-chi, an official.

2 Teng Ssu-yu and John K. Fairbank, *China's Response to the West*, p. 19, and in Michael Loewe, *Imperial China*, p. 213–4.

3 The emphasis on Holland probably arises because Holland traded with China in the seventeenth century, and the confusion with England because of William of Orange's succession.

4 In 1829, for instance, of twenty-one million dollars' worth of British commerce in China, ten million was in opium; of the United States' trade that year, (four million dollars' worth) a quarter was in the drug. Hosea Ballou Morse, *International Relations of the Chinese Empire*, Vol I, pp. 37, 82–4, 89–91 for opium figures).

5 Teng and Fairbank, *China's Response to the West*, 1970, pp. 42–3 quoting Hsu Chi-yu's *Acceptance of World Geography*, 1848.

6 Timothy Richard, *Forty-Five Years in China, Reminiscences*, 1916.

7 Vincent Shih, *The Taiping Ideology*, 1967, p. 9.

8 Walter Henry Medhurst, *Pamphlets issued by the Chinese Insurgents at Nanking*, 1853, p. 33.

9 Medhurst, *Pamphlets*. Quote from Book of Imperial Decrees of the Imperial Will, 1852, p. 34.

10 Many writers have attributed to Tz'u-hsi the appointments of Tseng-Kuo-fan and Li Hung-chang to the Taiping campaign, and claimed to see in them a freedom from prejudice against Chinese, for they were both granted military commands such as Manchus would normally have been given. But while Tz'u-hsi probably appreciated their forthright measures and supported them later, she can have had nothing to do with their appointments. Tseng was ordered to raise the Hunanese braves in 1852, when Tz'u-hsi had barely arrived at court; Li was chosen and recommended by Tseng.

11 Charles George Gordon's Diary for December 1860, quoted in Henry William Gordon, *Events in the Life of Charles George Gordon*, 1886, p. 49.

12 Donald Hurd, *The Arrow War*, 1967, p. 131–2.
13 Christopher Hibbert, *The Dragon Wakes*, 1970, p. 210.
14 Andrew Wilson, *The Ever-Victorious Army*, 1908, p. 310.
15 Stanley Lane-Poole, *Sir Harry Parkes*, 1901, p. 209.
16 Hurd, *Arrow War*, p. 103.
17 *Ibid.*, p. 117
18 Hummel, *Eminent Chinese*, p. 905.
19 J. O. P. Bland and E. Backhouse, *China under the Empress Dowager*, p. 24.
20 Medhurst, *Pamphlets*.
21 *Ibid*,.

CHAPTER 4
1 W. A. P. Martin, *A Cycle of Cathay*, 1896, p. 163.
2 Dr D. F. Rennie, *Peking and the Pekingese*, 1865. Vol. I, p. 30.
3 Martin, *Cycle*, p. 171
4 Hurd, *Arrow War*, p. 127.
5 Wilson, *Ever-Victorious Army*, p. 310.
6 Hurd, *Arrow War*.
7 Morse, *International Relations*, Vol. I, p. 536.
8 Hurd, *Arrow War*, p. 166.
9 Morse, *International Relations*, Vol. I, p. 576.
10 Martin, *Cycle*, p. 193.
11 Hurd, *Arrow War*, p. 179.
12 Correspondence re China 1859–60 (Blue Book). Found by Parkes, August 12 1860, p. 117.
13 Correspondence, August 26 1860, Parkes to Elgin, p. 126.
14 Bland and Backhouse, *Under the Empress Dowager*, pp. 25–6.
15 Mary C. Wright, *The Last Stand of Chinese Conservatism*, 1967, p. 12.
16 Correspondence 1859–60 (Blue Book). Found at Yuan Ming Yuan, dated 7 Sept. on 8th Oct. 1860, p. 271.
17 Lane-Poole, *Harry Parkes*, pp. 232–3.
18 Correspondence 1859–60 found at Yuan Ming Yuan 8 Oct., p. 262.
19 Henry B. Loch, *Personal Narrative of Occurences during Lord Elgin's Second Embassy to China*, 1869, p. 148.
20 Loch, *Personal Narrative*, p. 97.
21 Correspondence 1859–60, Parkes to Elgin, Oct. 20, 232.
22 *Ibid.*, Loch to Elgin, Oct. 9, p. 193.
23 *Ibid.*, Elgin to Prince Kung n.d. but clearly Oct. 13, p. 217.
24 *Ibid.*, Prince Kung to Elgin, Sept. 29, p. 183.
25 Rennie, *Peking and Pekingese*, Vol. I, p. 42.
26 Martin, *Cycle*, p. 346.
27 A. B. Freeman Mitford. (Lord Redesdale) *Memoirs*, 1948, Vol. I, pp. 361–2.
28 Wright, *Last Stand*, p. 13.
29 Daniele Varé, *The Last of the Empresses*, 1938, p. 30.
30 Correspondence 1859–60 Prince Kung to Elgin, Oct. 3, p. 186.
31 Oswald Siren, *The Imperial Palaces of Peking*, Vol. I, p. 46.
32 Hibbert, *The Dragon Wakes*, p. 271.
33 Robert Swinhoe, *Narrative of the North China Campaign of 1860*, 1861, p. 298.
34 *Ibid.*, p. 299.
35 *Ibid.*, p. 305.
36 Rev. R. J. L. M'Ghee, *How we got to Peking*, 1862, pp. 212–3.

37 Correspondence 1859–60, Prince Kung to Elgin, Oct. 12, p. 216.
38 *Ibid.*, Elgin to Sir John Russell. Oct. 25, p. 215.
39 *Ibid.*, p. 215.
40 Hurd, *Arrow War*, pp. 235–6.
41 Jonathan Spence, *The China Helpers*, 1969, pp. 74–5.
42 Henry McAleavy, *The Modern History of China*, 1969, p. 100.

CHAPTER 5
1 Mrs. Archibald Little (Alicia M. Bewicke) *Round About My Peking Garden*, 1905, p. 76.
2 Bland & Backhouse, *Under the Empress Dowager*, p. 47.
3 *Ibid.*, p. 30.
4 Rennie, *Peking and Pekingese* Vol. II, p. 235.
5 *Ibid.*, Vol. I, p. 220.
6 Juliet Bredon, *Sir Robert Hart*, 1909, pp. 121–2.
7 Rennie, *Peking and Pekingese*, Vol. I, p. 223.
8 Te-ling, *Two Years*, p. 252.
9 Henri Cordier, *Historie des relations de la Chine avec les puissances occidentales*, 1860–1902, 1900.
10 Bland and Backhouse, *Under the Empress Dowager*, p. 43.
11 *Ibid.*, p. 43.
12 *Ibid.*, p. 42.
13 Cordier, *Relations*, Vol. I, pp. 124–8; Rennie, *Peking and Pekingese*, pp. 134–8.
14 Wright, *Last Stand*, p. 17.
15 Bland and Backhouse, *Under the Empress Dowager*, p. 48.
16 I have called the Empress Tz'u-hsi throughout, although she first received this title in 1861. Although Niuhuru was called Tz'u-an at the same time, I continue to call her by her clan name Niuhuru to keep the distinctions between the two empresses clear.
17 At the end of her life the Empress Dowager was called Tz'u-hsi Tuan-yu K'ang-yi Chao-yin Chuang-ch'eng Shou-kung Ch'in-hsien Ch'ung-hsi Huang Tai-hou: Motherly, auspicious, orthodox, heaven-blessed, prosperous, all-nourishing, brightly-manifest, calm, sedate, perfect, long-lived, respectful, reverend, worshipful, illustrious, exalted Empress Dowager. She received two more titles on her thirtieth birthday, two more on T'ung-chih's majority, two more as he lay dying, two more on her fortieth birthday, two on her fiftieth, two on the Kuang-hsu Emperor's marriage, two on her sixtieth birthday, and she refused four more on her seventieth birthday.
18 Bland and Backhouse, *Under the Empress Dowager*: pp. 54–5.
19 Wright, *Last Stand*, p. 45.
20 Rennie, *Peking and Pekingese*, Vol. II, p. 163.

CHAPTER 6
1 McAleavy, *Modern History*, p. 100.
2 Wilson, *Ever-Victorious Army*, p. 283.
3 Spence, *China Helpers*, pp. 60–1.
4 *Ibid.*, pp. 81–2.
5 Wilson, *Ever-Victorious Army*, p. 316.
6 Morse, *International Relations*, Vol. II. p. 97.
7 Gordon, *Events*, p. 87.
8 *Ibid.*, p. 84.

9 J. Bland, *Li Hung-chang*, 1917, p. 86.
10 Bland and Backhouse, *Under the Empress Dowager*, p. 72.
11 *Ibid.*, p. 74.
12 Wright, *Last Stand*, p. 122, quoting Thomas W. Kingsmill, Retrospect of events in China and Japan during the year 1865, in *Journal of N. China, Branch of the Royal Asiatic Society*, 1865, p. 143.
13 Wright, *Last Stand*, p. 163.
14 Teng and Fairbank, *China's Response*. p. 48.
15 *Ibid.*, p. 55.
16 Wright, *Last Stand*, p. 22.
17 A. B. Freeman Mitford, *The Attaché at Peking*, 1900, p. 240.
18 Teng and Fairbank, *China's Response*, p. 53–4.
19 Martin, *Cycle*, p. 362.
20 Teng and Fairbank, *China's Response*, p. 98.
21 Freeman-Mitford, *Attaché*, p. 226.
22 Cordier, *Relations*, Vol. I, p. 282.
23 Bland, *Li Hung-chang*, p. 85.
24 Wright, *Last Stand*, p. 286.
25 *Ibid.*, pp. 262–3, quoting China no. 9 (Blue Book), 1870, pp. 10–11.
26 Paul A. Cohen, *China and Christianity*, 1963, p. 76.
27 The Protestants had not braved the interior before 1860, as the Catholics had done. During the 1860s, about two hundred and fifty priests were issued with passports for the interior and Catholic converts increased from 369,441 to 404,530; but by 1869, only 5,753 Chinese were Protestants. (Cohen, *China and Christianity*, p. 76).
28 Martin, *Cycle*, pp. 552–3.
29 Cohen, *China and Christianity*, pp. 48–58.
30 Cordier, *Relations*, p. 365.
31 Bland and Backhouse, *Under the Empress Dowager*, p. 78.
32 Teng and Fairbank, *China's Response*, p. 105.

CHAPTER 7
1 Freeman-Mitford, *Attaché*, p. 72.
2 Bland and Backhouse, *Under the Empress Dowager*, p. 71.
3 *Ibid.*, p. 439.
4 *Ibid.*, pp. 77–8.
5 Pierre Loti, *Les Derniers Jours de Pékin*, 1901, p. 261.
6 Morse, *International Relations*, Vol. II, p. 371.
7 Parker, *John Chinaman*, p. 165.
8 Lo Jung-pang (ed.), *K'ang Yu-wei*, (including K'ang's autobiography). p. 49.
9 Cyril Pearl, *Morrison of Peking*, 1970, p. 81.
10 Weng T'ung-ho, *Diaries*, 1871.
11 Bland and Backhouse, *Under the Empress Dowager*, p. 89.
12 *Ibid.*, pp. 92–3.
13 Te-ling, *Imperial Incense*, 1934, p. 161.
14 Cordier, *Relations*, pp. 458–9.
15 *Ibid.*, p. 486.
16 Hope Danby, *The Garden of Perfect Brightness*, 1950, p. 218.
17 Cordier, *Relations*, p. 566.
18 Wu Yung, *Flight of an Empress*, 1957, p. 200.
19 Te-ling, *Two Years*, p. 252.

20 Bland and Backhouse, *Under the Empress Dowager*, p. 125.
21 Te-ling, *Two Years*, pp. 252–3.
22 Bland and Backhouse, *Under the Empress Dowager*, p. 127.
23 *Ibid.*, p. 127.
24 *Ibid.*, pp. 145–6.
25 Hummel, *Eminent Chinese*, p. 731.

CHAPTER 8
1 Weng T'ung-ho, *Diaries*, Dec. 21 1883, quoted in Eastman, Lloyd, *Throne and Mandarins*, 1967, p. 211.
2 McAleavy, *Modern History*, p. 130.
3 Bland, *Li Hung-chang*, p. 112.
4 Morse, *International Relations*, Vol. II, p. 335.
5 Stanley F. Wright, *Hart and the Chinese Customs*, p. 486, quoted by Emily Hahn, *China Only Yesterday*, 1963, p. 180.
6 Morse, *International Relations*, Vol. II, p. 351.
7 Eastman, *Throne and Mandarins*, p. 105, quoting the diary of Li Tz'u-ming.
8 Bland and Backhouse, *Under the Empress Dowager*, pp. 155–6.
9 Eastman, *Throne and Mandarins*, pp. 128–35.
10 Teng and Fairbank, *China's Response*, p. 119.
11 Eastman, *Throne and Mandarins*, p. 201.
12 Bredon, *Sir Robert Hart*, p. 188.
13 Teng and Fairbank, *China's Response*, p. 121.
14 Bland and Backhouse, *Under the Empress Dowager*, p. 79.
15 Teng and Fairbank, *China's Response*, p. 106.
16 *Ibid*, p. 122.
17 *Ibid*, p. 101.
18 Eastman, *Throne and Mandarins*, pp. 192–3; Weng T'ung-ho's *Diaries* for 22nd Jan. 1885.
19 Chester Tan, *The Boxer Catastrophe*, p. 15.
20 Karl A. Wittfogel, *Oriental Despotism*, 1957, pp. 307 & 335.
21 Wright, *Last Stand*, p. 163.
22 Richard, *Forty-Five Years in China*, p. 130.
23 Morse, *International Relations*, Vol. II, p. 404.
24 Te-ling, *Two Years*, p. 252.
25 Bland and Backhouse, *Under the Empress Dowager*, p. 439.
26 Yun Yu-ting, *Stories relating to Kuang-hsu*, quoted in Maurice Collis, *New Sources for the Life of Empress Tz'u-hsi*, 1957, p. 5.
27 Philip Sergeant, *The Great Empress Dowager of China*, 1910. p. 131.
28 Bland and Backhouse, *Under the Empress Dowager*, p. 165.
29 Reginald F. Johnston, *Twilight in the Forbidden City*, 1934, pp. 369–71.
30 Tz'u-hsi covered her tracks skilfully when she embezzled the Navy funds. One definite piece of evidence did however come to light: an official copy of the regulations of the Nei Wu Fu (Imperial Household Department) for the summer palace stated that the Navy Board had petitioned that, as all building had been completed, maintenance should now be handed over to the Nei Wu Fu and the money required per annum for maintenance should be secured on the internal revenue tax and the riverine *likin*.

CHAPTER 9
1 Wu Yung, *Flight*, p. 179.

2 Weng T'ung-ho, *Diaries* (1897); Hummel, *Eminent Chinese*, p. 385.

3 Ho Ping-ti, *Weng T'ung-ho and the Hundred Days*, 1962, quoting Sir Claude MacDonald in *China*, N. I (1899).

4 Pearl, *Morrison*, p. 81.

5 Te-ling, *Two Years*, p. 64.

6 *Ibid.*, pp. 167–8.

7 Siren, *Imperial Palaces*, 1926, Vol. I. p. 26.

8 *Ibid.*, p. 27.

9 Te-ling, *Imperial Incense*, p. 248.

10 Headland, *Court Life*, 1909, p. 87.

11 Johnston, *Twilight*, p. 362.

12 Te-ling, *Two Years*, p. 17.

13 Headland, *Court Life*, p. 206.

14 Te-ling, *Two Years*, pp. 321–2.

15 Te-ling, *Ibid.*, p. 99.

16 Jung-ling, *Recollections of the late Ch'ing Palace*, 1903.

17 Te-ling, *Two Years*, p. 86.

18 Te-ling, *Imperial Incense*, p. 78.

19 Mrs Archibald Little (Alicia M. Bewicke), *Intimate China*, 1899, p. 507.

20 Katharine Carl, *With the Empress Dowager in China*, 1906, p. 106.

21 Te-ling, *Two Years*, p. 260.

22 *Ibid.*, p. 113.

23 Te-ling, *Imperial Incense*, p. 272.

CHAPTER 10

1 Richard C. Howard, 'K'ang Yu-wei 1858–1927: His Intellectual Background and early Thought', in Arthur F. Wright and Denis Twitchett, *Confucian Personalities*, pp. 306–7, quoting K'ang, *Autobiography* in Lo, *K'ang Yu-wei*, pp. 41–2.

2 Lo, *K'ang Yu-wei*, (Autobiography), p. 34.

3 Robert Hart, letter to J. D. Campbell 1894 quoted in Hahn, *China Only Yesterday*, p. 188.

4 Morse, *International Relations*, Vol. III, p. 35.

5 Bland and Backhouse, *Under the Empress Dowager*, pp. 168–9.

6 Pearl, *Morrison*, p. 81.

7 Bland and Backhouse, *Under the Empress Dowager*, p. 172.

8 George Nye Steiger, *China and the Occident*, 1927, p. 65.

9 *Ibid.*, pp. 65–6.

10 Pearl, *Morrison*, p. 83.

11 Lo, *K'ang Yu-wei*, (Autobiography), p. 83.

12 Bland and Backhouse, *Under the Empress Dowager*, pp. 186–7.

13 Teng and Fairbank, *China's Response*, p. 177–9; Lo, *K'ang Yu-wei*, (Autobiography) pp. 93-9.

14 Hummel, *Eminent Chinese*, p. 705.

15 T'an Ssu-t'ung, *Treatise on Benevolence*, quoted in David S. Nivison, 'The Problem of Knowledge and Action in Chinese Thought since Wang Yang-ming', in Arthur F. Wright *Studies in Chinese Thought*, p. 135.

16 Spence, *China Helpers*, p. 156.

17 Liang Ch'i-ch'ao, *Intellectual Trends in the Ch'iang Period*, p. 110.

18 Teng and Fairbank, *China's Response*, p. 164.

19 Tan, *Boxer Catastrophe*, p. 22.

20 Little, *Intimate China*, p. 589, quoting *China Mail* interview, 1898.

CHAPTER 11

1 Lo, *K'ang Yu-wei*, (Autobiography), p. 126.
2 Roger Pélissier, *The Awakening of China*, 1967, p. 257, quoting Paul S. Reinsch, *An American Diplomat in China*, pp. 1–3.
3 Jerome Chen, *Yuan Shih-k'ai*, p. 54.
4 Pélissier, *Awakening*, p. 186, quoting Lord Charles Beresford, *The Break-up of China*, pp. 270–3.
5 Ch'en, *Yuan Shih-k'ai*, p. 57.
6 *Ibid.*
7 Lo, *K'ang Yu-wei*, (Autobiography), p. 126.
8 Ch'en, *Yuan Shih-k'ai*, p. 59.
9 *Ibid.*, pp. 59–60.
10 *Ibid*, p. 60.
11 In later years when his betrayal of the reform movement brought obloquy upon him, Yuan tried to clear himself by claiming that the *coup* took place at dawn on 22 September, and he only arrived in Tientsin late on the twentieth, and only saw Jung-lu on the morning of the twenty-first, too late for his revelations to have influenced Tz'u-hsi's actions in Peking. The version he told to Morrison, the *Times* correspondent who later became his adviser when Yuan aspired to the throne after the fall of the Ch'ing dynasty, went like this: 'Next morning [21 September] Jung-lu called on Yuan and said "Lately friends from Peking have repeatedly informed me of the reformers' minutest movements. Their daring is astounding. We must rescue the Emperor from their clutches." In the evening he sent for Yuan and told him that the plot had been exposed in Peking.' (Pearl, p. 91).
   In effect Morrison, usually a shrewd observer, swallowed Yuan's whitewash whole. For the *Tientsin Times/Peking Gazette* recorded that Yuan's train from Peking arrived at 3pm on 20 September at Tientsin, and he therefore had plenty of time to tell Jung-lu that day. Also, Te-ling claims that Kuang-hsu told her that Yuan Shih-k'ai was present when he was arrested on 22 September in the Forbidden City. (*Old Buddha*, p. 211.)
12 Bland and Backhouse, *Under the Empress Dowager*, p. 440.
13 Te-ling, *Old Buddha*, 1929, p. 211.
14 *Ibid*, 211–2.
15 Bland, *Li Hung-chang*, p. 223.
16 Bland and Backhouse, *Under the Empress Dowager*, p. 236.
17 *Ibid*, p. 234.
18 Lo, *K'ang Yu-wei*, (Autobiography), p. 127.
19 *Ibid.*, p. 128.
20 T'an, 'Treatise on Benevolence', in Wright *Studies* p. 135.
21 Richard, *Forty-Five Years*, p. 267.
22 Tan, *Boxer Catastrophe*, 1955, p. 26.
23 Wu Yung, *Flight*, p. 178.
24 Steiger, *China and the Occident*, p. 85.
25 *Ibid.*, p. 50.
26 W. A. P. Martin, *The Siege in Peking*, p. 51.
27 Steiger, *China and the Occident*, p. 95.
28 Tan, *Boxer Catastrophe*, p. 32; Headland, *Court Life*, pp. 61–3.
29 Little, *Intimate China*, p. 596; Cordier, *Relations*, Vol. III, p. 424.

CHAPTER 12

1 Pélissier, *Awakening*, pp. 218–9, quoting Commandant Harfeld, *Opinions chinoises sur les Barbares d'Occident*, pp. 234-6.
2 Teng and Fairbank, *China's Response*, p. 190.
3 Allen, *Siege*, p. 25.
4 Te-ling, *Old Buddha*, p. 227.
5 Sarah Pike Conger, *Letters from China*, 1969, p. 42.
6 Bland and Backhouse, *Annals of the Court of Peking*, pp. 444–5.
7 Te-ling, *Old Buddha*, p. 241.
8 Bland and Backhouse, *Under the Empress Dowager*, p. 304.
9 Bowra, *Papers*.
10 Sergeant, *Great Empress*, pp. 222–3 (author's italics)
11 Tan, *Boxer Catastrophe*, p. 55.
12 *Ibid.*, p. 63.
13 Bland and Backhouse, *Under the Empress Dowager*, pp. 248–50.
14 Nigel Oliphant, *A Diary of the Siege of the Legations in Peking*, 1901, p. 24.
15 *Ibid.*,
16 Pearl, *Morrison*, p. 114.
17 Tan, *Boxer Catastrophe*, p. 72.
18 *Ibid.*, p. 73.
19 Bland and Backhouse, *Under the Empress Dowager*, p. 265.
20 Pearl, *Morrison*, p. 116.
21 Martin, *Siege*, pp. 110–2.
22 Bland and Backhouse, *Under the Empress Dowager*, p. 274.

CHAPTER 13

1 Teng and Fairbank, *China's Response*, p. 105.
2 Tan, *Boxer Catastrophe*, p. 95.
3 Allen, *Siege*, p. 129.
4 Steiger, *China and the Occident*, pp. 236–7.
5 Tan, *Boxer Catastrophe*, p. 65.
6 Victor Purcell, *The Boxer Uprising*, 1963, p. 256.
7 Tan, *Boxer Catastrophe*, p. 114.
8 Peter Fleming, *The Siege at Peking*, 1959, p. 227.
9 Tan, *Boxer Catastrophe*, p. 114.
10 Fleming, *Siege*. p. 227.
11 Bland and Backhouse, *Under the Empress Dowager*, pp. 331–3.
12 *Ibid.*, p. 289.
13 Allen, *Siege*, pp. 226–7.
14 Oliphant, *Diary*, p. 128.
15 Tan, *Boxer Catastrophe*, p. 105.
16 Mary Hooker, *Behind the Scenes in Peking*, 1910, p. 176.
17 Fleming, *Siege*, p. 207.
18 Conger, *Letters*, p. 161.
19 Wu Yung, *Flight*, p. 210.
20° I met in Hong Kong a Manchu of the Tatala clan now called Miss Tang, who was the first wife of P'u-chieh, brother of the last Emperor of China P'u-i. She was also the niece of the Pearl Concubine, and of the Lustrous Concubine, and joined the latter in the palace from 1911 to 1924. The Lustrous Concubine told the story of her sister's murder at Tz'u-hsi's orders many times, but without rancour. Indeed, when Miss Tang was describing the court to me, she kept on praising Tz'u-hsi's kindness and

dignity and greatness. I eventually interrupted her to ask: 'But didn't you believe then that your aunt had been thrown down the well at Tz'u-hsi's command?' Miss Tang replied: 'But there was such confusion. . . . Soldiers everywhere. It was done in the heat of the moment, and afterwards she was very very sorry.'

CHAPTER 14

1 Te-ling, *Two Years*, p. 362.
2 Fleming, *Siege*, p. 236; Bland and Backhouse, *Under the Empress Dowager*, pp. 348-9.
3 Robert Hart, *These from the Land of Sinim*, 1901, p. 59.
4 Pearl, *Morrison*, p. 131.
5 Oliphant, *Diary*, p. 215.
6 MacAleavy, *Modern History*, p. 166.
7 Steiger, *China and the Occident*, p. 261.
8 Hart, *These from the Land*, pp. 49-50.
9 Mary C. Wright, *China in Revolution* (Introduction), p. 11.
10 Steiger, *China and the Occident*, pp. 293-6; Tan, *Boxer Catastrophe*, pp. 150-1.
11 Bland and Backhouse, *Under the Empress Dowager*, p. 375.
12 *Ibid.*, pp. 422-3.
13 Wu Yung, *Flight*, p. 237.
14 *Ibid.*, p. 281.
15 Little, *Round About*.
16 Headland, *Court Life*, p. 98.
17 Robert Hart, Correspondence to J. D. Campbell, 26 May 1906.
18 *Ibid.*, 27 October 1903.
19 Ts'en Chun-hsuan, *Autobiography*, p. 15.
20 Teng and Fairbank, *China's Response*, p. 227-8; quoting manifesto of the T'ung-meng-hui, 1905.
21 Pélissier, *Awakening*, p. 245, quoting Paul Linebarger, *The Gosepl of Chung Shan*, pp. 51-2.
22 Tsou Jung, *The Revolutionary Army*, pp. 20-1, 12-3.
23 Te-ling, *Two Years*, pp. 280-90.
24 Bland and Backhouse, *Under the Empress Dowager*, p. 465.
25 *Ibid.*, p. 460.
26 *Ibid.*, pp. 468-9.
27 Ch'u Kuei-t'ung, Diagnosis of the Illness of Kuang-hsu privately recorded. I-Ching No. 29, May 1937.
28 Hart, Correspondence to Campbell, 19 February 1905.
29 Morse, *International Relations*, Vol. III, p. 442.

EPILOGUE

1 Pélissier, *Awakening*, p. 256.
2 Henry McAleavy, *A Dream of Tartary*, 1963, p. 186.

INDEX

Pinyin spellings appear in brackets

Marina Warner

IN A DARK WOOD

'Marina Warner's prose is gracefully analytical, her meanings are distinct, and the structures of the novel carefully modulated… This is an elegant novel, and it signals a major talent'
Peter Ackroyd, *Spectator*

'This a satisfying, challenging book'
Anthony Thwaite, *Observer*

VINTAGE

Marina Warner

THE SKATING PARTY

'This sensitive and forceful novel exposes the
complexities of each person's character and their
different needs as each strives for recognition and
reassurance'
The Times

'Marina Warner's literary terrain is already her own
but her characters would find themselves at home in
Iris Murdoch's fictions'
New Statesman

'Recalls writers like Elizabeth Bowen and Rosamond
Lehmann... Marina Warner is a novelist of real
talent and fine discrimination'
Scotsman

'Immaculately wrought'
Observer

V I N T A G E